Retrieving the Ancients

An Introduction to Greek Philosophy

David Roochnik
Boston University

Blackwell
Publishing

© 2004 by David Roochnik

BLACKWELL PUBLISHING
350 Main Street, Malden, MA 02148-5020, USA
108 Cowley Road, Oxford OX4 1JF, UK
550 Swanston Street, Carlton, Victoria 3053, Australia

First published 2004 by Blackwell Publishing Ltd.

Library of Congress Cataloging-in-Publication Data has been applied for

Roochnik, David.
  Retrieving the ancients : an introduction to Greek philosophy / David
Roochnik.
    p. cm.
  Includes bibliographical references and index.
  ISBN 1-4051-0861-4 (hardback) — ISBN 1-4051-0862-2 (pbk.)
  1. Philosophy, Ancient.   I. Title.

  B171.R66 2004
  180—dc22
                                                      2003024555

A catalogue record for this title is available from the British Library.

Set in 10.5/13 pt Galliard
by Graphicraft Limited, Hong Kong
Printed and bound in the United Kingdom
by MPG Books Ltd, Bodmin, Cornwall

For further information on
Blackwell Publishing, visit our website:
http://www.blackwellpublishing.com

Contents

Introduction

Two Reasons to Study Ancient Greek Philosophy

Ancient Greek philosophy began with Thales, who correctly predicted an eclipse that occurred in 585 BCE, and culminated in the monumental works of Aristotle, who died in 322.[1] (Unless otherwise noted, all dates in this book are BCE.) The simple fact that these thinkers lived over 2,000 years ago should provoke a question: in the age of the microchip and the engineered gene, why bother with them?

One good answer immediately springs to mind: to become educated. The Greeks were the intellectual ancestors of western culture. They laid the foundations for all future developments in the natural sciences, medicine, mathematics, history, architecture, sculpture, tragic and comic drama, lyric and epic poetry, as well as philosophy. To the extent that one must know one's heritage in order to know oneself, it is imperative to study the ancient Greeks.

This is particularly true in the field of philosophy. Alfred North Whitehead famously said, "the safest general characterization of the European philosophical tradition is that it consists in a series of footnotes to Plato" (Whitehead 1969, p. 63). Even if he exaggerated, it is undeniable that in his some 25 dialogues Plato (429–347) addressed an extraordinary range of questions that remain alive and well (and unanswered) even today. What is knowledge? What is courage? What is the best possible political regime and the best possible human life? Can one know that an action is wrong but nevertheless perform it? What makes language meaningful? Are values relative? Should one obey a law even if it is unjust? What does mathematics tell us about the world?

Even if he had influenced no one else, Plato's impact on western culture would be huge simply because he taught Aristotle (384–322), who was a student in his school (the Academy) from 367 to 347. In turn, Aristotle became far and away the dominant thinker for at least the next 1,500 years. Thomas Aquinas, for example, and other medieval philosophers (Arab, Christian, and Jewish) simply had to say "The Philosopher," and their readers knew Aristotle was being named. In the middle ages European universities first came into being, and their curricula were decisively shaped by the works of Aristotle.

Even if Plato and Aristotle were the unmatched giants of Ancient Greek Philosophy, they did not arise in a vacuum. In the sixth and fifth centuries thinkers powerful in their own right set the stage for their emergence. The "Presocratics," who lived before or contemporaneously with Socrates (469–399), made remarkable leaps in what today we call natural science. Democritus (born ca. 460), for example, formulated a rudimentary version of atomic theory. Empedocles (493–433) planted the seeds of a theory of biological evolution. Pythagoras (living in the sixth century) arrived at the insight fundamental to the development of modern physics, namely that the universe has a mathematical structure. He understood that the "book of nature," as Galileo said, "is written in mathematical characters."

A curious feature of ancient Greek philosophy, which will be discussed at some length in chapter 1, is that in critical ways these Presocratics were more modern in their outlook than their successors, Plato and Aristotle. Indeed, to put the point anachronistically, and as chapter 4 will elaborate at length, Aristotle criticized the Presocratics precisely for being too modern in their thinking. In a parallel fashion, when the great proponents of the "scientific revolution" (such as Bacon, Galileo, Descartes, and Spinoza) in the sixteenth and seventeenth centuries began to develop their new vision of philosophy and science, they did so by attacking Aristotle, who had dominated European intellectual life for centuries. In doing so they were often turning back, both explicitly and implicitly, to the Presocratics.

Another group of innovative thinkers crucial to the emergence of Plato and Aristotle, and significant on their own, were the Sophists, especially Protagoras (born ca. 485) and Gorgias (483–376). As chapter 2 will show, their views are stunningly similar to many professed today. They believed, for example, that ethical values were relative, and that neither objective knowledge of the external world nor a definitive interpretation of a given text or event were possible. For the Sophists language was responsible for constructing our relationship to the world. As such, they prefigure the segment of twentieth-century thought that originated with Nietzsche and came to be known as "postmodernism." Just as Aristotle argued against the Presocratics, much of Plato's work is an attempt to overcome the Sophists. Strangely enough, even though he lived over 2,000 years ago, Plato was in a position to criticize Postmodernism.

In sum: a good reason to study ancient Greek philosophy is to become educated about thinkers who were enormously influential in shaping western culture. This book will help the reader begin this task.

There is, however, a second, and better, reason to study the Greeks, especially Plato and Aristotle: in order to retrieve and revitalize their views. In other words, one can, and should, turn back to the Greeks not only to become knowledgeable about the venerable past, but because the Ancients may still have much to teach us today. They may have come up with better answers to the urgent questions human beings, in every age, invariably face.

This reason may be especially appealing to those who, like myself, often find themselves deeply troubled by the very nature of the modern world in which we live. To many of us, something seems to have gone wrong. Often this feeling is sparked by witnessing the enormous level of destruction technological development has caused. Seeing pictures of the Amazon jungle going up in smoke, or the ice-cap melting in the Arctic, or learning the number of animal species becoming extinct by the day, often trigger a feeling of despair. Perhaps even more troubling is the thought of weapons of mass destruction, all of which were produced by the very scientific techniques of which we are so proud. The image of highly trained technicians, dressed in the clean white garb we associate with laboratories and hospitals, working together to produce "weapons-grade" bacteria is revolting. Something, we often feel, has gone wrong in a scientific culture capable of producing, but not knowing how to use or being able to control, the awesome tools of modern technology. We wonder if human cloning will in fact be attempted, and if the chemistry of the brain will become so well understood that a feeling of well-being will be easily attained by the taking of a pill.

A sentiment distantly but importantly related to this was expressed by Edmund Husserl in a lecture titled "Philosophy and the Crisis of European Humanity," written in 1935. Even if his prose was forbidding, Husserl's message was clear. "The European nations," he wrote, "are sick. Europe itself, it is said, is in crisis" (Husserl 1970, p. 270). Husserl was specific in identifying what had gone wrong: "The European crisis has its roots in a misguided rationalism" (p. 290).

A materialist, mechanistic conception of nature, studied by a mathematically based science, which in turn spawned the powerful technologies we now both take for granted and occasionally dread, has come to dominate not only all modes of human reasoning, but western culture itself. This is the crisis. Like a giant shadow, modern science and technology have blotted out all other forms of human knowledge and inquiry. Most important, the hegemony of modern science, based always on the paradigm of mathematical physics, has obliterated the possibility of gaining knowledge of the "meaning" of human life itself. For this "meaning" requires natural or ordinary language, and resists mathematical or scientific articulation.

Facing this crisis, Husserl refused to succumb to a common twentieth-century temptation, namely to abandon western rationalism altogether. In fact, his love of reason was steadfast, and he denied that "the European crisis . . . [means] that rationality as such is evil" (p. 290). Instead, the task he undertook was to reform reason, to expand it so that it could not only account for material bodies in motion, but also for the meaning of human life. He called his new science "phenomenology," a word composed of two Greek words, *phenomena*, "the appearances," and *logos*, "rational account."

What Husserl said about Einstein typifies his critique of modern European rationality and gives some inkling of what he meant by phenomenology:

> Einstein's revolutionary innovations concern the formulae through which the idealized and naively objectified physics is dealt with. But how formulae in general, how mathematical objectification in general, receive

meaning on the foundation of life and the intuitively given surrounding world – of this we learn nothing; and thus Einstein does not reform the space and time in which our vital life runs its course. (p. 295)

To make the same point, Husserl says this: "the scientist does not become a subject of investigation" (p. 295). In other words, modern science, always speaking the language of mathematics, "objectifies" the world. It understands how material things work and can predict and thereby manipulate their movements, but has nothing whatsoever to say about the unique "meaning" or "the vital life" human beings, including the scientists themselves, actually experience. "No objective science can do justice to the very subjectivity which accomplishes science" (p. 295). Modern science is in this very specific sense dehumanizing. It presents the technician with the opportunity to manipulate the natural world, but says and knows nothing about what it is like for a human being actually to live in it.

Consider the simplest possible example. Since Copernicus we have known that the earth revolves around the sun and so is not, as Aristotle thought, the center of the universe. On the one hand, this scientific fact forbids dissent. On the other, it also conceals a compelling truth: for human beings, the center of our daily lives will always be the earth. It is where we live. In order to see the stars we must look upwards, out and away from ourselves. To describe the dawn, we invariably say "the sun has risen," even though, from an astronomical perspective, this is false. Ordinary life, as well as ordinary language, speak against the Copernican revolution.

By contrast, the purpose of Aristotle's physics, as we will see in chapter 4, is precisely to speak for ordinary life; that is, to articulate the phenomena and explain how the natural world appears from a human perspective and to the naked eye. Therefore, when in his work *On the Heavens* he argues that the earth is the center of the universe around which the stars move eternally in fixed circular orbits, the reader should resist the temptation to dismiss him as a primitive or a quack. His argument is, from a phenomenological perspective, far more powerful than one may think. What Aristotle achieves is exactly what Husserl called for, namely a *logos*, a rational account, of how the world presents itself to earth-bound human beings. Unlike the modern scientist, Aristotle can explain what the world means *to us*. For him, the scientist, as well as the ordinary human being, is indeed "a subject of investigation."

Recall a point made above: in crucial respects the Presocratics were far more modern in their philosophical views than Plato or Aristotle. Democritus, for example, intuited the possibility of a mathematically based science able to explain atomic motion. Just as contemporary neuroscientists try to explain consciousness by reducing it to the firings of neurons in the brain, Democritus thought that what was then called the "soul" was actually just the motion of tiny particles moving at the speed of fire. Therefore, when Plato and Aristotle criticize Democritus on this score, as we will see them do in chapters 3 and 4, they are also criticizing a broad and basic tenet of modern thought. And this criticism should be taken seriously, even today.

In his comments about Einstein, Husserl uses the word "meaning." It is important to recall exactly what this word itself means. It has at least two different senses: (1) "to intend," "to have a purpose," as in "I meant to do it;" (2) "to signify," as in "the word 'table' means a piece of furniture with a flat top placed horizontally on legs."

If these two senses are combined, the statement, "human life has meaning," implies that life has a purpose which can be signified or explained in ordinary language. To reiterate, this is precisely the possibility the modern scientific view rejects. It denies that the way ordinary human beings, speaking ordinary language, experience their daily lives is epistemically useful or informative, and so is, in this regard, dehumanizing.

A major thesis of this book, developed especially in chapters 3 and 4, will be that the philosophical views of Plato and Aristotle are worth retrieving today because of their profound appreciation and attempt to comprehend the meaning of human life. They think from within and remain faithful to the geocentric, naked-eye, perspective articulated by ordinary (as opposed to mathematical) language. They think from within the confines of human experience and so they can, even today, still teach us much about what it means to be a human being. Perhaps at no other time in the history of western culture has their tutelage been more needed. This is the second, and the better, reason to study ancient Greek philosophy.

The Organization and Strategy of This Book

This book will be organized in a straightforwardly chronological manner. Chapter 1 will cover the Presocratics, chapter 2 the Sophists and Socrates, chapter 3 Plato, and chapter 4 will focus on Aristotle.

There is an obvious problem in trying to cover this much material in a book as short as this: the subject is vast. Perhaps the most well-known work (in English) in this field is W. K. C. Guthrie's *A History of Greek Philosophy* (1962), and it runs for six long volumes. The present book is, by contrast, quite modest. As a result, some sort of principle had to be invoked according to which a selection could be made of what portions of ancient Greek philosophy to discuss. This book will use what will be called the "dialectical principle."

"Dialectical" comes from the Greek *dialegesthai*, "to converse." To describe the history of Greek philosophy as "dialectical" is thus to say it is like a conversation. Each thinker we will study will be conceived as responding to, and is in this sense as being shaped by, a previous one. These responses typically have both a positive and a negative side. In other words, when a thinker responds to a predecessor's thought, he affirms what he takes to be positive and so worth preserving, but then also criticizes what he takes to be inadequate and in need of revision. So, for example, the early Presocratic philosopher Anaximander affirmed the most general belief of his predecessor Thales – namely that the world is rationally organized around a single, unifying source or origin – but he disagreed entirely as to what this origin actually was. His criticism moved the conversation forward. Soon, however, Anaximander faced a "dialectical negation" of his own. He was criticized by his follower, Anaximenes.

There is more than one sense to the word "dialectical." It can, for example, refer to the kind of conversation that goes back and forth between the partners. It can also suggest a more linear discourse that develops over time. The latter is often associated with the German philosopher Hegel, and is the one adopted in this book. It implies, above all else, a sense of progress. Anaximander moved beyond Thales, and Anaximenes beyond Anaximander. Greek thinking gradually became more complex and comprehensive. For this reason, then, Aristotle is the "hero" of this book. He wove together the conceptual threads bequeathed to him by the two previous centuries of philosophical activity. He retained what was positive and rejected or revised what he thought negative. He tied up the loose ends, and finally put his own stamp on what became an immense conceptual project. (See Collobert 2002 for a good discussion of Aristotle's relationship to his predecessors.)

The goal of this book is to tell the story of this dialectical development. In turn, this goal provided the principle used to select the texts to be discussed. Simply put, we will concentrate on those aspects of a philosopher's work in which he is most directly responding to his predecessors and thus participating in the conversation. So, for example, chapter 3 will emphasize those dialogues in which Plato is most critical of the Sophists. The Sophists were ethical relativists; Plato was not. It will take a major portion of chapter 3 to explain exactly what this means. Doing so will obviously require us to ignore a huge chunk of Plato's writings. As the quote from Whitehead suggests, the dialogues cover a vast terrain, only a small fraction of which can be covered in this short book.

In addition to giving this book an economical structure and a sense of narrative development, the "dialectical principle" of text selection will bring another benefit. By approaching the history of ancient Greek philosophy as a conversation, this book will invite its readers to participate. The conversation we are about to begin deals with basic philosophical questions. Not only have these questions inspired the entire tradition of western philosophy, but they are also ones that most readers, even if they have never officially studied a work of philosophy, have probably already asked themselves. Is the world orderly or chaotic? Is it a projection of our minds, or does it exist independently on its own? Can something come from nothing? Is anything stable, or is all in flux? In the face of death does human life have meaning, and how should we go about living it well?

As the conversation progresses, readers will not only learn much about the history of Greek philosophy, but they should increasingly be able to probe and progress in developing their own thoughts. In other words, and as mentioned above, studying Greek philosophy entails more than learning about the dusty past. It is a philosophical experience. For this reason, I will use the present tense as often as possible, even when I am discussing thinkers of the past. (This is often called "the historical present" by grammarians.) In addition, especially in the last two chapters, I will occasionally call upon the reader to perform "thought experiments," to imagine certain situations that they might actually face and to use them as a way of reflecting on the works we are discussing.

The strategy of this book carries with it some risk. Because it is "An Introduction to Greek Philosophy," and aims to be informative, one of its primary obligations is to be historically and textually accurate. What is said about any given philosopher must be "philologically sound"; it must be supported by an objective reading of the works written by that philosopher. On the other hand, since this is not a comprehensive treatment of Greek philosophy like Guthrie's, it has a far more limited goal, namely to tell a "dialectical story" about the history of Greek philosophy. As just explained, this goal will determine the choice of texts to be discussed. Here is where the danger lies. Because only some aspects of a thinker's work will be discussed, and a comprehensive (and therefore completely objective) analysis of his thought cannot be offered, the risk is that the version of Greek philosophy this book presents will be truncated in such a way as to reflect the prejudices of its author. More specifically, because the dialectical story about to unfold will culminate in Aristotle, the risk is that the views of his predecessors, especially the Presocratics, will be colored by his interpretation of them.

In this context the reader should be alert to the way in which the word "useful" will be employed in the chapters to follow. In chapter 1, for example, it will be stated that it is "useful" to think of Parmenides as a critic of Heraclitus. "Useful" in this context means "useful in organizing a historical narrative about the dialectical development of Greek philosophy." It must be admitted, however, that it is impossible to prove that Parmenides actually was criticizing Heraclitus. Nonetheless, he will be treated as if he were doing so. This assumption is defensible for two reasons. First, even if it is not demonstrable, it is not philologically implausible; it does no violence to the texts. Second, this assumption will generate a fruitful conversation with an intrinsic philosophical value.

In a similar vein, the discussion of Empedocles will emphasize the extent to which he offered a theory of nature, specifically of evolution, for this is largely the way Aristotle read him. Recently such an interpretation has been passionately denounced. "There is no disputing the fact that Aristotle tortured Empedocles' teaching, twisted his words, abused his meaning," Peter Kingsley (2002, p. 356) has written. It is possible he is not wrong. Still, as part of the dialectical story developed in this book, the Empedocles who is presented will indeed be one much influenced by Aristotle. Because this book aims to be fair and faithful to the texts that it discusses, the reader will always be informed whenever comments are made that venture beyond what can be confidently secured by textual evidence. Throughout the chapters to follow, in either the body of the work or in the notes, alternative interpretations and suggestions for further reading will be given.

There are a great many English translations of the Greek philosophers. This book will use either my own or ones that I have found to be as readable and accurate as possible. The translations cited, as well as the original Greek texts used, will be indicated in the notes.

Note

1 The source of all dates and biographical information mentioned in this book is *The Oxford Classical Dictionary* (1970). The source of all lexical information is Liddel and Scott's *Greek-English Lexicon*. A preliminary version of this book was produced in audio and video form for the Teaching Company in 2001.

1

The Presocratics

Preliminaries

The writings of the Presocratics are substantial – the standard edition of their works (by Hermann Diels, 1922, revised by Walther Kranz, 1961) contains three large volumes – and so we are immediately faced with the problem of text selection discussed in the Introduction. There is, in addition, another significant problem when it comes to the source material of Presocratic philosophy: it is fragmentary in nature. Furthermore, the fragments are of two kinds (at least according to Diels): some (the "A" fragments) are reports about the Presocratics given by other ancient thinkers, while others seem to be original to the thinkers themselves ("B"). Trying to defend a coherent interpretation of these fragments is a monumental challenge for a philological detective.

The "A" fragments pose a unique difficulty. For example, several of the most extensive of them come from Aristotle. But, as one scholar, echoing the complaint made by Kingsley cited in the Introduction, says, "Aristotle focuses narrowly on exactly that aspect of [his predecessors'] theories which is of relevance to his own intellectual concerns" (Inwood

2001, p. 73). In short, Aristotle may not give us an objective or accurate account of the Presocratics.

In this chapter, all my citations of the Presocratics will be from Diels and will be indicated by using his notation (for example, A12, B34). Unless mentioned otherwise in the notes, translations are my own. Before beginning, however, a small step backwards must be taken. The first author to be discussed in this book will not be a philosopher at all. Instead, he will be a poet, a myth-maker: Hesiod.

Before the Beginning: Hesiod

Thales of Miletus (a town on the far eastern or Ionian side of the Hellenized world, in what today is western Turkey) is generally regarded the first philosopher in the west. Very little is known about his life, but since many scholars believe that he correctly "predicted an eclipse which took place in 585" (Kirk, Raven, & Schofield [hereafter KRS] 1983, p. 76), this is a convenient, albeit contrived, date to pinpoint the beginning of western philosophy.[1]

Even if Thales was the first philosopher, he surely was not the first person to think in ancient Greece. Nor was he the first to write. (Indeed, it is possible that Thales himself did not actually write a book of his own. See KRS 1983, p. 88.) Homer composed his extraordinary epics, the *Odyssey* and the *Iliad*, around 700, and these are rich with profound reflections on war, courage, friendship, honor, fate, mortality, marriage, personal identity, and a host of other themes.[2] Hesiod wrote the *Theogony* about the same time, and in it he told a story about the beginning and then the development of the world itself. During the seventh century the lyric poets Sappho, Alcaeus, and Anacreon gave exquisite voice to the human emotions. With all this intellectual and literary activity before 585, what makes scholars so sure that Thales was the first to philosophize?

The answer is simple: "Thales evidently abandoned mythic formulations; this alone justifies the claim that he was the first philosopher" (KRS 1983, p. 99). Thales occupies the throne because unlike his predecessors he did not make up stories, write poems, or retell myths. To use the Greek word that encapsulates all these creative activities, Thales did not engage in *muthos* (the ancestor of our word "myth"). Instead, he was a practitioner of *logos*, of rational thought or speech, which is, in turn, the lifeblood of philosophy.

But what exactly is *logos* and what differentiates it from *muthos*? To suggest an answer, this section will take a peek at passages from Hesiod's *Theogony*. The hope here is that by identifying what philosophy is not – namely the work of a storyteller or myth-maker – we will be in a better position in the next section to discuss what it actually is, and thus why Thales, rather than any of the poets, is traditionally counted as the first philosopher. (See Hyland 1992, pp. 29–33 and 38–44 for a good discussion of this theme.)

Hesiod begins the *Theogony* by invoking the Muses:

> From the Heliconian Muses let us begin to sing, who hold the great and holy mount of Helicon, and dance on soft feet about the deep-blue spring . . .
>
> And one day they taught Hesiod glorious song while he was shepherding his lambs under holy Helicon, and this word first the goddesses said to me – the Muses of Olympus, daughters of Zeus who holds the aegis:
>
> "Shepherds of the wilderness, wretched things of shame, mere bellies, we know how to speak many false things as though they were true; but we know, when we will, to utter true things."
>
> So said the ready-voiced daughters of great Zeus, and they plucked and gave me a rod, a shoot of sturdy laurel, a marvellous thing, and breathed into me a divine voice to celebrate things that shall be and things that were aforetime. (*Theogony*, 1–33)[3]

The Muses, daughters of Zeus and Memory, are the goddesses of inspiration. They "breathe into" (the literal meaning of "inspire") the poet; they fill him up with creative energy and enable him to sing. Without them he would be mute.

On the one hand, invoking the Muse is merely a convention traditionally employed by ancient poets. On the other hand, it signifies something basic to the act of literary creation: it cannot be fully explained. By invoking the Muses the poet denies ultimate responsibility for, and therefore knowledge of, his own poem. He needed the Muses, and they came to him from outside of himself. He did not make his poem up entirely by himself, and so he cannot quite understand it.

Hesiod tells a story: one day he was shepherding his animals when, for no apparent reason, he was visited by the Muses on Mount Helicon. They began by insulting him. A "mere belly," a thoughtless and voiceless blob of desires, is what they called him. Even worse was what they said next. They warned Hesiod that even though they are capable of speaking the truth, they could well be telling him "a false thing," and if so, he would have no way of finding out. After all, these are the goddesses of creative activity, and so their lies seem "as though they were true." They are, in other words, plausible and effective.

As a "mere belly" Hesiod is utterly dependent on the Muses. They "breathed into him a divine voice" without which he would not have been able to "sing." The situation implied by the invocation is therefore quite grim. Hesiod is in the grip of confessed liars, and he does not have the rational power to determine the truth of what they say. His is a precarious enterprise for the story he tells can never be fully verified.

To anticipate the next section and the transition to *logos*: the philosophical project, unlike the poetic or mythic one, will demand verification. The philosopher, unlike the storyteller, must accept full responsibility for his *logos* and will not be allowed to invoke a Muse. He must offer an argument, a set of reasons he himself conceives and articulates, for the views he presents. He must defend what he says. If he fails to do so, he may be deemed a "mere" poet.

After the invocation, Hesiod begins his actual song:

> At the first Chaos came to be, but next wide-bosomed Earth, the ever-sure foundation of all the deathless ones who hold the peaks of snowy Olympus, and dim Tartarus in the depth of the wide-pathed Earth, and Eros [Love], fairest among the deathless gods, who unnerves the limbs and overcomes the mind and wise counsels of all gods and all men within them. From Chaos came forth Erebus and black Night; but of Night were born Aether and Day . . . (*Theogony*, 116–24)

In the beginning there was "Chaos." The English is misleading. While it is phonetically identical to the word it translates, namely the Greek *chaos*, the latter has a different meaning. Our "chaos" is a confused mass of disordered parts, while the Greek means "the abyss," or even better, the "gap." It is the empty space in-between.

This is crucial. In the beginning there was an abyss from which, for no apparent reason, came Earth, Tartaros (the underground), and Eros (sexual desire). According to Hesiod's Muse-inspired *muthos*, the beginning of the world is unintelligible. Unlike the creation story in the biblical Genesis there is no supreme being who brought the universe and all its inhabitants into existence. Unlike the big-bang theory, there is no explanation of the beginning. For Hesiod, the world just popped up.

The first generation of beings to emerge from the abyss included the Earth, on which most of the subsequent developments in the poem will take place, Tartarus, the place below the earth, and Eros. Note the descriptions of Eros. It "unnerves the limbs," it masters minds, and it subdues wills. These phrases ring true: sexual desire can make us weak at the knees and drive us (and other animals) crazy. We fall madly in love and then, despite the fact that we know better, often act in stupid and self-destructive ways.

Eros plays an essential role in the poem because the *Theogony*, which literally means "the birth or generation of the gods," is a kind of family history. In the beginning there was the empty abyss. Then came the first generation, which was composed of three members. Then came Night. And then Earth gave birth to Sky and Hills and the Sea. She then coupled with Sky and gave birth to all the gods and other beings that eventually populate the world with which Hesiod was familiar. In short, the *Theogony* is a genealogy, a family tree whose branches grow and are progressively occupied. Since the process by which this development takes place is sexual reproduction, Eros must be present at the outset to make all these future births possible.

These three features of the *Theogony* – Hesiod's invocation of the Muses, the fact that no reason is given why Earth emerged from the primordial abyss, and the crucial role Eros plays in the subsequent sexual generation of the various inhabitants of the world – together express the poet's basic conviction: the world in which we live is a shaky place. At its core it is not fully intelligible. It began in the abyss and this cannot be rationally comprehended. *Chaos*, after all, is some sort of empty space and so comes close to meaning "nothingness," and no one can comprehend nothingness. (See Miller 2001 for an alternative interpretation of this passage.) This is because to understand or rationally grasp something requires that the something be determinate or distinct. It must be some thing, and not no-thing. To be intelligible is to be determinate, to be this rather than that. Because the abyss is indeterminate, nothing can be said or understood about it.

By contrast, the world, as Hesiod (and everybody else) actually experiences it, is essentially differentiated and intelligible. A tree is a tree and not a rock, and so we chop the former and not the latter. This tree is not that one. The door is not the wall, and so we walk through it rather than into the latter. This rabbit is not that bird and so we do not expect it to fly.

The trajectory of Hesiod's *Theogony* is now clear. It moves from an incomprehensible one to an organized and thus comprehensible many; from a formless and indeterminate abyss to the determinations or differentiations of ordinary experience. Because "at first Chaos came to be," the origin of our intelligible experience is itself unintelligible. This means that the intelligibility we take for granted is itself not entirely reliable. We are reminded of this every night when the bright light of day, in which distinctions between trees and rocks, rabbits and birds, can easily be seen, gives way to a darkness in which such clarity disappears. Night is a vestige of the abyss, from which it is directly descended. ("From Chaos came forth Erebus [another underworld] and black Night.") Despite the trust we invest in the intelligibility of our daily lives – we are confident that we will walk through doors and not into walls – night often shakes us to the core.

To summarize: Hesiod's *muthos* is a genealogy whose undifferentiated and hence unintelligible beginning gradually develops into a world occupied by all the many divine, natural, and human entities with which we are so familiar. However distinctly delineated and well formed these entities might seem to be, their origin is blank and formless. The world, as our dreams and nighttime agonies too often remind us, is not quite as clear-cut as it seems during the day.

In a similar vein, the fact that mind-mastering and "unnerving" Eros is the energy source powering the genealogical development, implies that this development is also not completely intelligible or rational. After all, Eros makes those it attacks do stupid things and no one can predict or control it. Indeed, because Hesiod's story is a genealogy, contingency or chance is given a crucial role to play in the coming into being of the world and its inhabitants. All family histories are testimony to this. Why exactly did your grandparents get married and give birth to your parents?

Given Hesiod's basic conviction that the intelligibility of the world is precarious, it makes perfectly good sense for him to appeal to the Muses. The genealogy he retells is not fully amenable to *logos*. The only reason Hesiod can, for example, report that "at first Chaos came to be," when *Chaos* itself is not rationally comprehensible, is because the inexplicable and unreliable Muses decided, for no apparent reason, to help him. As a result, the invocation to the Muses with which he begins his poem fits together beautifully with what his story actually says. The way Hesiod expresses himself, the form of his story, namely Muse-inspired *muthos*, coheres with the content of the story, namely a world beginning in *Chaos* and fueled by Eros. In this important sense, Hesiod's *muthos* has its own kind of internal coherence and integrity.

These three features of Hesiod's *Theogony* – the invocation of the Muse, the world's beginning in *Chaos*, and the centrality of Eros – are characteristic of *muthos* itself. In other words, *muthos* is a worldview, a conception of what it means to be a human being in the world. It is a powerful intellectual option, one which has never ceased to be attractive and compelling to human beings eager to express their own experience of life. It is not, however, philosophical. For this, we must turn to Thales.

The Ionian Philosophers of the Sixth Century

a) The beginning: Thales of Miletus

Thales may well have been responsible for impressive breakthroughs in engineering, astronomy, and other areas. But far and away his most significant contribution to the history of western culture is revealed in the following statement by Aristotle, listed by Diels as an "A" fragment:

> Of those who first philosophized, most believed that the first principles of all beings are only first principles in the form of matter. For that of which all beings are and that from which they originally come into being and that into which they finally perish, the Being persisting but changing in its attributes, this they state is the element and first principle of beings. And on account of this they believe that nothing comes to be nor is destroyed since this sort of nature is always preserved . . . Thales, the originator of this kind of philosophy, declares [the first principle] to be water . . . Perhaps he got this idea from seeing that the nourishment of all things is moist, and that the hot itself comes to be from this . . . and also because the seeds of all things have a moist nature, and water is the first principle of the nature of moist things. (A12)

This passage typifies the problem of Presocratic source material discussed above. No writings attributable to Thales himself survive, and, to reiterate the complaint, many scholars believe that "Aristotle was not necessarily conscientious in using original sources" (KRS, p. 87). In fact, it is possible that Aristotle has translated Thales' *logos* into his own philosophical terminology. Even so, this passage is so rich and it is extremely useful to assume it does represent Thales' position (an assumption that is not implausible and cannot be disproven), for doing so will help account for, and give shape to, the subsequent philosophical developments of the sixth century. For these reasons, and fully cognizant of the grain of salt with which it must be taken, we will treat the passage above as if it accurately reflected Thales' views.

There are several critical terms in the passage that will appear repeatedly throughout the Presocratic period, and will establish a general conceptual framework or worldview, which will be called "The Milesian Picture."

1) The phrase "philosophize" translates the Greek *philosophein*, which literally means "to love [*philein*] wisdom [*Sophia*]."

2) "First principle" translates the Greek *archê*, but it could also be rendered as "origin," "source," "beginning," and, significantly, "ruler." The *archê* is thus the origin that persists and continues to exert authority.

3) "Beings" translates *ta onta*, which derives from the verb "to be" (*einai*). The tree, rock, door, wall, rabbit, and bird are all "beings." Together they constitute the world. "Things" can also be used to translate *ta onta*.

4) "Beings" are all the particular items in the world that "come into being." This verb translates *gignesthai*, "to become." After "beings" come into being, they change; they become different. And then they perish; they cease to be. This entire sequence of activities can be encapsulated by the single word "Becoming."

5) Like *ta onta*, *ousia* is also derived from *einai*, "to be." It is a noun that in ordinary usage means "that which is one's own, one's substance or property," but for the philosophers it comes to signify "Being" understood as what is most real and enduring.[4] Why it is useful to capitalize "Being" in order to contrast it with "beings" will be explained shortly. Note that the Greek *to on*, which is the singular version of *ta onta*, can be used synonymously with *ousia*. Our word "ontology," which means "the study of Being in general," has its roots in *logos* and *to on*.

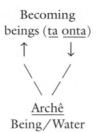

Becoming
beings (ta onta)

Archê
Being/Water

Figure 1.1   Thales

6)   "Nature" translates *phusis*, the origin of our words "physics" and "physical." In the passage above, it comes close to being a synonym of "Being."

Why Thales' *logos* was so extraordinarily influential, and why its departure from the prevailing worldview of the past centuries (from *muthos*) is genuinely revolutionary, can be explained by using these terms and by referring to figure 1.1, a diagram of "the Milesian Picture."

Thales (and other Milesian philosophers) believed that there was an *archê*, a first principle that is the origin of, and so is responsible for, all beings. It itself persists: it does not come into being nor does it cease to be. It is not itself a being nor does it participate in Becoming. Instead, it is that which is most real and enduring: it is Being or Nature. It is the unifying principle of all reality.

The things of this world come into being, and then pass out of being. They are finite. Everything that comes into being eventually passes out of being. My pet rabbit, for example, was born, came into being, in 1996 and went out of being in 2001. Everything that comes into being changes while it is in being. My rabbit began life as a bunny and after a while became a mature adult. By contrast, the *archê* neither changes nor does it come into being and perish. It always just IS.

Thales drew a distinction between Being and beings, between the one enduring principle that is most real, and all the many little beings in the world that are here today and gone tomorrow. Despite these differences, Being and beings are inextricably related, precisely because the former is the *archê*, and thus the origin of the latter. To reformulate this point: Thales was an ontological dualist who divided reality into two categories, Being and Becoming. Again, the former is the origin of, and so more real than, the latter.

At this stage "the Milesian Picture," the general worldview with which philosophy began in the west, may seem similar to Hesiod's *muthos*. After all, in his poem Hesiod also identified what is first or at the beginning, namely *Chaos*, and this functions as a kind of *archê*. There are, however, radical differences between the philosopher's beginning and the poet's.

Thales' *archê* is an ordinary, observable substance: water. Unlike the abyss it is determinate and so it can be recognized. It is intelligible and can be understood. Furthermore, Thales (at least as presented by Aristotle) arrived at his conception of the *archê* (his "archaeology") through a thoroughly rational process. Without a Muse to assist him, he observed that all living beings need water, that the ocean on whose shore he lived seemed to stretch forever and that the earth seemed like a flat disk floating on its surface. He noticed that through the processes of evaporation and condensation water underwent various transformations. When it boils, it becomes more like air; when it cools, it returns to liquid form. During all these changes, however, it always remains what it is, namely water. (See KRS 1983, pp. 89–95 for a good discussion.)

These observable characteristics of water provided evidence that water is the basic and unifying element of all reality. In general, the Ancient Greeks conceived of the material world as composed of four basic elements – earth, air, fire, and water – and perhaps Thales thought that through evaporation and condensation each of the other three elements somehow came from water. This, plus its power to sustain life on earth and in the sea, and its apparently permanent supply, makes water an attractive and empirically plausible candidate for the *archê*.

At first blush, Thales' identification of water may well seem primitive to our sophisticated eyes. After all, we know that water itself is composed of hydrogen and oxygen, and so cannot possibly be the first principle. Nonetheless, Thales' rational articulation and empirical defense of his conception of the *archê* is such a stunning break with Hesiodic *muthos* that the year 585 is as significant as any other in the history of western culture. For the first time human beings attempted to penetrate reality with reason alone. No longer was a Muse needed to supply inspiration. No longer was the heart of reality indeterminate and mad Eros its driving force. Instead, human reason, unaided by external (and unreliable) assistance, could work hard and figure out what the *archê*, the grounding principle of all things, is, and then take responsibility for giving good reasons why it should be so. Philosophy has begun.

Two points need to be made before moving forward. First, in this early period there was no distinction between what we call "philosophy" and "natural science." Second, the Milesian Picture betrays a fundamental conviction (which to some might seem a prejudice): that which is permanent and changeless, namely the *archê*, is ontologically superior to that which is temporary and changeable. Being is prior, is "more real," and in some significant sense, better than Becoming, than those beings which come into being, change, and then perish.

b) The first debate: Anaximander v. Anaximenes

Anaximander
It is possible that Anaximander of Miletus (ca. 610–540) was Thales' student. Such, at least, was the view of the fourth-century philosopher Theophrastus, who described him as "the 'successor and pupil' of Thales" (KRS, p. 101). Even if this assertion cannot be proven, it will be useful nonetheless to think of the relationship between the first two Milesian thinkers in this manner. To be more specific, think of Anaximander as the very best of students, the one who exhibits the qualities every teacher seeks: he was a good and intelligent listener who understood and affirmed much of what his teacher had to say. But he was anything but a passive disciple. Instead, Anaximander was willing to criticize Thales. His doing so pushed western philosophy forward, into its first great debate.

Anaximander, who almost certainly wrote a book, was perhaps the first Greek to construct a map of land and sea. He probably did significant work in meteorology, zoology, and cosmology. But what makes him crucial in the history of philosophy, and what shows him to be just the kind of loyal yet critical student described above, is found in his one remaining fragment:

> Anaximander . . . said that the indefinite [*to apeiron*] was the first principle and element of beings, and he was first to give this name to the first principle. He says that it is neither water nor any other of the so-called elements, but some other nature which is indefinite, out of which come to be all the heavens and the worlds in them. It is that from which beings come to be, and into which they come to perish

Becoming
beings

↑   ↓

\ /

\ /

Archê
Being/The Indefinite

Figure 1.2   Anaximander

according to necessity. For they pay a penalty and reparation to each other for their injustice and according to the order of time. (A9)

Anaximander affirmed the general conceptual structure represented by "the Milesian Picture" he had inherited from Thales, but he also revised it critically. His worldview looks like figure 1.2.

Like his teacher, Anaximander conceived of the many beings constituting the world, those coming into being and passing away, as originating from and returning to a stable and unifying *archê*. Being underlies and organizes becoming. But Anaximander offered a fundamental criticism of Thales as well. The *archê*, he reasoned, cannot be a determinate substance like water. Instead, it is "the indefinite." (The Greek word *apeiron* is composed of *a*, the "alpha privative," which is a negative prefix, and the noun *peras*, "end, limit, boundary.")

Anaximander agreed with Thales that Being, or the *archê*, must be different from beings. His criticism was that water, Thales' candidate, was not different enough. Water is, after all, an ordinary, identifiable substance. But precisely because it is so readily identifiable it is like other things. What is characteristic of beings is their definiteness. A being is a "this" and not a "that." A rabbit is not a bird because it has certain definite features that the bird does not. Because Being differs essentially from beings it must be stripped of all definition. It must be utterly indefinite.

To reach the same conclusion, Anaximander's thought may also have proceeded like this: the *archê* is the source of everything else. It is the "one" underlying the "many." But a definite thing cannot perform such a task. Because it is definite, it is limited. As the word itself suggests, to be de-finite, is to be finite. But the *archê* cannot be finite, for its job is to be the origin of everything. Therefore, Anaximander reasoned, while the Milesian Picture discovered by his teacher was fundamentally sound, Thales was wrong to identify the *arché* with a definite substance. Even though water has qualities making it attractive as a candidate for the first principle – it is in every living thing, the earth is surrounded by it, and it goes through the transformations of evaporation and condensation – it is still too limited. Water does not seem, for example, to be present in fire. As fluid as it is, it is still too determinate, too chunky, to be responsible for and somehow present in everything. The Milesians agree that the first principle is material, but according to Anaximander it must also be indeterminate. (This is, at least, Aristotle's rendition of Anaximander's argument. See *Physics* 204b22–30.)

One last version of Anaximander's criticism of Thales: the *arché* is Being. It endures, neither coming to be nor passing away, even as all things change. But, the argument goes, it stands to reason that all definite things, because they are finite, do come into being and pass away. Therefore, no determinate substance, no thing, can be permanent or qualify as the *arché*.

We can now see that at the very beginning of western philosophy there was a conflict between two competing conceptions of how human thought understands reality, between what came to be known as "empiricism" and "rationalism." If Thales was an empiricist, someone who thinks that human knowledge comes from observations made by the senses, then Anaximander was a rationalist. For him, the *arché* could not be observed. What we see with our eyes is limited and definite. The "indefinite," by contrast, cannot be seen, touched, heard, etc. It can only be thought. For Anaximander reason, unaided by the senses, could penetrate to the heart of reality.

The last chunk of Anaximander's fragment is strange, and so is worth repeating: "[The indefinite] is that from which beings come to be, and into which they come to perish according to necessity. For they pay a penalty and reparation to each other for their injustice and according to the order of time." The terms "penalty," "reparation," and "injustice" seem to jump out of nowhere. What do they mean in the context of Milesian ontology? The key lies in the notion of negation.

Imagine a piece of wood that is placed into a roaring fire. After a few minutes it is consumed by the flames, and becomes ash. When this happens the wood ceases to be. Coming to be ash requires the negation of being wood. When the bunny becomes a mature rabbit, the bunny is no more. Anaximander conceives of the process of Becoming as necessitating such negations, and he expresses this in terms of "injustice" and "retribution." The ash must be punished for having negated the wood. It must eventually pay the same penalty. When the wind blows, the ash will scatter and end up in the ocean. The ash, like the wood whose negation gave rise to it, will meet the same fate. Eventually, it too must be negated.

To put the point generally, Becoming is a strictly temporal affair. No being, no thing, is permanent, for it will eventually cease to be. Such, says Anaximander, is the "order of time." In other words, time itself is nothing but a sequence of negations. Every moment or "now" will, upon arriving, become not-now. Time continuously flows from the future, through the present, into the past. The flow never ceases; the negations never stop. Time is the relentless negator, and everything temporal is victim to its cruel logic. If something comes to be it commits an "injustice": it negates. And then it must face equivalent retribution.

Only the first principle, which can be conceived of as purely positive, is immune from this relentless stream of negations. It is one, unlimited, impervious to the ravages of time.

Anaximenes

Diogenes Laertius, an ancient historian writing in the third century CE, reported that "Anaximenes son of Eurystratus, of Miletus, was a pupil of Anaximander" (KRS 1983, p. 143). This cannot be proven, but once again it will be useful to think it to be the case. Imagine that Anaximenes studied with Anaximander because, like others of his generation, he was inspired by the radically new forms of rational investigation that were being practiced in Miletus. At first, he was deeply impressed by Anaximander's criticism of Thales. He recognized the power of his teacher's argument: if there is to be a first principle, then there must be an essential difference between it (Being) and all the many beings for which it is responsible. Since every thing (including water) is definite, the first principle must be "the indefinite."

The logic seemed impeccable. Soon, however, a problem surfaced: the "indefinite," precisely because it is not a thing, is unintelligible. To think is to think something, and not no-thing. Anaximenes had a disturbing realization: Anaximander's *archê* was uncomfortably close to Hesiod's *Chaos*, his "gap," his "nothingness." His teacher thus ran the risk of betraying the fundamental philosophical commitment to the intelligibility of Being, and so had to be criticized. (For a different view of Anaximander, and a comprehensive interpretation, see Kahn 1960.)

Anaximenes' solution was simple: "air," he asserted, "is the *archê* of beings" (B2). Air is a determinate, empirically observable substance, and so in this sense Anaximenes returned to Thales' essential intuition. But air is far less determinate than water, and so with it Anaximenes could preserve some of the force of Anaximander's critique. Air, unlike water, is boundless but not indeterminate. While water cannot be present in fire, air can run through earth, water, and fire. It can go anywhere. It is invisible and as such is the least determinate of the determinate substances.

The first great debate in western philosophy has begun. Is Being definite and thing-like, as Thales and Axaximenes proposed? Or is it indefinite, as Anaximander insisted? There are advantages to both positions. Anaximander has on his side the force of reason. His *logos* was driven by a purely rational argument that looks something like this:

If X is definite thing, then X is finite.
If X is finite, then X comes into being and passes away.
The first principle neither comes into being nor passes away.
Therefore, the first principle is indefinite.

As powerful as such pure reasoning is, it culminates in a conclusion that cannot be empirically verified and so rests on the shaky foundation of logic alone. By contrast, Anaximenes insisted that Thales was headed in the right direction. The first principle must be a definite, observable substance. Because it is the most indefinite of the definites, air is the best candidate.

c) Sixth-century rationalism: Xenophanes and Pythagoras

Before moving forward to the fifth century, when powerful objections were raised against the Milesian Picture, two additional thinkers need to be briefly discussed. Both are best construed as rationalists who reason in a spirit similar to that of Anaximander.

Xenophanes
Like the Milesians, Xenophanes (ca. 570–475) was an Ionian. He came from Colophon, a city north of Miletus. Apparently he wandered

around quite a bit, and perhaps he ended up in Elea, a city on the far western side of the Greek world, which later became the home of the great philosopher Parmenides.

A single insight animates Xenophanes' thought: Being must be essentially different from the beings of which it is the origin. Xenophanes develops this thought in theological terms. He begins with a critique of standard Greek polytheism, the religious view held by the poets Homer and Hesiod. It is, he argues, absurdly anthropomorphic.

> Homer and Hesiod have attributed to the gods everything that among human beings is shameful and blameworthy: stealing, adultery, and deceiving each another. (B11)

> Ethiopians say that their gods are flat-nosed and dark, Thracians that theirs are blue-eyed and red-haired. (B16)

> If oxen and horses and lions had hands, or could draw with their hands and do the things men do, horses would draw figures of the gods that look like horses, and oxen would draw figures of the gods that look like oxen. (B15)

Xenophanes' point is that human beings project an image of themselves onto what they call the divine. As a consequence, the Greek gods are no more than inflated versions of ourselves. As depicted by Homer, for example, Zeus falls in love, gets angry with his wife, and desires revenge. Such projections, however, tell us nothing about the divine itself. Instead, they only disclose information about those who do the projecting. If the gods are conceived as being dark, then the human beings who made them up are probably dark. If the gods have blue eyes, then rest assured that fair Thracians did the telling. To emphasize how absurd this sort of anthropomorphism is, and how little it tells us about the actual nature of the divine, Xenophanes says that if horses were able to draw a picture of the divine, it would look like horses. In other words, religious people are narcissists who see an image of themselves wherever they look.

From this scathing critique of polytheism comes Xenophanes' own teaching:

> One god, greatest among gods and human beings, not like mortals in body and thought. (B23)

> All of him sees, all of him thinks, all of him hears. (B24)

But without labor he shakes all things by the thought of his mind. (B25)

Always in the same place [god] remains moving not at all. Nor is it fitting [for god] to go here and there at different times. (B26)

God is the *archê* and "shakes all things." God is essentially different from everything else. God is "one" while all "mortals," indeed all things, are many, i.e., are composed of more than one part. A human being has eyes, ears, etc. God, however, does not. When God sees, "all of him sees." By contrast, when a human being or an animal sees, only a part does the seeing. Indeed, everything we do – seeing, hearing, thinking – is complex and thus requires motion over time. When we think, we think a series of thoughts. When we walk, it is a step at a time. All "mortal" beings as well as the activities they perform can be divided into parts.

Xenophanes' God somehow moves ("shakes") everything else, while "moving not at all." What exactly this means is unclear. Nonetheless, of this we can once again be sure: God is fundamentally unlike mortals. In order to move something else, a mortal thing must itself move. My hand moves the book by itself moving over the desk. By radical contrast God is, to use a phrase Aristotle will later make famous, an "unmoved mover."

Xenophanes' theology can be represented as a version of the Milesian Picture (figure 1.3).

Because God is essentially different from the mortal beings that it "shakes," because God has an ontological unity unavailable to any empirical entity, it is knowable only by an act of thought. For this reason, there is an affinity between Xenophanes' God, his version of the *archê*, and Anaximander's "indefinite." Both are accessed through a form of reasoning whose conclusion must be formulated negatively.

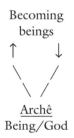

Figure 1.3 Xenophanes

Just as the "indefinite" is precisely what all things are not, so too is Xenophanes' God "not at all like mortals in body or thought."

(For an alternative interpretation of Xenophanes, which argues that God is not some one original Being, but instead "is identical with the world," see KRS 1983, p. 172.)

Pythagoras

Pythagoras was born in approximately 570 in Samos, which is near Miletus in the easten Aegean. He moved to Croton, a city located in what is now southern Italy, where he "founded a community that was philosophical, religious, and political" (Cohen, Curd, & Reeve 2000 [hereafter "Cohen"], p. 15).[5]

"The Pythagorean Theorem" is still taught today, but there is no evidence that Pythagoras himself discovered it. In fact, no writings whatsoever can be attributed to him. All of his work is shrouded in mystery, for his community of disciples was probably cultic in nature and its members sworn to secrecy. (See Burkert 1972 for a thorough discussion.) What we today call "Pythagoreanism" is based on a series of fragments collected over a long period of time and apparently written by Pythagoras' followers. Three in particular express the central insight most relevant to the history of Greek philosophy. The first two come from Aristotle, the third from Philolaus (born ca. 470), the earliest Pythagorean whose work survives.

> They [the Pythagoreans] supposed the elements of numbers to be the elements of all existing things. (Cohen, p. 19)

> The elements of number are the even and the odd, and of these the latter is limited and the former unlimited The One is composed of both of these (for it is both even and odd) and number springs from the One; and numbers, as I have said, constitute the whole universe. (Cohen, p. 18)

> And indeed all things that are known have number. For without this nothing whatever could possibly be thought of or known. (Cohen, p. 20)

Simply put, the Pythagoreans believed that number constituted the intelligible structure of all reality. To borrow a metaphor used much later in western history, they held that "the book of nature" was written in the characters of mathematics. What makes "all existing things" into what they are, and what makes them knowable, is their arithmetic structure.

One of the best examples of this, and according to legend the first discovery made by Pythagoras, comes from music. The difference between mere noise and the harmonious sound produced by a lyre (the ancestor of the guitar) can be explained in terms of the numerical ratios of the musical scale. The beauty of music, which seems to be strictly a sensory phenomenon, can in fact be explicated mathematically. Under or behind music, then, lie ratios. This, for the Pythagoreans, is the great clue to reality itself. The order and harmony of the sensible world is grounded on the purely intelligible world of numbers.

Why the Pythagoreans might well have been a religious cult should now be clear. For them, the sensible things we touch and see and hear are but a superficial and temporary manifestation of a much deeper and enduring "spiritual" reality. The individual lyre playing this piece of music, and the flute playing that one, and the boy over there whistling, are all but instances of an intelligible arithmetic structure that itself can not be heard. Invisible, changeless, and utterly pure, numbers are more real than lyres, flutes and boys. In this sense, they are "spiritual," and as such they can be virtually worshipped.

The Greek word for number is *arithmos*, the root of "arithmetic." While it is properly translated as "number" it also means "count." This nuance reveals an important difference between the Greek conception of number and our own. For the Greeks, *arithmos* implies plurality. A number is a number of things because when we count we count more than one thing. If there is a single book on my desk, nobody would ask, "how many things are on your desk?" Instead, the question would be, "what's that on your desk?" Only when there are two or more books would the question arise, "how many?"

To count requires the identification of a unit to serve as the basis of the count. So, if there are several books on my desk, as well as several pencils, and you ask, "how many?", I would respond, "how many what?" "How many books?" you say. Now I can count, for the unit has been established. When the count is not of sensible objects, when I simply count 4–5–6 or add 7 and 5, the unit being used is pure and not the least bit sensible. It is impossible to touch, see or smell the number 3. Instead, it is strictly intelligible, thoroughly immaterial, entity.

The above implies that, quite unlike our own version of arithmetic, two is the first number. *Arithmos* is a count, and thus requires units to be counted. One is not itself an *arithmos* but is instead the "unit itself" and as such, as Aristotle puts it, is the "source (*archê*) of number" (*Metaphysics*, 1021a10). The One makes *arithmos* possible and in this sense "number springs from the One." This accounts for what, to a modern thinker, seems so strange in the second quotation above: the One is "both even and odd." All numbers, according to the Pythagoreans, were either even or odd. Since the One is the origin of and so participates in all numbers it must be both. As a result, it cannot itself be a number.

Because they conceived of *arithmos* strictly as whole positive integers beginning with two, the Pythagoreans would have obvious difficulty explaining (among other things) what today we call an "irrational number," say the square root of 2. This cannot be expressed as a ratio between whole numbers. Legend has it that the Pythagoreans themselves discovered irrational numbers, and when they did the discovery was so disruptive of the cult that they swore their members never to divulge it.

While it is significantly different from other versions of the Milesian Picture, Pythagoreanism nonetheless can be represented by using its basic terms (figure 1.4). Like Xenophanes' God and Anaximander's unlimited, the Pythagorean One is fundamentally different from all those things for which it is responsible. "All things that are known have number," but the One itself is not an *arithmos*. It is, to quote Aristotle again, the *archê* of all things arithmetical.

d) The crisis of sixth-century philosophy

The Milesian Picture dominated sixth-century thought and gave rise to all subsequent developments in western philosophy. It represents

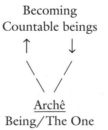

Figure 1.4 Pythagoras

a powerful yearning for intellectual order, for it demands that the multiplicity, variety, and tumultuous change of the sensible world be derived from a single source, which itself can be discovered and then articulated through the hard work of human reason. *Logos*, the Milesians boast, can do it alone. Unlike Hesiod's *muthos* no Muse is required. The human intellect, whether it operates on the basis of empirical observations (Thales, Anaximenes) or brilliant strokes of abstract theorizing (Anaximander, Xenophanes, Pythagoras) is a mighty tool and can penetrate, on its own, the heart of Being. Indeed, this lust for a theory of Being may well be the best way to characterize sixth-century thinking in general. It is also the source of its greatest problem: ontological dualism, the division of reality into two distinct categories.

Each of the thinkers discussed so far relies on a basic distinction between Being and beings, between what always IS and what is Becoming. Because Being is stable and enduring, while beings are constantly in flux, the dilemma repeatedly facing the Milesians is how to reconnect the two. For the empiricists, Thales and Anaximenes, the question becomes, how do water or air actually become the other elements? For Xenophanes, the problem is, how can a motionless God "shake" all things without itself moving? How can a single, utterly unified Being interact with the multiplicity of beings without losing its self-identity? The question haunting Anaximander is similar: if all things are definite, then how can they derive from a first principle said to be indefinite? To put the question in metaphorical terms, how can the first principle, upon making contact with the things for which it is responsible, avoid becoming polluted by them? The *archê* is, after all, meant to be that which is impervious to all change.

The crisis embedded in the Milesian Picture, then, is that after having succeeded brilliantly in distinguishing the ontological categories of Being and Becoming, it is not clear how philosophers can possibly bring them back together again.

Heraclitus and Parmenides: Extreme Solutions

a) Heraclitus: lover of flux

Before beginning this section, two warnings: first, the interpretation of Heraclitus to follow will be controversial. To some extent, it is influenced by Plato's critique of Heraclitus as found in the dialogue *Theaetetus*, and as Kirk points out, Plato "may not have known as many of the actual sayings of Heraclitus as even we do" (Kirk 1954, p. 82). As will be explained shortly, it is also inspired by Nietzsche's commentary on the Presocratics in his early work *Philosophy in the Tragic Age of the Greeks*, a book which is hardly objective and clearly reflects the author's own intensely-held philosophical convictions. It would thus be reasonable for the reader to consult alternative readings of Heraclitus (Kirk 1954 and Kahn 1979 are good places to start, as well as KRS 1983, pp. 181–213. Also, see Hyland 1992, pp. 145–69.)

Second, throughout this section the word "fragments" will be used to describe the various sayings of Heraclitus. This implies that they were part of a larger whole, perhaps an entire book. It is possible, however, that Heraclitus fully intended his work to be fragmentary. If so, "aphorism," a concise, deliberately crafted statement or maxim, would be more accurate than "fragment" to describe his writings. Given the interpretation to be presented below, it is tempting to use "aphorism" to characterize Heraclitus' writings. Since, however, the exact status of Heraclitus' text cannot be established, this section will use the more conventional "fragment."

Translations below are my own, and as usual will be indicated only by their standard Diels number.[6]

With a single, insanely bold stroke, Heraclitus of Ephesus (who probably did his writing early in the fifth century) resolved the crisis of Milesian philosophy: he eliminated Being. With no Being in the picture, the enormous problem of accounting for the relationship between the things of Becoming and the *archê* vanishes. (See figure 1.5.)

Heraclitus expressed his essential insight imagistically: "Into the same river it is not possible to step twice" (B91). This is not merely

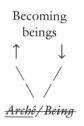

Figure 1.5 Heraclitus

an empirical observation about the continual flow of water molecules. It is an image of what always goes on everywhere. Nothing is stable, nothing endures. Heraclitus is thus an "anarchist," which literally means one who denies the existence of a first and ruling principle, or *archê*.

No one has loved Heraclitus more than the nineteenth-century philosopher Friedrich Nietzsche. His affinity with the "obscure one," as Heraclitus has been called since antiquity (see KRS 1983, p. 183), was so deep that Nietzsche effortlessly imagined himself speaking in Heraclitus' own voice.

> Heraclitus proclaimed: "I see nothing other than becoming. Be not deceived. It is the fault of your myopia, not of the nature of things, if you believe you see land somewhere in the ocean of coming-to-be and passing away. You use names for things as though they rigidly, persistently endured: yet even the stream into which you step a second time is not the one you stepped into before." (Nietzsche 1962, pp. 51–2)

The key to this passage is Nietzsche's notion of the "myopia," the weakness of sight, which is reflected in ordinary language. Language, especially its nouns, misleads, for it suggests the existence of stable entities in the world. The word "rabbit," for example, apparently refers not just to this particular animal right here, but to all rabbits. Like all beings, an individual animal is continually changing and soon will perish, but the noun might seem to promise that the species (or the "form" as Aristotle will later put it) "rabbit" will endure. The unreflective use of ordinary language might, therefore, suggest the sort of ontological dualism intrinsic to the Milesian Picture. One may be tempted to think that a species endures and just IS, even as individual members of that species come-into-being and cease to be. But to believe this is to suffer from myopia. Nothing, neither this rabbit right here nor "rabbit" in general, endures.

The realization that it is impossible to step into the same river twice – which will be called the "flux" doctrine – is potentially awful. If nothing endures, then one may well conclude that nothing has meaning or value or importance at all. As Nietzsche puts it:

> The everlasting and exclusive coming-to-be, the impermanence of everything actual, which constantly acts and comes-to-be but never is, as Heraclitus teaches it, is a terrible, paralyzing thought. Its impact on

men can most nearly be likened to the sensation during an earthquake when one loses one's familiar confidence in a firmly grounded earth. (Nietzsche 1962, p. 54)

Perhaps Heraclitus' elimination of Being is most terrifying on a personal level. If nothing is stable, then neither am "I." In other words, if he is right, then there is no enduring self uniting all the many experiences "I" go through, and so, in the deepest sense, "I" do not exist at all.

In a similar vein, Heraclitus' insight plays havoc with the very possibility of *logos* itself. If ordinary language is deceptive, and nothing is stable, how can there be a rational account of this ever-changing state of affairs? Consider the following sentence: "everything is constantly changing." If it is true, then presumably the meaning of the very words within the quotation marks are changing. But if so, then they do not have a fixed meaning. As a result, the Heraclitean elimination of Being might undermine the basic philosophical project of offering a meaningful, rational articulation of the world.

It is striking, however, that far from abandoning *logos*, Heraclitus seems to affirm it enthusiastically.

This *logos* always is but human beings fail to understand it. (B1)

Thus it is necessary to follow what is common. But even though the *logos* is common, most live as if they had their own private wisdom. (B2)

Listening not to me but to the *logos* it is wise to agree that all is one. (B50)

These fragments sound positively Milesian. But how can there be a unifying *logos* if everything flows and nothing abides? Given Heraclitus' "flux," how in the world could "all be one?"

There is a Heraclitean *logos* – he is a philosopher – but it is very strange and radically different from any belonging to a previous (or subsequent) Greek philosopher. This is because his *logos* embraces contradiction. For example: "The road up and the road down are one and the same" (B60). This translation, like so many, actually adds a bit to the original Greek. A literal version of the fragment would be, "road up down one and the same." The first "and" in the translation does not appear, and there is no verb. (The latter feature is not unusual: Greek often omits inflections of "to be.") Instead, what Heraclitus does is place two words with opposite meanings – "up" and "down" – side by side. In the original fragment, there would not even have been a space between them, just this: roadupdownoneandthesame.

Heraclitus likes to do this. "Changing it rests" (B75) is an example. So too is "into the same rivers we both step and do not step, we are and we are not" (B49). And this: "The same thing living and dead, and awake and asleep, and young and old" (B78). These are contradictions, the attribution of opposite predicates to a subject. In formal terms, a contradiction is expressed as "S is P & not-P," and at least since Aristotle, it has been declared illogical, illegal, and an affront to reason itself. If S can be both P and not-P, then S can also be Q or not-Q, R or not-R. S can be anything at all. If contradictions are allowed, then the possibility of a truth-giving *logos* (the root of "logical") seems to be destroyed. A basic requirement of logical reasoning, and hence of philosophy itself, seems to be that if "S is P" is true, then "S is not-P" must be false.

The logical situation is not quite as simple as suggested above. The "Principle of Noncontradiction" (PNC), the rule prohibiting contradictions as illogical, includes at least two conditions. First, S cannot be P & not-P "in the same way." Sue, for example, may be both intelligent and unintelligent if "intelligent" is used differently in the two instances. Sue may be intelligent when it comes to mathematics, but unintelligent when it comes to poetry. The PNC only prohibits her from being both intelligent and unintelligent "in the same way."

It is also possible, sadly enough, that Sue's mathematical intelligence may decline precipitously when she gets very old. She thus can be intelligent and unintelligent at different times of her life. This indicates the other crucial condition placed on the PNC: S cannot be P and not-P "at the same time."

This second condition is central to understanding Heraclitus' thought. The phrase "at the same time" implies the possibility of a "moment" frozen in time. In other words, the sort of *logos* governed by the PNC is a timeless one. If Bob says "I am sitting at my desk" and he insists that the statement "I am not sitting at my desk" is false, it is because he thinks he is sitting at his desk right now. If Sue says "three is odd and not even" she believes her statement always has been and always will be true. By contrast, for Heraclitus no thing, no statement, and no truth can resist the relentless flow of time. There is no timeless truth; there is no "right now." In this sense, for Heraclitus the PNC is simply irrelevant. For him, a philosophical *logos* must consist of opposites predicated of a single subject, for only they express the true logic of time. "The wise alone is one; it is willing and unwilling to be called by the name Zeus" (B32).

To explain a bit further, recall the perplexing statement made by Anaximander.

> [The indefinite] is that from which beings come to be, and into which they come to perish according to necessity. For they pay a penalty and reparation to each other for their injustice and according to the order of time.

The temporal flow of becoming is a continuous series of negations. The wood, having been thrown into the fire, becomes ash. Coming to be ash requires the negation of being wood. In a metaphorical sense this implies an injustice and as a result the ash must be punished for what it has done. It must also suffer negation. When the wind blows it into the sea, it will become water. To put the point most generally, time itself is nothing but a continuous sequence of negations. Every moment or "now" will, upon arriving, immediately become "then" or "not-now." Time continuously flows from the future into the past, with the present as no more than a gateway, which itself has no magnitude or duration of its own, in-between. The flow never ceases. Time is the relentless negator, and everything temporal is victim to its unforgiving logic.

In good Milesian fashion, Anaximander conceives of the *archê*, which for him was "the indefinite," as timeless. As opposed to the negativity of time and Becoming, Being simply and always is; it is purely positive. Heraclitus, by contrast, is an anarchist: for him, nothing is permanent, nothing is stable, for "Into the same river it is not possible to step twice."

Because it embraces contradictions, Heraclitus' *logos* is inherently at odds with itself, and so it is no wonder that "Timon of Phlius, the third-century B.C. satirist, called [him] *ainiktês*, 'riddler'" (KRS 1983, p. 183). (*Ainigma*, the root of our word "enigma," means "riddle" in Greek.) KRS characterizes this description of him as a "legitimate criticism" (p. 183). But on this they miss the point entirely. The enigma, the riddle, the self-contradiction, is in its own way truth-giving for Heraclitus. For only such a *logos* gives voice to the ceaseless flow of time. Consider the following fragment:

> Human beings are deceived about the knowledge of things that are apparent, like Homer who was wiser than all the Greeks. For children who were killing lice deceived him by saying, "whatever we saw and grasped we have left behind, but whatever we neither saw nor grasped we carry with us." (B56)

Knowledge is like lice. If it is grasped, it is lost. Only if it is missed is it kept. There is a necessary elusiveness in Heraclitus' writing. It is meant to articulate the fluid alterations of temporal beings. It is designed to do justice to the negations of the temporal flow. His *logos*, therefore, must be enigmatic. Were it not, it would be false. Such, at least, seems to be the message implied by the following fragment: "An unapparent harmony than an apparent one is better" (B54). Literally, this fragment would read, "harmony unapparent apparent better." Or consider this one: "Nature loves to hide" (B123).

Heraclitean flux seems to shake the ground under our feet. Nothing endures. Such a thought may well cause despair. If nothing endures, then one might conclude that nothing matters. But Heraclitus' own writings do not suggest a trace of despondency. For example, he says, "One man to me is ten thousand if he is best" (B49). Indeed, the simple fact that Heraclitus wrote at all, and with such graceful and playful ingenuity, suggests a creative mind actively, perhaps happily, at work. The next question is why, given his conception of flux, didn't Heraclitus succumb to despair? Why did he bother to write at all?

Once again, Nietzsche offers a fruitful suggestion: "It takes astonishing strength," he says, to transform this potential for despair "into its opposite, into sublimity and the feeling of blessed astonishment" (1962, p. 54). But what sort of strength does Nietzsche have in mind? How can the thought of flux inspire such positive feelings? The clue lies in the following fragment: "A lifetime [or, eternity] is a child playing . . . the kingdom belongs to a child" (B52).[7] The Greek for "play" is related to "child," and so the fragment itself contains some word-play: "Child playing" translates *pais paizôn*.

The kingdom is in the hands of a child playing. And what characterizes child's play? It is free-flowing and imaginative, spontaneous and, most important, not bound by a strict set of rules or objectives. It thus stands in radical distinction to adult play, which mainly takes the form of clearly defined games. In basketball, for example, the players are not permitted to use their feet to move the ball, and a referee is employed to make sure this rule is enforced. By contrast, when young children play, there is no referee and either there are no rules or the rules keep changing. The child uses her feet, her hands, her nose to move the ball any way she likes. Bound by no predetermined goals, oblivious to the clock, constrained by no demands, child's play aimlessly moves forward. In doing so the *pais paizôn* is an image of Heraclitean flux itself. As Nietzsche puts it, "In this world only play, play as artists and children engage in it, exhibits coming-to-be and passing away, structuring and destroying, without any moral additive, in forever equal innocence" (Nietzsche 1962, p. 62).

The key phrase is "without any moral additive." Children do not play because they should. They play for fun and care not a bit about the health or social benefits of their activities. Their imaginations are constantly at work and are capable of transforming any object – the ball, the shoe, the shoelace – into a plaything.

"The kingdom is in the hands of a child." In other words, the world is unstructured, aimless flow. "The most beautiful cosmos is a heap of sand poured out at random" (B124).

Heraclitus' affirmation of play exerted a powerful influence on Nietzsche, and through him on his many postmodernist descendants (especially Derrida; see 1976, p. 50.) It is a delicious notion suggestive of a fluid, productive, joyful moving forward. Not surprisingly, however, Heraclitus himself seems to contradict it with the following: "War is of all things the father, of all things the king, and some he reveals as gods, others as humans; some he makes slaves, others free" (B53). Again the words are carefully chosen for their sound: *polemos patêr pantôn*, "war father of all things." (Each of the three Greek words are roots of English ones: "polemic," "paternal," and "pan," the prefix meaning "all.")

At first blush, no two activities could seem more dissimilar than child's play and war. The latter is the filthy work of deadly serious men, while the former is the province of happy, bubbling children. On reflection, however, the two share much. To illustrate, consider for a moment the lines on a map demarcating the borders of various countries. Most of these have been established by war. The United States, for example, has a long border with Mexico. This line between the two countries was the result of the Mexican-American War of 1846–8 when the Rio Grande was fixed as the southern boundary of Texas, which in turn became part of the USA.

Look at a map. The lines on it seem to suggest fixed structures. When one says "United States of America" one might well think of the shape formed by the borderlines. But to think this shape is some sort of stable form is to succumb to what Nietzsche called "myopia." These lines are contingent and temporary. They were the result of a battle which could have gone either way. The fact that the USA won this particular war only means that it might lose the next one. If "war is the father of all" then the "all" is in flux, temporary, unstable.

This is the connection between war and play. Both are unpredictable, not bound by a fixed set of rules. Both reveal the power of time. In both there is an element of chaos, of surprise.

Several of Heraclitus' fragments seem to have a similar theme:

Pigs take pleasure in mud more than pure water. (B13)

Mules would choose garbage rather than gold. (B9)

Pigs wash themselves in mud, birds in dust or ash. (B37)

These are not empirical observations made for the purpose of zoological classification. They are, once again, imagistic expressions of a philosophical idea. In this case, the idea is "ethical relativism," the view that the meaning and authority of ethical values are dependent upon the person or group holding those values. In other words, the ethical relativist denies that any value is absolute. "Absolute" comes from the verb "absolve," "set free from." What is "absolute" is absolved of all dependence on anything else. An ethical absolutist believes certain values are binding regardless of who holds them. In opposition, the relativist refuses to grant values this sort of independence.

Heraclitus denies absolutism precisely because he affirms the flux. If nothing is stable, then no value could be stable. Instead, as the fragments cited above are meant to suggest, values are relative to the ones who hold them. A mule thinks rubbish is good; a person thinks gold. Since individuals and groups are always changing, so too are values. In eighteenth-century America, slavery was widely considered to be morally defensible as a social good. In twenty-first century America, it is universally denounced as immoral. For the relativist, slavery is neither good in-itself nor bad in-itself. Instead, it depends. It was good for those living 200 years ago, it is bad today. Values, like all else, change.

Before closing this discussion of Heraclitus, we must look carefully at a series of fragments that could well be used to challenge the basic argument of this section.

> This cosmos, the same for all, not one of the gods nor of human beings made, but it was always and is and will be an ever-living fire being kindled in measures and being extinguished in measures. (B30)

> For fire going forward will decide and compel all things. (B66)

> All things are an exchange for fire and fire for all things, as goods for gold and gold for goods. (B90)

These fragments might seem to support an interpretation of Heraclitus as a Milesian thinker in the tradition of Thales and Anaximenes. On this reading, far from being an anarchist, he identifies the *arché* with one of the four standard elements, namely fire. There is, he might seem to be saying, an orderly "exchange" between fire, construed as the primal element of the world, and everything else. If this were the case, then fire would indeed play the role of Being. This is certainly the way Kirk and Kahn read the fragments, and the case they make is not implausible. Nonetheless, these "fire fragments" must be balanced with one already cited: "The most beautiful cosmos is a heap of sand poured out at random." In other words, there is no orderly exchange, no structure to reality, only anarchy. In fact, the very nature of fire itself may suggest why.

Of the four elements, fire is the least likely candidate for the *arché*, which, after all, is required to be stable, enduring, the intelligible source of all the many beings in the realm of becoming. But fire is uniquely ill-suited to perform this task. This is because it is inherently and visibly in motion. And its motion, as every fire-watcher knows, is unpredictable. A fire dances. It plays. This is why it is so visually alluring and speaks so forcefully to the pyromaniac within.

Furthermore, there is an inherent contradiction lying at the heart of fire. While it is life-giving and, as the myth of Prometheus has it, the source of civilization itself, it is also terribly dangerous. It cooks our food and burns down our homes. It is both creative and destructive. Or, as Heraclitus puts it, "Fire is need and fullness" (B65). The dance of the flames becomes the roar of the inferno. For this reason, and not because it is suitable as a traditional Milesian *archê*, Heraclitus puts such emphasis on fire. In other words, just as he invokes the river, the child playing, and war, fire is an image of the ever-moving flux, of the astonishingly anarchic movement of all things.

b) Parmenides: champion of being

Even though he agreed with Heraclitus that the Milesian Picture was fatally flawed and so had to be thoroughly revised, Parmenides (born around 515) despised his enigmatic colleague. Utterly opposed to Heraclitus, he was the consummate rationalist, the purely logical man for whom the Principle of Noncontradiction was absolutely binding.

(*Warning*: as KRS 1983, pp. 182 and 244, notes, there is only a hint in Parmenides' writings to suggest that he may actually have known, or been responding to, Heraclitus at all. The opening statement of this section is thus quite possibly exaggerated. Nonetheless, it is a useful way to organize the material at this stage of the story.)

Parmenides' critique of the Milesian Picture looks like figure 1.6. With an extremism every bit as intense as Heraclitus', Parmenides eliminated the ontological category of Becoming and all the many beings that come-into-being, continually go through changes, and then pass away. As opposed to the dualism characteristic of the Milesians, Parmenides, who came from the other side of the Greek world (Elea, in present day Italy) was an ontological monist. For him, Being was one, indivisible, changeless, and eternal.

Even if Heraclitus' anarchy is difficult to swallow, Parmenides' elimination of Becoming may prove even more so. After all, what could be more obvious in all of human experience than the fact of

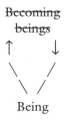

Figure 1.6 Parmenides

flux and change, of motion and generation? We open our eyes and we immediately seem to be looking at many things moving around. Who in his right mind could deny this?

Parmenides' position is, as we shall see, deeply "paradoxical." This word comes from the Greek *para*, "to the side of" or "contrary to," and *doxa*, often translated as "opinion," but better conceived more broadly as "what seems to be the case." Most generally, *doxa*, an altogether crucial word in the history of western philosophy, means "the appearances." At times, especially in Aristotle, it can come close to meaning something like "commonsense" or "what people commonly say." Parmenides' ontological monism is paradoxical because nothing seems to manifest itself or appear as clearly as Becoming. What sort of reasoning led him to make his extraordinary denial?

The first step of Parmenides' argument is found in the following fragment. (Parmenides, by the way, wrote in the form of poem in which a Goddess was addressing him. Despite this, he was in no way a practitioner of *muthos* as, say, Hesiod or Homer were. His is a thoroughly, indeed obsessively, rational *logos*. See Lombardo 1982, pp. 1–9, for a quite different interpretation.)

> Come now, I will tell you, and having heard my story, you must carry it away with you, these are the only paths of inquiry to be thought: the one, that it is and that it is not possible for it not to be, is the way of Persuasion (for it accompanies Truth); the other, that it is not and that it is necessary for it not to be, this I say to you is a path completely unlearnable, for you can neither know that which is not (for it cannot be done) nor can you say it. (Fr. 2)[8]

The first step of the argument concerns "nonbeing." This English phrase, which will be used consistently in this section, will cover several Greek phrases, including "it is not" and "that which is not." (It is important not to be misled by these verbal phrases. Greek verbs are "synthetic": they have their subject built into them and so do not require a separate pronoun. Thus, the one word *estin*, with no subject specified, can indeed be translated as "it is." No "it," however, is actually used. The phrase *to mê eon* is formed from a participle derived from *einai*, "to be." *Eon* is just a slight variation in spelling of the word *on*, which is the root of "ontology.")

As paradoxical as Parmenides' thought may ultimately be, his initial step is quite straightforward: nonbeing, he explains, is unthinkable.

To discover what this means, simply try to prove him wrong: try to think nonbeing. No matter how hard you concentrate, it is impossible to summon "nonbeing." To make this point more clear, substitute the word "nothing" for "nonbeing." (Even if "nothing" is somewhat misleading as a way of translating *to mê eon*, it is nonetheless helpful as a way of appreciating the fundamental dynamic of Parmenides' argument.) Note again what happens: it is impossible to think nothing. To think, in other words, is to think something. Or, as Parmenides puts it, "The same thing is for thinking and being" (Fr. 3). He makes much the same point in more concrete terms in the following fragment: "But gaze upon things which although absent in the mind are securely present" (Fr. 4).

Think about your friend Sue. She's not in the room with you right now. But when you think of her, perhaps by summoning a clear visual image from your memory, you do not, because you cannot, think her as absent, but only as present. She is, to use the familiar metaphor, "in your head." Or reflect upon your own childhood. It is past. But you cannot think it as past, because when you bring your childhood to mind you bring it into the present. This is why we so commonly say "time flies," and why Parmenides' argument has such power. Upon thinking the past the gap between it and the present is obliterated. As a result, the passage of time, and so Becoming itself, may well seem to have no substance at all.

The Greek for "things absent" is *apeonta*, formed by the prefix *apo* – "away from, off" – and *eonta*, which like *eon* is a participial form of *einai*, "to be." "Present" translates *pareonta*, literally "being right here at hand." (Note that both English words have "ent" in them, which derives from the Latin *esse*, to be. *Abesse* means "to be away from," while *praeesse* is "to be present.") To put the point most generally, thinking for Parmenides is presencing. An absent object, like Sue or your childhood, can be thought of only as present. For this reason, nonbeing, or being-absent, is unthinkable.

However unexpected, this first step of the argument may seem plausible. But the second step, which follows directly from the first, will generate a conclusion even more difficult to swallow.

What is said and what is thought must be. For it is possible for it to be, but not possible for nothing to be. I ask you to consider this. For I bar you from this first path of inquiry, but next from the path on which mortals, knowing nothing, two-headed, wander. For helplessness in their breasts steers their wandering mind. But they are carried on equally deaf and blind, muddled, undiscerning swarms, for whom both to be and not to be are judged the same and not the same, and the way of all is backward-turning. (Fr. 6)

Some scholars "see a particular reference to Heraclitus" (Wright 1985, p. 81) in the statement, "for whom both to be and not to be are judged the same and not the same," and so he may well be the "two-headed" know-nothing Parmenides scorns. In any case, from this passage the basic logical critique Parmenides brings to bear against Becoming can be extracted.

Becoming is an ontological category. It is a concept, and a complex one, for contained within it are the additional concepts of both being and nonbeing. The most obvious sense of Becoming is coming-into-being and then ceasing-to-be. But both of these concepts are themselves complex and they too require nonbeing. Before something comes-into-being it must not have been, and when it ceases-to-be it, to put the point awkwardly, goes-into-nonbeing. As the first step of the argument dictated, however, nonbeing is an impossible concept: it cannot be thought. Therefore, since it is implicit in the concept of Becoming, the latter cannot be thought either. Upon analysis, Becoming is revealed as conceptually impossible.

To illustrate this argument by means of an image, think of nonbeing as a deadly computer virus that destroys any hard-drive it enters. Nonbeing is infectious. If it enters into any concept, it destroys it. It enters into Becoming, and so Becoming is annihilated.

One last way to put this point: the concept of Becoming is self-contradictory. As Parmenides puts it, "both to be and not to be are judged the same and not the same" by those who, like Heraclitus, would affirm Becoming. This is because Becoming requires and implies a temporal process, and time itself is a self-contradictory. A "moment" in time is what we call the present. But time's moment has no duration for it is nothing but the gateway between the past and the future, both of which are not here now, i.e., are absent. The moment, therefore, is both present and absent, both now and not-now. It is precisely this sort of contradiction, which is the very life-blood of the enigmatic Heraclitean *logos*, that Parmenides condemns as an affront to reason itself. As a consequence, he is obligated by the force of his own reasoning to sacrifice Becoming. Indeed, Parmenides is above all else a strict rationalist. More specifically, he is a conceptual analyst.

He dissects ideas and only if they are free from the nonbeing virus and pass the test of a logic governed by the PNC are they allowed to stand. Because of his commitment to this conception of rationality, he rejects the testimony of *doxa*. Consider the following:

> For in no way may this prevail, that the things which are not, are. But you, bar your thought from this way of inquiry, and do not let the habit that comes from much experience force you along this path and direct your sightless eye and your ringing ear and your tongue, but decide by reason [*logos*]. (Fr. 7)

Recall that Thales was described above as an "empiricist." He seemed to draw his conclusions about the world on the basis of observation. He saw that water was found in all living things, was seemingly inexhaustible, and that the earth seemed to float on it, and concluded that water must be the *archê*. The root of "empirical" is the Greek *empeiria*, which is related to *polupeiron*, translated above as "much experience." Unlike Thales, Parmenides dismisses all who would claim to learn anything true on the basis of their experience of the sensible world. The eye, far from providing information, is "sightless," and so the worst "habit" one could fall into would be to accept what one sees as actual knowledge. Instead, a thinker must rely solely on pure reasoning, on what Parmenides here calls *logos*, to arrive at the truth.

(This is an excellent example of just how flexible the Greek word *logos* is. Both Heraclitus and Parmenides claim to champion it, but what it means is radically different for each thinker. Indeed, what a philosopher means by *logos* goes a long way toward characterizing him in general.)

To put the same point in slightly different terms, for Parmenides there is a radical disjunction between *doxa* and Truth. As he puts it, "You must learn all things – both the unshaken heart of well-rounded Truth [*alêtheia*] and the opinions [*doxas*] of mortals in which there is no true conviction" (Fr. 1).

There is, for Parmenides, only one coherent line of thought: Being is. In the longest remaining fragment of his writings (Fr. 8), Parmenides, by means of the most careful argumentation, attributes four characteristics to Being.

1) First and foremost, "Because it is ungenerated it is also imperishable" (8.3). Being cannot come-to-be. If it did, it would have to

come-to-be from something other than Being. It would have to come-to-be from nonbeing. Nonbeing, however, is not, so nothing could possibly come from it. Therefore, Being is "ungenerated." Or as Parmenides puts it, "I will not allow you to say or to think that it came from nonbeing, for that nonbeing is can neither be said nor thought" (8.7–9).

In a similar vein, Being cannot cease-to-be. If it did, it would have to "go into" nonbeing, and this it cannot do. Therefore, Being is imperishable. More generally, from this line of argument "coming to be has ceased to be and destruction is unheard of" (8.20–21).

2) Being has no future: "How could what is be in the future?" (8.18). In other words, Being is only in the present tense. The phrase "it will be" implies that it is not now, and Being is now. In a parallel vein, the phrase "it was back then" implies that it is not now. Being has no past. As Parmenides puts it, "Nor was it ever nor will it be, since it is now" (8.5). In short, Being is pure presence. To reformulate using a term of enormous significance in the history of western culture, Being is "eternal." It is important to be clear what this word means. The eternal is not the same as the immortal. Greek gods, for example, were conceived as being immortal. They were born, but they did not die. They existed just as we do, in the passage of time – they had a past and could anticipate the future – but for them time never ran out. By contrast, time does not pass in the eternal. Instead, it is presence without past or future. The immortal is the endless, the eternal is the timeless. (Of the philosophers we have studied so far, Xenophanes' God, which moves without being moved, comes closest to the eternality of Parmenidean Being. It is not surprising, therefore, that Parmenides was reputed to have been a student of his [KRS 1983, p. 240]).

3) As (2) clearly implies, Being is "unchanging" (8.26) and "remains the same in the same and by itself" (8.29).

4) Being is "all together, one, continuous" (8.5–6). "Nor is it divided, since it all is alike" (8.22). In other words, Being is indivisible. Parmenides' reasoning here is that division implies difference, and that difference implies the impossible concept, the deadly virus, of nonbeing. To illustrate imagine Being is a circle (figure 1.7):

Figure 1.7

Now, imagine that Being were divided into four parts (figure 1.8):

Figure 1.8

This apparently simple maneuver generates a big problem: what makes one quadrant of the circle different from another? Presumably, the top right is not the same as the bottom left. As such, it must not be the bottom left. But the entire circle is meant to symbolize Being. Therefore, if the top right is not the bottom left, then it is not Being. Nonbeing, however, is impossible. Hence, Being cannot be divided.

To make the same point, consider what the lines on the diagram might represent. Their function is to divide one quadrant from another. They themselves, however, are not part of any of the four quadrants. Hence, they must be nonbeing.

The basic point is that division implies difference, and difference – being able to say "this is not that" – requires negation. Because Being cannot be negated, it cannot be divided. It is one, continuous, and indivisible.

Parmenidean Being is accessible only to pure thinking, to *logos* understood in this sense of the word. By contrast, Becoming is the essential ingredient of *doxa*. It is important to emphasize that Parmenides would not disagree with this statement. Indeed, it is possible that in the second half of his poem he articulates the very structure of *doxa* as a self-contradictory movement between opposites (e.g., "all things have been named light and night" [Fr. 9]). No one could deny that human beings typically are aware of a multiplicity of being in constant change. What Parmenides does deny is that this ordinary empirical awareness contributes anything to our understanding of the Truth.

Because of this radical distinction between *doxa* and Truth, Parmenides is the first thinker in the west to don "the philosopher's hat." What this means is that he is the first to separate his work as a conceptual analyst from the ordinary living of his life. When Parmenides says, Being is "now, all together one, continuous," he is speaking strictly as a philosopher. So, if you were standing on the railroad tracks, and a train were approaching, he would not advise you to stay there. If you argued that because Being is one the train could not possibly break you into lots of little parts, you would be making a big mistake. *Doxa* has its own kind of validity. Our experience is, of course, always based on the assumption of change, multiplicity, and Becoming. So, as an ordinary person, you would be well advised to get off the tracks. But donning the philosopher's hat, one is compelled by the demands of strict logical analysis to admit that Becoming is an impossible concept.

Perhaps because of the purity of his conception of *logos*, his willingness to abide by the dictates of reason alone, Plato once used the phrase "Father Parmenides" (*Sophist* 241d) to describe his Presocratic predecessor. Far more than Thales or Anaximenes, whose work actually is of a piece with what today we might call physics or cosmology, Parmenides, the first great rationalist who discovered the concept of Being and argued that it must be eternal, changeless, and one, is the father of western rationalism.

Recall how warmly Nietzsche expressed his affection for Heraclitus. Not surprsing, then, is what he says about Parmenides.

> All sense perceptions, says Parmenides, yield but illusions. And their main illusoriness lies in their pretense that the non-existent coexists with the existent, that Becoming, too, has Being. All the manifold colorful world known to experience, all the transformations of its qualities . . . are cast aside mercilessly as mere semblance and illusion. Nothing may be learned from them. (Nietzsche 1962, p. 79)

> One's sympathy towards phenomena atrophies; one even develops a hatred for phenomena including oneself, a hatred for being unable to get rid of the everlasting deceitfulness of sensation. Henceforward truth shall live only in the palest husks of the most indefinite terms, as though in a house of cobwebs. And beside such truth now sits our philosopher, likewise as bloodless as his abstractions. A spider at least wants blood from its victims. The Parmenidean philosopher hates most of all the blood of his victims, the blood of his empirical reality which was sacrificed and shed by him. (Nietzsche 1962, p. 80)

Nietzsche's distaste for "Father Parmenides" can be countered by an admiration for the astonishing intellectual strength it takes to methodically think through concepts like Being, Becoming, and nonbeing, and the courage to be willing to abide by the result of one's analysis regardless of how massively paradoxical it may be. It can also be countered by the often sad realization that because the past can only be thought by having been made present, time does indeed fly and its passage may really amount to nothing at all.

Fifth-Century Elementalism

The extreme philosophical positions of Heraclitus and Parmenides emerged in the fifth century as responses to the essential dilemma of the Milesian Picture, namely ontological dualism and the problem of reconnecting Being and Becoming. Some readers may find the extremism of both thinkers attractive in itself. Heraclitus and Parmenides each have the courage to think a single thought through to its end and they do not shirk from the conclusions they reach. However admirable this may be, neither could be ultimately satisfying, and Greek philosophy could not help but move forward. The Heraclitean denial of Being, while perhaps faithful to our experience of change, generates an elusive, self-contradictory, and enigmatic *logos*. Surely, one might object, something must BE stable out there, and philosophers can do better than make statements like "roadupdownoneandthesame." By contrast, the Parmenidean *logos* concludes that Being is one, eternal, motionless, and indivisible. Even if its logical rigor is deeply impressive, its comprehensive denial of the truthfulness of *doxa* seems outlandish. Surely, one might object, the appearances cannot be all wrong.

The history of philosophy must continue, and its path is clear. There must be some sort of reconciliation between Heraclitus and Parmenides. This is precisely what later thinkers in the fifth century tried to provide. They were "elementalists." They were persuaded by Parmenides' arguments about Being. It must, they agreed, be eternal, changeless, and indivisible. But for them Being was not just one. Instead, they conceived of "bits of Being," or elements, each of which had the features Parmenides attributed to Being. This move allowed them to offer a far more generous account of Becoming than Parmenides and thereby to preserve the ordinary experience of multiplicity and change. In a qualified sense, the elementalists maintained, beings do come into being, change, and go out of being. But they do not do so simply or absolutely. Instead, when things seem to come into being what really happens is that elements are combined. When they change or go out of being elements separate.

My pet rabbit came into being in 1995. Various elements, such as the carbon atoms that are essential to all organic matter, combined to form her. She died in 2001. When she did, her carbon atoms did not cease to be, even if she did. Instead, they scattered, eventually to be recombined to form some other organic compound.

This insight, that while the basic constituents of the universe remain unchanged, they do move around and enter into and go out of various combinations, is fundamental to all forms of fifth-century elementalism. In this way Becoming is retained as an ontological category, albeit at a much lower level than Heraclitus would allow, while much of what Parmenides said about Being is retained, but only as a description of the elements.

One fifth-century thinker, Anaxagoras, succinctly expressed the elementalist credo:

> The Greeks incorrectly believe that there is coming to be and perishing, for nothing comes to be, nor does it perish, but from things that are they are mixed together and are separated apart. Thus it would be correct to call coming to be "being mixed together," and perishing "being separated apart." (B17)

On the level of the elements, which is the ultimate level of reality itself and is, as we shall see, microscopic, nothing perishes or comes to be. On the macroscopic level of ordinary objects, things do, in a qualified sense, come to be and perish. The power of this ingenious reconciliation of Heraclitus and Parmenides will soon become evident.

There were three great elementalist thinkers, Anaxagoras (500–428), Democritus (born approx. 460), and Empedocles (493–433). We will begin with Democritus who, although not the earliest in a chronological sense, offers the most basic elemental scheme of all, namely atomism.[9]

a) Democritus: atomic theory

Democritus' theory is not only brilliant, but also resoundingly familiar.

> Democritus believes that the nature of the eternal things is small beings unlimited in multitude. He posits another place for these which is unlimited in magnitude, and he calls the place by these names: the

void, the nothing, and the unlimited . . . He thinks that these beings are so small that they escape our perception. All sorts of shapes and all sorts of forms and differences in magnitude belong to them. From these, just as from elements, he generates and compounds visible and perceptible objects. (A37)

[Democritus] said that the principles are unlimited in multitude, and believed them to be atoms and indivisible . . . These atoms, which are separate from one another in the unlimited void and differ in shape and size and position, and arrangement, move in the void, and when they overtake one another they collide, and some rebound in whatever direction they may happen to, but others become entangled in virtue of the relation of their shapes, sizes, positions, and arrangements, and stay together, and this is how compounds are produced. (A14)[10]

The Democritean universe is composed of atoms – miniscule, invisible, and indivisible bits of Being – moving through the void (or empty space). The Greek word *atomos*, composed of the alpha-privative and the word derived from the verb "to cut," means "uncuttable." Because they cannot be subdivided, they cannot fall apart and so they are imperishable. Furthermore, these atoms are qualitatively homogeneous (a notion we will explore shortly). They do, however, differ in quantitative senses such as shape, size, position, and arrangement, and they are in motion (and so would have velocity). As they are moving through the void some "collide" and become "entangled." This is the way in which visible objects "come into being." Again, this coming-into-being is not quite literal. Instead, it is, as Anaxagoras put it, a "mixing together."

Because he endorses these views, Democritus is rather like Parmenides in being a "paradoxical" thinker, one who strictly separates *doxa* and Truth. Ordinary experience suggests that the book you are holding in your hand is a real object in and of itself. As a result, if someone asked you, "what is it you are holding?," you would quickly answer, "a book." (Always keep in mind how closely intertwined *doxa* is with ordinary language.) But according to Democritus, you would be wrong. What you hold in your hands is not really a book at all. Instead, it is a collection of atoms moving through the void that happened to clump together and will soon separate. To reach this conclusion Democritus explicitly rejects the testimony of *doxa*. "There are two kinds of judgment," he declares, "one legitimate and the other bastard. All the following belong to the bastard: sight, hearing, smell, taste, touch" (B11). Ordinary sight cannot reveal the atomic structure of the book you are now holding: the atoms are, after all, invisible. Instead, as the first citation above indicates, Democritus "posits" or hypothesizes or infers the existence of atoms. He concludes that only atoms and the void, neither of which can be empirically observed, are truly real by constructing a theory.

Unlike Parmenides' account of Being, Democritus' atomism is, at least in principle, empirically verifiable. Even if he rejects the testimony of ordinary "sight, hearing, etc.," he would, for example, welcome the powerful observational tools used by scientists today. Democritus would have been delighted to learn that there are electron microscopes able to detect entities as seemingly elemental as molecules, or cloud-chambers which generate images of the tracks of fundamental particles. Nevertheless, even if theoretically compatible with a modern form of empiricism, Democritean atomism is still quite paradoxical. Consider the following, all-important statement:

> By convention sweet; by convention, bitter; by convention, hot; by convention, cold; by convention, color; but in reality, atoms and void. (B125)

The terms Democritus uses here are critical. The Greek for "in reality" is a participle derived from "to be" (*einai*), and so could also be translated as "in Being." Atoms REALLY ARE. They are bits of Being. By contrast, qualities such as sweet or cold are a matter of "convention." The word here is *nomos*, and it can also be translated as "custom" or "law." Each of these signifies some sort of human agreement. It is, for example, customary in our culture to shake hands upon being introduced to someone. This gesture has no intrinsic, natural, or permanent significance. It is strictly symbolic, and its meaning has been determined by the culture. In another culture, or at a different time, a different gesture, such as gently rubbing noses, might well perform the same function that shaking hands does for us today.

The preceding paragraph alludes to one of the great oppositions in the entire history of philosophy, namely that between *nomos* and *phusis*, "convention" and "nature." Nature is what is real all by itself. The fact that, for example, Mount Everest exists and is the tallest mountain in the world has nothing to do with human agreement. It got there all by itself. By contrast, the name of the geological entity standing close to the intersection of the meridian 87° E longitude and the parallel 28° N latitude, "Everest," is a strictly human affair. The mountain was named by specific English-speaking human beings who decided and then agreed to recognize the achievement of Sir George Everest, who surveyed it in 1841.

Democritus does not use the word *phusis* in the citation above. Instead, his choice is "reality" or "Being." But the point is the same. Atoms really are, regardless of what human beings say or think about them. By contrast, sweet and hot belong to human experience alone. Recall that atoms have no qualitative features whatsoever. They are neither sweet nor bitter, neither hot nor cold. They are imperceptible and have only the quantitative characteristics of size, shape, and position, etc. So, for example, my tongue is composed of, say, 936 rectangular atoms. These numerical features constitute its nature or reality. The honey in the jar is composed of 472 atoms which are, as Democritus says about the sweet, "round and good-sized" (A129). When the honey atoms interact with the tongue atoms there is an "entanglement" of some sort and the result is the sensation of sweetness (which reaches my brain by being communicated from the tongue by neurological atoms). But this sensation, which lies in the realm of *doxa*, provides no information about the honey itself. In reality, and like everything else, the honey is nothing but atoms moving through the void.

In this sense Democritus is a paradoxical thinker. If I ask you, "how does that honey you're eating now taste?," you might well say "it's very sweet." From the perspective of atomic reality your answer is meaningless. The truth is 472 "round and good-sized atoms" have bumped into 936 rectangular atoms and produced a certain atomic motion traveling through your nerves to your brain. "Sweet" tells us nothing about what is really happening or what exists. It is simply a name, an appearance which conceals the Truth about the honey.

Implicit in Democritus' declaration "sweet, by convention . . . in reality, atoms and void," is not only the distinction between nature (or Being) and convention, but also that between what later philosophers will call "primary and secondary qualities." The former belong to objects in the world independently of any human cognizance of those objects. The roundness of honey atoms is an objective and quantitative fact and does not depend on human perception or observation. By contrast, the perception of sweetness is a consequence of the interaction of the object and the perceiving subject who tastes it.

Sweetness is thus a secondary quality. The statement "the honey is sweet" is false about the honey itself even if the statement "the honey tastes sweet to me" is true.

One way to appreciate the force of this idea is to perform an experiment. Put a cube of sugar into your mouth for 10 minutes. Then have a taste of the honey. It will no longer seem quite as sweet. Next, put a lemon in your mouth for ten minutes before tasting the honey. It will seem extremely sweet. On the basis of experiments like these one can conclude that the honey is not sweet in itself. Instead, its sweetness depends on the one perceiving it. By contrast, regardless of how the honey tastes to you, or even whether you taste it at all, it will still be composed of 472 atoms.

As the above suggests, a decisive difference between primary and secondary qualities is that the former are expressible only in the language of mathematics. Recall Democritus' assertion that atoms are qualitatively homogeneous; that is, they are "not different in kind," but only in size, position, shape, etc. The only true statements to be made about them, and hence about reality itself, are those formulated in the language of mathematics. Secondary qualities, by contrast, require ordinary language (the medium of *doxa*) for their articulation. "Sweet," "bitter," "hot," "cold" – Democritus' examples – are all adjectives.

It is difficult to overstate the magnitude of Democritus' discovery. Some 2,000 years later Galileo would reach similar conclusions.

> I think, therefore, that these tastes, odors, colors, etc., so far as their objective existence is concerned, are nothing but mere names for something which resides exclusively in our sensitive body, so that if the perceiving creatures were removed, all of these qualities would be annihilated and abolished from existence. (Galileo 1960, p. 18)

By contrast, what is really real and does not depend on "perceiving creatures" are "material bodies continually resolving themselves into tiny particles," precisely what Democritus calls "atoms." What Galileo describes as "mere names" is what Democritus refers to when he says "by convention." To declare that "the honey is sweet" is merely a conventional naming of a microscopic event which has nothing whatsoever to do with sweetness. If there were no tongue with which to taste the honey, there would still be honey, but it would not be sweet. It would just be 472 atoms.

David Hume, writing in the eighteenth century, believed that this distinction between primary and secondary qualities was fundamental to modern (post-1600) philosophy in general:

> The fundamental principle of [modern] philosophy is the opinion concerning colors, sounds, tastes, smells, heat and cold; which it asserts to be nothing but impressions in the mind derived from the operation of external objects, and without any resemblance to the qualities of the objects. (Hume 1975, p. 226)

Even if Hume is correct in characterizing modern philosophy in this fashion, he neglected to note that the distinction between primary and secondary qualities was already present, however incipiently, in the ancient world in the form of Democritean atomism. As mentioned in the Introduction to this book, the views of the Presocratics, especially the elementalists, were far more "modern" than those of their successors Plato and Aristotle. Indeed, it is precisely this feature of Presocratic thought that, as we will see in some detail in chapter 4 below, Aristotle criticized and believed that he had defeated. It will be useful here to get ahead of ourselves a bit and preview a few of his criticisms of Democritus in order to gain a better grasp of atomism as well as the sorts of objections that might be brought to bear against it.

First: atomism, according to Aristotle, destroys what might be called the "ontological integrity" of individual objects. Things are no longer unified wholes with a being of their own. As Simplicius, one of Aristotle's followers, put it, Democritus "does not make any thing out of them that is truly one" (A37). This becomes a particularly damning complaint when applied to living beings, for these above all else seem to have a very strong kind of identity. They can, after all, maintain their organic unity through metabolic activity and can reproduce themselves. For Democritus, however, a rabbit is not really a singular being with its own ontological integrity. (The word "integrity," by the way, comes from "integer," a "whole number.") Indeed, a rabbit is not, on the atomist account, really a rabbit at all. Instead, it is an entanglement of, say, 6,418 square atoms. But this is at complete variance with our ordinary experience of living beings, which in fact present themselves to us as unified and with a very powerful sense of ontological integrity. My pet rabbit had a name, Ginger, and what seemed to be a strong personality. At least according to my everyday experiences of her, she was not merely an entanglement of atoms which can only be explicated mathematically. She was a living being whose nature and value required ordinary language for their articulation. This strong sense of the ontological integrity of living beings is destroyed by Democritean atomism.

As we will see in chapter 4, according to Aristotle (but not Galileo or other modern thinkers) this implication of atomism counts as a damning indictment against Democritus. He is, to use a contemporary term, an "eliminativist," one who eliminates everyday concepts in favor of materialist ones that can be explicated scientifically (or mathematically). For example, atomism eliminates all familiar psychological concepts. In Democritus' system the notion of a mind or soul is replaced by atoms moving through the void. In a striking, even if primitive, prefigurement of contemporary neuroscience, he says the mind "consists of primary and indivisible bodies, and its power of producing movement is due to the smallness of its parts, and its shape; for . . . the spherical [is] the most easily moved of all shapes; and this characteristic is shared by mind and fire" (*De Anima*, 405a7–13).[11] As we will see, both Aristotle and Plato will strongly object to replacing the mind or soul with a chunk of matter, even one as complex and dynamic as the human brain.

A second Aristotelian complaint against atomism is that "Democritus leaves aside purpose, but refers all things which nature employs to necessity" (A66). "Necessity" (*anangkê*) signifies that which cannot be otherwise than it is. If, to conjure up an imaginary example, a rectangular shaped atom collides with a round one, they cannot become entangled but they must bounce off each other. By contrast, if two triangular shaped atoms collide, they will have to stick together. The world of objects is, for Democritus, a necessitated one. Atoms are perpetually in motion and their movements and entanglements strictly obey the laws of physics. Such a view eliminates all aspects of purposiveness or goal-directed activity.

Once again, from Aristotle's perspective the great limitation of atomism comes sharply into focus when it is applied to living beings. So, for example, he argues that human teeth have a purpose, namely to chew food. Democritus, by contrast, would claim that the teeth are composed of a bunch of atoms which, because of their random motions, just happened to clump together, and proved to be useful. For reasons to be elaborated at length in chapter 4, Aristotle argues that such "necessity" cannot possibly do justice to the orderliness and regularity of organic nature.

Another objection, which actually encapsulates the previous two, is this: the atomist doctrine places a wall between ordinary human experience and reality. As Democritus puts it, "a person must know that he is separated from reality" (B6). Reality as it is presented in *doxa* is composed of objects, especially living ones, which do have ontological integrity and whose parts often do exhibit purposiveness. Reality, at least as we ordinarily experience it and talk about it, looks this way to us. By contrast, Democritean reality is nothing but invisible, quantitatively determined atoms moving through the void and combining or separating according to the necessary laws of motion. Reality is, in sum, divorced from us. The only way to overcome this separation is by an act of thought, namely to hypothesize or construct a theory about the existence of atoms one cannot see. For Aristotle, such a procedure, such a thorough debasement of *doxa*, is philosophically unacceptable.

A final comment about Democritus: in addition to his atomic doctrine, he wrote a great deal about how one should lead one's life, or about what today we would call ethics. Indeed, "over four-fifths of his surviving *verbatim* fragments are concerned with ethics." Most of these reflect a concern "with our subjective well-being" (KRS 1983, p. 431), that is, with how human beings actually feel. For example, some of Democritus' writings recommend practical strategies for coping with grief and anger, and in general they aim to teach us how to achieve contentment. A representative statement is this: "Best for a person is to live his life being as cheerful and as little distressed as possible" (B189).

This fragment may well prefigure the thought of later ethicists like Epicurus (341–270) and, most famously, Lucretius (94–55), who were both atomists and hedonists: they identified pleasure as the highest good for human beings. Their reasoning – which perhaps can be read back into Democritus – was essentially this: nothing should distress a human being precisely because nothing really exists in its own right. Take, for example, the most distressful of all eventualities, namely death. For the "atomic-ethicist," to fear death is a big mistake. After all, death, like all forms of Becoming, is not quite real. Yes, the body will decompose and its elements will separate. The elements themselves, however, which are the truest reality of all, do not die and so in this sense nothing really dies. Human beings become upset because they fear they will lose what they have – their family, friends, wealth, or finally their lives. But since nothing really exists on its own, nothing can really be lost, and so nothing should cause us to worry or fear. The atomic nature of reality is the great constant on which we may all rely, and understanding this is the key to a pleasurable existence.

The kind of hedonism Democritus may have had in mind (and which Lucretius certainly did have in mind) is hardly the familiar sort that recommends luxurious eating or drinking or sexual pleasure. In fact, Democritus urges us to stay away from just these sorts of pleasures: "All those who make their pleasure from the belly, exceeding the right time for food, drink, or sex, have short lived pleasures . . . but many pains" (B235). The best form of pleasure is intellectual. When one thinks clearly about a world of purposeless atoms moving through the void one realizes it is pointless to get emotionally distraught over anything. The optimum psychological state, which arises when this realization is thoroughly integrated into one's thinking, is what later Greek thinkers called *ataraxia*, "tranquility," or more literally, the "absence of distress." Because the greatest source of human unhappiness is anxiety or stress, and this can be eliminated through a proper understanding of reality, a pleasurable life is within our reach.

Aristotle would object to atomic-ethics. He is, in stark contrast to the elementalists, fundamentally wedded to *doxa*. Human beings typically fear death, and for Aristotle they have good reason to: it represents the end of life. And life, for Aristotle, has meaning, purpose, and integrity. Tranquility is therefore not equivalent to human happiness. What it is will be the subject of chapter 4.

According to some scholars, atomism is "in many ways the crown of Greek philosophical achievement before Plato" (KRS 1983, p. 433). It is a comprehensive doctrine and, as modern developments clearly suggest, one that could be adopted without embarrassment today. It combines Parmenides' insights about Being with ordinary sense perception. It offers a comprehensive view of the world. Democritus, however, was neither the first, nor the only, elementalist of the fifth century. Next we turn to Empedocles. If Democritus prefigures Galileo, then Empedocles prefigures Darwin.

b) Empedocles: evolution

Like Democritus, Empedocles (495–435) preserves the essential insights of Parmenides, but refuses to abide by his notion of the singularity of Being. Instead, he divides Being into elements, which in turn mix and separate and thereby generate the macroscopic objects of *doxa* comprising the realm of what appears as becoming. Much like Anaxagoras, Empedocles declares "There is coming to be of not a single one of all mortal things, nor is there any end of deadly death, but only mixture and separation of what is mixed" (B8).[12]

(*Warning*: Empedocles, like Parmenides, wrote in verse, which I do not indicate in my citations below. This is in keeping with what Aristotle says: "Homer and Empedocles have nothing in common except for their meter. Therefore, it is proper to call the one a 'poet,' and the other a 'natural philosopher' rather than a poet" [*Poetics*, 1447b17–20]. For an alternative view that makes poetry central to Empedocles' project see Lombardo 1982 and Kingsley 2002. Also, new papyrus material containing some texts by Empedocles has recently been discovered. These will not be discussed here, for, as Inwood [2001, p. 78] concludes, "The impact of the papyrus materials on the intepretation of Empedocles' poetic work . . . is not as great as one might have expected" [Kingsley 2002 elaborates].)

Empedocles' version of elements are what he calls the "four roots of all things" (B56), namely earth, air, water, and fire. In addition, there are two powers at work on these elements, which he names "Love" and "Strife" (B17), and which can be construed as symbolic of attraction and repulsion. Equipped with these six entities, Empedocles constructs a sort of proto-chemistry. Objects "come into being" when the strong force of Love attracts the required number of elements, and they "perish" when Love gives way to Strife and the elements are repelled from each other and so go their separate ways. As in Democritus, there is no Becoming in the strict sense of the word: "From what is altogether not it is impossible to come to be, and it is inconceivable that what is perish" (B12). Or, as he also puts it about the roots, "at different times they come to be different things and yet are always and continuously the same" (B17).

Empedocles holds a rather obscure doctrine of cosmic history. At one stage, the strong force of Love was totally ascendant and as a result, "at this point all these things come together to be one single thing" (B35). With only Love at work, there was no differentiation; there were no things. At a subsequent point, Strife did intervene, and elements began to separate from the one glob. Empedocles seems to have had some sort of cyclical conception of history in mind: "I will tell a double story," he says. "For at one time they grow to be only one out of many, but at another they grow apart to be many out of one" (B17). This may well suggest that Love and Strife take turns at the driver's seat and so the cosmos oscillates back and forth between being one, undifferentiated mass, and being a collection of separate things. Again, what he means by this is quite obscure and will not be discussed further. (For discussions of these cycles see KRS 1983, pp. 289–94 and Inwood 2001, pp. 42–9.)

What is most important here is that Empedocles had some inkling of what today we would call the "evolution" of animal life and the theory of natural selection. Inwood cautiously makes this point: "Though the resemblance of Empedocles' theories of animal generation to Darwinian evolution is very slender, they nevertheless represent for us the clearest and best-attested attempt in early Greek thought to give a rule-governed and nontheological account of the origin of animal species" (2001, p. 73).

As explained by Furth (1987, pp. 30–7), who largely follows Aristotle's reading of his predecessor, Empedocles conceived of six distinct stages in the evolution of animal life.

Stage 1:   As mentioned above, before the emergence of the four elements, Love was totally dominant and so there was only an undifferentiated unity: "at one time all coming together into one by Love" (B17).

Stage 2:   Strife intervened and the elements separated: "they grew apart to be many out of one: fire and water and earth and the immense height of air, and deadly strife apart from them, equal in all directions and Love among them" (B17).

Stage 3:   Love then became operative on a local basis, and so elements were drawn together to form compounds. So, for example, "white bones came into being" from "Pleasant earth, two parts of bright Nestis [god of water] out of the eight, and four of Hephaestus [god of the forge, i.e. fire]" (B98). Furth translates this imagistic statement into a chemical formula. Bone can be represented as $E_2W_2A_0F_4$ (Furth 1987, p. 35). Two parts earth, two water, zero air, and four fire comprise a bone "molecule." Such a "molecule" has an elemental structure and "comes into being" only when the right proportion of each element happens to be present.

Stage 4:   Bits of organic matters were mixed into miscellaneous animal parts. "By her [Love] many neckless faces sprouted, and arms were wandering naked, bereft of shoulders, and eyes were roaming alone, in need of foreheads" (B57).

Stage 5: These parts in turn randomly combined to form various combinations. Some were quite strange. "Many came into being with faces and chests of both sides, man-faced ox-progeny, and some to the contrary rose up as ox-headed things with the form of men, compounded partly from men and partly from women, fitted with shadowy parts" (B61). Such beings were poorly adapted and did not survive. (See Aristotle's *Physics* 198b29–32.)

Stage 6: "In a very small fraction of cases, creatures were thus mixed together that happened to be both well adapted and reproductively viable" (Furth 1983, p. 39).

In this evolutionary process animal life emerged "from the bottom up." Beginning with inorganic, elemental bits, organic compounds were formed, and then large-scale parts, and finally living beings. Only a few of the latter managed to survive and then reproduce on a consistent basis.

Throughout this process chance plays a pivotal role. In describing how blood and flesh came to be, Empedocles says "earth came together by chance in about equal quantity to these" (B98). "When . . . these things began to fall together, however they chanced to meet, and many others besides them arose continuously" (B59).

The Empedoclean story, sketchy as it is, is now complete. It is a thoroughly materialist account in which the elements are the fundamental level of reality. Evolution takes place because of random mixtures and, ultimately, survival is the sole determinant of what sort of animal life exists.

As he does in his criticism of Democritus, Aristotle brings two basic objections to bear against Empedoclean evolution. First, it deprives animals, which for Aristotle are the paradigmatic instances of beings or what he calls "substances," of their ontological integrity. According to the evolutionary story, a rabbit is a chance conglomeration of organic chunks of matters that happened to be able to survive and reproduce. There is nothing qualitatively unique about a rabbit to differentiate it essentially from a turtle. Their differences would be captured instead by the sort of chemical formula used to articulate the molecular structure of bone. Furthermore, because there is continual motion of the elements, because Love and Strife oscillate cyclically, and chance is forever at play, no given animal species is genuinely stable or permanent. Rabbits may well evolve into a different sort of animal in the future.

Aristotle's second objection is that there is no purposiveness in the Empedoclean evolutionary scheme. Animals, just like all other beings in the universe, are comprised of random conglomerations of elements, and that is all. By contrast, for Aristotle, as we will see in chapter 4, biological beings have a level of organization that requires them to be understood precisely in terms of their purposes. The human teeth, for example, are for the sake of chewing food. To explain the teeth in a formula such as $E_2W_2A_0F_4$ will not suffice. Teeth are a far too regular and predictable part of the human animal to have been caused by chance.

To repeat again a point made in the Introduction: of all the Presocratics, the fifth-century elementalists Democritus and Empedocles are most modern in their basic conceptual framework. Thus when Aristotle criticizes them a century later, he will actually be criticizing doctrines as current and familiar to us as atomism and evolution. While the contemporary versions of these theories are of course vastly more sophisticated than their ancient predecessors, the basic ideas were nonetheless latent in antiquity, and so were on the table when Plato and Aristotle entered the scene in the fourth century.

c) Anaxagoras

Like Democritus and Empedocles, Anaxagoras (500–427) is a complex thinker whose work merits an analysis far more detailed than what this book provides. As has been the case throughout this chapter, only those portions of his text that help position him in the dialectical development of ancient Greek philosophy will be discussed. In this regard, what is critical in selecting passages from Anaxagoras' writings is the fact that Plato was both influenced by and critical of his ideas.

As a good elementalist, Anaxagoras conceives of bits of Being, which he calls "seeds." "It is necessary to believe," he states, "that there are many things of all kinds, and seeds of all things, in everything that has been compounded" (B4).[13] There is, unfortunately, much dispute among scholars about what exactly this means. (See KRS 1983, pp. 368–70.) Nonetheless, even without knowing exactly what these seeds are, it is still possible to suggest how they figure into Anaxagoras' scheme. Simply put, they play a role similar to that of Empedocles' "roots" and Democritus' "atoms." They are the unchanging elements whose mixture and separation cause the appearance and disappearance of macroscopic objects.

Somewhat like Empedocles, Anaxagoras has some sort of notion of cosmic development. In the beginning, "all things were together" (B1) and there was no differentiation. Then there was separation and the world as we know it (as composed of distinct objects) began to come into being. Anaxagoras' bold innovation was to assign the cause of this separation to what he called "Mind."

> And when Mind began to cause motion, out of everything that was moved there came to be setting apart, and to the extent that Mind caused motion, there was that much separating. While the things being moved were separating, the rotation caused much more separating. (B13)

> And Mind ruled the entire rotation, so that it rotated at the beginning. (B12)

Again, it is quite unclear what this "rotation" was and hence exactly what these statements actually mean. The key point here is only that Anaxagoras claims Mind is ultimately responsible for the emergence of distinct macroscopic objects. As such, it performs much the same function as Love and Strife did for Empedocles. "In place of Empedocles' Love and Strife Anaxagoras substitutes the single intellectual motive force of Mind" (KRS 1983, p. 364).

Anaxagoras' description of Mind is striking (and to some extent reminiscent of Xenophanes' description of God). It is assigned the role of first cause of all things, but at the same time it is not itself one of those things. As he puts it, "All else has a share of everything, but Mind is unlimited and self-ruled and has been mixed with no other thing, but alone itself by itself it is" (B12). This last phrase, "itself by itself," is especially significant and will prove to be influential in the development of the Greek philosophical vocabulary.[14] It is composed of two different types of pronouns. The first "itself" is intensive: it modifies "Mind." The second is reflexive: it is the object of the preposition "by," and forms a prepositional phrase that modifies (and so reflects back on) the first "itself."

The phrase "itself by itself" attributes to Mind ontological independence. Unlike everything else, it is capable of being on its own. For reasons to be discussed in detail in chapter 3, this description is appealing to Plato. He was impressed that Anaxagoras, somewhat like

Parmenides (whom Plato also admired), seemed to have had a notion of a nonmaterial being (Mind) whose ontological status was superior to, because responsible for, ordinary material beings. As a result, Anaxagoras was by his lights the most promising of the fifth-century elementalists. Unlike Democritus or Empedocles, he did not appear to be a strict materialist. Ultimately, as we will see, Plato became disenchanted with Anaxagoras, for Mind was not the thoroughly nonmaterial substance for which he had hoped, and the process by which Mind initiated the separation of things was actually more mechanical than intelligent. Nevertheless, because he seemed to intuit the possibility of an intelligent force in the universe, to which he attributed ontological independence, Anaxagoras helped to push Plato into developing his own ideas.

To conclude this chapter: the fifth-century elementalists are the culmination of the period of Presocratic philosophy that began in 585 with Thales' identification of water as the *archê*. They were astonishingly prescient thinkers whose ideas prefigured some of the most important conceptual developments of the modern age, especially atomic physics and evolutionary biology. While what remains of their writings is fragmentary, and so none of them have attained the stature of Plato or Aristotle, their importance in the history of Greek philosophy is considerable. They set the stage for the emergence of the two giants of the fourth century, and because their ideas contain the seeds which later sprouted into modernity, when Plato and Aristotle respond to the Presocratics in general, and to the elementalists in particular, they are also responding to us.

Notes

1   Kirk, Raven, & Schofield 1983 is a basic reference text for the study of Presocratic philosophy, and will be cited throughout this chapter.
2   It is safer to speak of the "Homeric poems" rather than of "Homer," for about the latter we know next to nothing.
3   Translation is from Evelyn-White 1977.
4   The more common translation of *ousia* is "substance."
5   All translations of Pythagoras are taken from Cohen et al. 2000, and will be indicated only by "Cohen" and a page number from this book.

6   I have consulted Cohen 2000 on all of my translations, and have also benefited from Wright 1985, which I also consulted for translations of Parmenides.
7   I leave out a phrase from this fragment, namely, "playing checkers."
8   The Greek text is KRS 1983, and the translations offered are guided by theirs. I use their abbreviation, "Fr.", to indicate fragment numbers.
9   I leave out Leucippus, the putative founder of atomism. SEE KRS 1983, pp. 402–3 for a brief discussion.
10 Fragment A37 is from Diels, and is my own translation. A14 is from Cohen, p. 67. All subsequent translations of Democritus will be from this book, but will indicated only by the Diels number.
11 Translation is from Hett 1957.
12 With only slight exceptions, my translation comes from Cohen.
13 Translation is my own.
14 A similar phrase is used by Parmenides. Being, he says, is "unchanging" (8.26) and "remains the same in the same and by itself" (8.29).

2

The Sophists and Socrates

A New Beginning: The Sophists

Parmenides might seem to be a terribly idiosyncratic thinker. After all, he argued for the paradoxical view that the Truth resides solely in the one, indivisible, motionless Being. Still, however extreme his thinking was, Parmenides was no outsider. In fact, he could even be conceived as the purest distillation of Presocratic thought in general. In other words, in one way or another all Presocratic thinkers were concerned with the Truth about Being. They were, in this literal sense, ontologists, i.e. philosophers who offered a *logos*, "a rational account," or even a theory, of *to on*, "what is" or Being.

The Milesians – Thales, Anaximander, and Anaximenes – began the tradition by trying to figure out what remained constant in the midst of all the change in the world. They attempted to discover and articulate an *archê*, a "first principle" underlying all the multiplicity of Becoming. This *archê* was stable, changeless, the source of all reality, and permanent. While all other things in the world – rabbits, trees, people – come into being, change, and then perish, the first principle just plain IS.

Xenophanes too sought the basic source of all reality. He found it in the "One God," changeless and eternal, which, like a Milesian *archê*, somehow got all things moving without itself being moved. In a similar vein, the Pythagorean "One" was the *archê* of number, which in turn makes all things intelligible. For Democritus, the *archê* took the form of atoms; for Empedocles it was the "roots" and the forces of Love and Strife; for Anaxagoras the "seeds" and the "Mind" that organizes them. However diverse they may be, all of these conceptual developments, all of these contributions to the Presocratic conversation, were engaged in a common theoretical endeavor: to understand the nature of Being. Furthermore, they were linked by a common conviction: because it is stable and enduring, Being is prior and superior to the beings of Becoming.

(The one great exception to this characterization of early Greek philosophy is Heraclitus, the wild man of Becoming. Nevertheless, even if he rejected Being, it is arguable that he was still engaged in the same sort of project as his nemesis Parmenides: the attempt to give a *logos* of reality, which he located in the flux of Becoming.)

The Presocratic obsession with Being eventually wore thin. Something was missing from the conversation. Humanity, in its uniqueness, had been neglected. Ask a thinker like Thales what it means to be human, and he answers by using exactly the same terms he would use to account for a rabbit or a tree: they all come from water, and so only by referring to it can one speak the Truth. Thinkers like the Milesians and the Elementalists homogenized reality. Even if specific beings differed quantitatively (three parts water, two parts air versus two parts water, three parts air) all were ultimately the same, namely derivatives of the fundamental reality or compounds of the basic elements.

But human beings cry out to be recognized as unique. Human life – at least as it appears to those of us experiencing it – is profoundly different from the reality of the rabbit or the tree, for we take ourselves to be more than our material constituents. We are acutely conscious of our lives and our loves, our suffering and our impending deaths. We live together in communities regulated by certain values, which we intensely care about and discuss at great length. We reflect on the meaning of our own existence and try to give it a voice. As such, a human being is no ordinary thing. Or so, at least, we tell ourselves. Because their goal was to achieve a theoretical articulation of the nature of Being, what was missing in Presocratic philosophy, then, was any sustained and focused concern with what it means to be human.[1]

A group of thinkers known as the "Sophists" changed all this. They pushed the conversation forward by demanding that human being, and not just Being, take center stage. They changed the subject, and thereby became the first "humanists" in the West. (See Guthrie 1988 and Kerferd 1981 for general introductions to the Sophists.)

The word "sophist" is derived from the Greek *sophia*, which is usually translated as "wisdom." In the fifth century, however, this word did not carry with it the highfalutin connotations ours does. A "sophist" can simply mean someone who is skilled. The Sophists of the fifth century were itinerant teachers who traveled from city to city in ancient Greece and charged a fee for their instruction. What they were skilled in, what they taught and believed, and why they are so important to the history of western thought, will be the subject of this section.

Protagoras

With a single sentence Protagoras of Abdera (ca. 485–415), the first great Sophist of the fifth century, altered the course of Ancient Greek Philosophy:

> Of all things human being is the measure; of those that are, that they are, and of those that are not, that they are not. (B1)[2]

For the Presocratics, Being is the measure of all things, and human being is just one more thing among the many others. For Thales, my wife, my city, my friends are beings centered around, "measured by," water, the most fundamental of all realities and thus the source of Truth. In striking contrast, for Protagoras, the first humanist in the West, human being (*anthrôpos*) does the measuring.

What remains of Protagoras' work is sparse – his extant corpus consists of only four major fragments – and so it is impossible to know exactly what he means in his famous saying. Specifically, two of its crucial terms are ambiguous. "Human being," for example, could refer to individuals, to people as they join together in political communities, or to the species as a whole. "Things" might mean literally every thing, i.e. every entity in the world (trees, rocks, rabbits), or it might be restricted to "human things" such as laws, rules, and values.

(This latter interpretation, which I think is correct, comes from Versényi 1963, pp. 11–13.)

Despite these ambiguities, one point is clear. Protagoras is some sort of relativist. For him, "things," whatever exactly they are, are measured by "human being," whatever that is. It is, yet again, not quite clear precisely what "measure" means here. Presumably it means "determine the extent of." When human beings do the measuring, they are determining the extent of, the reality of, even the truth of, "things." Assume "things" does refer to "human things," especially values. If so, then Protagoras' view would be some sort of "ethical relativism," the view that ethical values depend on (are measured by) the group or individual holding those values.

To clarify, consider the following question: is it ethically permissible for a pregnant woman to have an abortion if she so chooses? For the sort of ethical relativist we are imagining, the answer would be "it depends." If someone is a member of a traditional Catholic community, which firmly maintains the immorality of abortion, then the answer is an emphatic "no." By contrast, if someone is a member of a group that affirms freedom of choice above all else, then the answer might well be "yes." For the relativist, there is no one right answer. Instead, it depends on the group giving the answer.

As mentioned, it is possible that in saying "human being is the measure of all things," Protagoras has individual human beings in mind. If this were so, and "things" does mean "human things," or values, then his position would be that values are dependent upon individuals. If Bob believes it is right and proper to worship rabbits, then it is right and proper . . . for Bob. If Sue believes it is good to chop off the toes of everyone taller than 6 feet then, despite her view being wildly out of tune with those of her fellow citizens, such is the good . . . for Sue. If you believe they are both wrong, then you are right . . . for you.

As the silly examples above are meant to suggest, this radically individualistic version of ethical relativism is neither plausible nor interesting. Furthermore, such individualism was quite foreign to Ancient Greek thinking in general.[3] Indeed, the Greeks were intensely political beings. In other words, they strongly identified their own interests with that of their *polis* (often translated as "city-state"). As Pericles, the great statesman of fifth century Athens, puts it in his famous funeral oration (reported by Thucydides), "the very men who take care of public affairs look after their own at the same time . . . For we think that a man who does not take part in public affairs is good for nothing.''[4] Much more likely, then, with "human being" the Sophist refers to human beings as grouped together in a political community.

To reiterate, it is unclear what "things" means. It is possible Protagoras literally means every thing: this dog, the rock over there, the moon, and so on. If so, then he would be "an ontological relativist," someone who believes reality itself is relative. If an individual or group believes rabbits do not exist, then rabbits do not exist . . . for them. "Ontological relativism" of this extreme sort is, like the ethical individualism sketched above, difficult to take seriously and probably not Protagoras' view.

For these and other reasons to be developed throughout this section, it is much better to think of Protagoras as an ethical relativist who believes values are relative to human beings conceived as members of communities. This is not only an inherently plausible view, it is also one widely held today. In fact, for many people it simply counts as commonsense.

The second Protagorean fragment is this:

> About the gods I am unable to know either that they are or that they are not, or what their form is like. For many things prevent our knowing: the obscurity [of the subject] and the fact that the life of human beings is short. (B4)

This fragment shows Protagoras to be an "agnostic," one who claims not to know, and hence not to take a stand on the question of whether the gods exist or not. But as Versényi has again shown, the meaning of this fragment can be extended considerably and taken to express two basic strands of the Sophist's thinking: his skepticism and his orientation to the practical life. The "gods" mentioned in this fragment, he argues, refer not only to the deities of ancient Greek polytheism, but to anything "absolute." Recall that this word describes something whose being is independent of, absolved of any relationship to, all other beings. An absolute being, to cite the language Anaxagoras used to describe "Mind," is "itself by itself." According to Versényi, Protagoras believes that, because the subject is obscure and life is short (and so our cognitive powers are limited), human beings have no intellectual access to the Truth about absolute objects whatsoever. Thales' water, Democritus' atoms, Empedocles' roots, and Parmenides' Being, are all absolute. About thoroughly nonhuman entities such as these, which exist in and of themselves, Protagoras is silent. He simply is not interested in the Truth, if by this one means a conceptual grasp of reality or Being as it is in and of itself. Instead, his fundamental concern is with "things" as they appear to, as they are experienced and measured by, human beings. His thinking, then, is guided by the practical, for it takes its bearings from what we do – "practical" is derived from *prattein*, "to act" – and the lives we actually live in our cities. Referring to the fragment above, Versényi puts this point as follows: it "is simply another expression of Protagoras' reluctance to deal with what we cannot know and what has, therefore, no relevance for practical life" (1963, p. 17).

There are two ways of reformulating this same point. The first invokes a distinction mentioned in chapter 1 and the discussion of Democritus. For the Sophist, *nomos* – "custom, agreement, convention" – and not nature or *phusis* is primary and the overwhelming context of human life and thought. Second, according to Protagoras what matters is not what the gods (or anything else) actually are in and of themselves, but what human beings take the gods to be. In other words, what really matters for Protagoras – and now we come to the heart of Sophistry – is what human beings say about the gods. This emphasis on language brings us to the final two fragments.

On every issue, there are two arguments (*logoi*) opposed to each other (A1).

To make the weaker argument the stronger. (A21)

In Protagoras' thoroughly anthropocentric worldview there is no absolute Truth. When it comes to "things," especially the human things by which we guide our lives, namely values, all is relative to the communities in which we live and the conventions that define them. One community may hold abortion to be morally reprehensible, while another may not. Neither side is objectively right or wrong, for the "truth" is relative. To use a device popularized by Richard Rorty (1980, p. 377; 1982, p. xiv), there is no single Truth with a capital "T." Instead, human beings have access only to a host of different "truths," which are local and subject to revision by the communities upholding them. This is the meaning of Fragment A1. Any given argument (*logos*) on any given subject can be equally countered by its opposite. Bob may argue, and argue well, for a pregnant woman's right to choose to have an abortion. Sue may argue equally well for the opposite view. Neither of two arguments can be counted as objectively superior, for there is no standard outside of the argument to determine (to measure) which of them captures the Truth. Instead, the only possible mode of adjudication is which of them is taken to be true, i.e. which of the two is persuasive and thereby succeeds in becoming a *nomos*.

What determines which "truth" will become authoritative in a specific community is the extent to which its advocate is effective. Before 1973, for example, abortion was illegal in the United States. From the perspective of the state it was counted as something very bad. After *Roe v. Wade* the verdict was overturned. In a variety of forums, an argument had been successfully mounted to defend the right to an abortion. In Protagorean terms, what had been the "weaker argument" – the one defending the moral permissibility of abortion – had become the "stronger." It's possible that views will change on this issue at some time in the future. What is now the weaker argument – abortion is morally wrong and should be completely prohibited – may become the stronger.

Because of this oscillation between weaker and stronger arguments, change is central to the Protagorean worldview. No truth, no agreed-upon value or regulation, is permanent. Or, to reformulate, truths are not "necessary," for they can be otherwise. They are, instead, "contingent." All the various truths and values by which we are guided depend upon the efficacy and power of those advocating for them. Such power waxes and wanes, depending on a variety of circumstances. Ultimately and in the broadest sense, what changes minds is rhetoric, and this is, finally, what the Sophists taught.

Rhetoric is traditionally defined as the "art of persuasion" or of "speaking well." In antiquity, before there was video, the essential form of communication was oral, and so for the Greeks "rhetoric" referred to the ability to make speeches. In our time, persuasion largely takes place through the manipulation of visual images, and so the skilled rhetoricians of today generally work in either TV, the movies, or on the internet. Regardless of whether it is ancient or modern, the first sense of "rhetoric" refers to a specific set of communication skills. To study this subject thus means to learn how to become an effective persuader.

"Rhetoric," however, has a second and much broader sense. Here it names not only a skill, but the worldview in which that skill becomes paramount. This worldview is precisely the humanistic one expressed by Protagoras. "Rhetoric" implies that, in the absence of absolute Truth, human communities are the measure of what is the case and what not, what should be and what should not be. It privileges *nomos* over *phusis*, the practical over the theoretical, and locates change and contingency at the core of the human experience, which in turn is shaped by human effort and constructed largely by language. (See Mendelson 2002 for a discussion of these themes.)

To reiterate, within such a worldview, rhetoric in the narrow sense – namely, technical skill in persuasive argument – takes on paramount significance. Given the Protagorean inversion of the Milesian Picture, articulating the objective Truth is no longer deemed possible or desirable. As a result, ontology is replaced by rhetoric as what we might call "the first science." For the Sophist, the issue is no longer Being, but what people say about Being and how they act in the world. In the Protagorean world nothing is more important than being able to speak well and persuasively about whatever it is that people are speaking about.

There is insufficient historical evidence to determine exactly what Protagoras actually taught as he wandered from city to city. One way or another, however, it surely had something to do with the use of language. Some of the Sophists (including the one we will meet in the next section, Gorgias) did teach rhetoric in the narrow sense. For this reason, among their most enthusiastic clients were young men interested in furthering their political careers. After all, rhetoric, whether in its ancient or modern guise, is essential in pushing oneself or one's agenda forward in any sort of political forum. For this reason, one Greek city, one *polis*, exerted the greatest lure for the Sophists: Athens. This was because Athens was not only wealthy but also intensely democratic. It both permitted and genuinely valued free speech. Many of the most critical political decisions were made in its Assembly, where all the citizens met, debated, and directly voted on specific policy questions. Other crucial issues were decided by the jury system. In both cases, the art of persuasion was at a premium, for both operate on the principle of majority rule. The issue before members of both the jury and the Assembly is not the Truth, but the Vote. Contestants speak and the matter is decided not by a wise judge, but by one's peers, fellow citizens who are often randomly chosen. The task for the good speaker is therefore not to articulate what is Good or Just "itself by itself," but to persuade a group of ordinary human beings.

This Sophistic migration to Athens will have important consequences for the history of Greek Philosophy, for it helps to establish this democratic and free-speaking *polis* as the future home of all significant philosophical developments in Greece. While the Presocratic story began in Ionia, and many of its most significant contributors came from the far western portion of the Greek world (what is today Italy), beginning in the late fifth century, philosophy will take hold in Athens. The significance of this move will be elaborated shortly, when we discuss Socrates, the first native-born Athenian in the history of Greek philosophy.

As mentioned in the Introduction, there is a deep similarity between the Sophistic movement and what today is called "postmodernism." To close this section, we will take a brief look at some comments by a contemporary thinker who is both a representative of the postmodern movement, as well as someone who understands its affinity with Sophistic rhetoric, Stanley Fish.

(*Warning*: the following discussion will be painfully brief and simplified. "Postmodernism" is a somewhat outdated term for a broad and unwieldy trend in contemporary thought. It has long been associated with "deconstruction," a mode of thinking devised by the French thinker Jacques Derrida [see Derrida 1976], as well as the work of the American philosopher Richard Rorty [see Rorty 1980 and 1982]. Among his other virtues, Fish explains Derrida in terms far more clear than those used by Derrida himself [see Fish 1989, pp. 37–67]. He also does a good job explaining how his own views recapitulate much of what the Greek Sophists had to say [see pp. 480–2, and pp. 525–6]. Mendelson 2002 is also a good source on this subject. His work aims to revitalize Protagorean rhetoric, and he devotes his first chapters to explaining its relation to contemporary thinking.)

A good way to begin thinking about postmodernism is first to consider what it opposes. As Fish puts it, the opponent affirms "an independent reality whose outlines can be perceived by a sufficiently clear-eyed observer who can then represent them in a transparent verbal medium" (p. 479). This description would fit Thales, for example. He "saw" reality, in the form of the *archê*, as absolute, and thus as independent of human thoughts or speeches about it. He was "clear-eyed." He surveyed the things in the world before him and concluded that they all derived from water, which he in turn identified as the fundamental reality. Finally, he believed he could communicate this Truth clearly in a *logos* that accurately and objectively "represented" this reality. For Thales, indeed for all the Presocratics, the implicit assumption is that philosophical "language faithfully reflects or reports on matters of fact uncolored by any personal or partisan agenda or desire" (p. 474). They are convinced that there is a "Truth that exists independently of all perspectives and points of view" (p. 474), and a philosophical "discourse must be measured against [such] a stable and independent reality" (p. 481). A "transparent" *logos* allows the listener (or reader) to see through it to the reality which it represents. If successful, it is counted as being true: it allows the object under discussion to be seen clearly as what it actually is in itself.

The several visual metaphors used in the previous paragraph can be encapsulated by a single Greek word: *theorein*, "to look at, to behold," which is the root of our word "theory." What Fish is saying, then, is that the postmodernist rejects the possibility of the kind of theorizing, the clear-eyed apprehension of Being "itself by itself," that was initially championed by the Presocratics. Instead, for the postmodernist, "the highest truth for any man is what he believes it to be" (p. 480). In other words, as Rorty puts it, there is no Truth, just truths. And these, far from being theoretical, are constructed by linguistic or interpretive communities. "Human activity," Fish tells us, "is itself always engaged in constructing the systems in relation to which its own actions and their meanings become at once possible and intelligible" (p. 226). Human beings have no direct access to an objective Truth. Instead, our entire experience is "mediated." In fact, "already-in-place interpretive constructs are a condition of consciousness" itself (p. 394). This means we never simply encounter Being or beings as they are in and of themselves. Instead, between us and them is always what the linguistic community has to say. On this view, we never experience or "see" nature or reality as raw or untouched. The best we can do is only talk about what other people say.

Given this sort of worldview, "the skill which produces belief and therefore established what, in a particular time and particular place, is true, is the skill essential to the building and maintaining of a civilized society. In the absence of a revealed truth, rhetoric is that skill" (p. 480). Quoting Richard Lanham, Fish states, "Rhetorical man is trained not to discover reality but to manipulate it. Reality is what is accepted as reality, what is useful" (p. 483).

Fish connects postmodernism (or as he here calls it "deconstructive thought") with rhetoric in the following: "This is why deconstructive . . . thought is supremely rhetorical: it systematically asserts and demonstrates the mediated, constructed, partial, socially constituted nature of all realities" (p. 492).

These concise statements about rhetoric and "postmodernism" can easily and usefully be applied to Protagoras, and indeed to Sophistry in general.[5] To elaborate, we turn next to the second of the great fifth century Sophists, Gorgias of Leontini.

Gorgias

Like Protagoras, Gorgias (ca. 483–376) was not a native of Athens. He was from Leontini, which is in modern day Sicily. But he too came to Athens (in 427).

One of Gorgias' three major fragments (and the only one to be discussed in this section) is an imagined defense of Helen of Troy. Helen was the cause of the Trojan War. After having been stolen by Paris, the son of the Trojan king Priam, the Greeks, led by Helen's husband Menelaus and his brother Agamemnon, laid siege to Troy for 10 years in order to get her back. Homer, you recall, composed the *Iliad* somewhere around 700. Regardless of how he depicted Helen, by the fifth century, she had become something of a stock figure, the loose woman *par excellence*, whose infidelity had caused the deaths of so many valiant soldiers. By writing a defense of this notorious trollop, Gorgias was showing off. It was as if he were boasting, "if I can persuade you to find Helen innocent, I can persuade you of anything at all."

Gorgias begins his *Encomium of Helen* by listing four possible reasons why she ended up in Troy. (1) It was fated by the gods that she be taken by Paris. (2) She was forced to go there; she was raped and abducted. (3) She had fallen so madly in love with the handsome Trojan that she lost control of her senses. (4) She was persuaded by speeches (*logoi*). In each of these cases, Gorgias argues to his imaginary jury, Helen was not responsible for, and hence should not be condemned or punished for, her actions.

Reasons (1) and (2) are reasonable enough. Helen surely should not be held accountable for actions caused by others. (3) is notoriously problematic: should those who commit a "crime of passion" be forgiven? Perhaps not. But (4) is the crux. What really concerns Gorgias is "speech," and his discussion of it forms not only the basis of his defense of Helen, but also provides a critical insight into his rhetorical worldview.

Logos, Gorgias tell us, "is a powerful master" (8).[6] Remember, this is arguably the single most important word in the history of Greek philosophy, and it assumes different shades of meaning depending on who is using it. Unlike Parmenides, for whom *logos* means "rational account," for Gorgias it tokens "speech" in a much broader sense (whose nuances will become increasingly clear as we progress).

Speech is a master that can overpower us. It can, for example, "put an end to fear, eliminate pain, instill delight, and increase pity" (8). With these remarks, Gorgias is asking his imaginary jury to reflect on the simple but remarkable power of language. A good storyteller, like Odysseus in Homer's *Odyssey*, can make us cry by telling us of his woes, even though we ourselves are actually unaffected by the story's events and have no idea of whether they are true or not. An inspiring leader, like Henry V in Shakespeare's play, can inspire his frightened, weary, and outnumbered troops to fight with mad valor against their enemies. He can, with words alone, "put an end to fear." For this reason, speech, says Gorgias, is like "witchcraft and magic" (10). Words fly invisibly through the air and somehow strike and impact their target. When they do the result is the production of a *doxa*, a word used regularly throughout the *Encomium of Helen*.

Doxa, like several other Greek words we have cited throughout this book, has both a narrow and a broad meaning. In the former sense, it means "opinion" or "belief," in the latter, "appearance" or "the way things seem to be." Speech, according to Gorgias, constructs *doxa*. If Bob tells you in painful detail the story of how his mother suffered in the hospital, you may well cry. An image of Bob's mother will appear before your eyes, and you will feel the pain of her suffering. Bob may or may not be telling the truth. Regardless, what matters is only whether the listener has been persuaded. This is the true power of speech. It creates images which in turn generate emotional responses. The ability to marshal this image-building power of language, and use it in a methodical and self-interested way, is, Gorgias suggests, something like magic.

How many men have persuaded and do persuade how many, on how many subjects, by fabricating false speech [*logos*]! For if everyone, on every subject, possessed memory of the past and [understanding] of the present and foreknowledge of the future, speech would be equally [powerful]; but as it is, neither remembering a past event nor investigating a present one nor prophesying a future one is easy, so that on most subjects most men make belief [*doxa*] an adviser to their soul. But belief, being fallible and unreliable, brings fallible and unreliable success to those who employ it. (11–12)

"Fallible" translates the Greek *sphalera*, which derives from a verb meaning "to fall" or "to cause to fall."[7] Something is "fallible" if it can rather easily fall down. Such precariousness and contingency is basic to the Sophistic worldview. Human being is the measure; there is no stable Being, no Truth, with which to anchor ourselves. Far from being able to achieve an enduring and objective Truth, we can barely manage to remember what happened yesterday. On most matters, then, most people have only a tenuous grip. We in fact know very little, if anything, for sure. What remains to guide us is *doxa*, which in turn is fashioned or produced by skillful speakers able to exert their linguistic expertise.

To illustrate the scope of *doxa* and the power of rhetoric, Gorgias uses an example we would not normally associate with either, namely astronomy.

To show that persuasion, when added to speech, also moulds the mind in the way it wishes, one should note first the speeches of the astronomers, who substituting belief for belief, demolishing one and establishing another, make the incredible and obscure become clear to the eyes of belief. (13)

The ancient astronomer Ptolemy thought the earth was the center of the universe. Copernicus radically disagreed, and developed what is now the standard heliocentric model. From Gorgias' highly relativist viewpoint, neither view is more True than the other. Both are beliefs. Copernicus managed to persuade the scientific community that the earth revolves around the sun, a theory which before him had seemed "incredible." But Copernicus does not represent a step closer to the Truth about nature (*phusis*). He was merely more successful in shaping convention (*nomos*). His theory, no less than his predecessors', stands poised only to be made weaker by the next, stronger contestant.[8]

Another comparison Gorgias offers is between speech and drugs.

> The power of speech bears the same relation to the ordering of the mind as the ordering of drugs bears to the constitution of bodies. Just as different drugs expel different humours from the body, and some stop it from being ill but others stop it from living, so too some speeches cause sorrow, some cause pleasure, some cause fear, some give the hearers confidence, some drug and bewitch the mind with an evil persuasion. (14)

Just as one drug can alleviate the pain of a headache, and another cause it, so too can one speech free us from grief and another make us cry. Like the expert physician, the well-trained rhetorician has a repertoire of speeches which he can systematically administer in order to achieve the results he wishes.

In sum: Helen is not guilty of a crime because she, having been persuaded by the power of masterful speech, was not responsible for her actions. Upon reflection, however, it quickly becomes clear that Gorgias' argument is not really about Helen at all. Because it would apply to anyone who has been persuaded by speech, and because all human beings are guided by their beliefs, which in turn are the products of persuasion, it applies to everyone. In general, then, just as there is no absolute Truth or Being, so too there is no "self" which exists "itself by itself" and can take complete responsibility for human action. The human self is nothing but a conglomeration of *doxai*. It is a product of external forces – specifically, linguistic and persuasive forces – acting upon it.[9] Such, at least, is the view of what Fish calls "the rhetorical man."

To conclude this section: the Sophists changed the subject. Unlike the Presocratics, their concern was not with the *arché* or with Being itself. Instead, theirs was a thoroughly anthropocentric world in which human beings only have access to, and live their lives by, *doxa* rather than the Truth. In such a world, rhetoric, the producer of *doxa*, replaces ontology as the most esteemed achievement of *logos*.

The Sophists pushed the conversation forward, but their contribution was bound to provoke criticism. Because they relinquished the quest for Truth and substituted their relativism for the "absolutism" characteristic of earlier thinkers, they betrayed the animating impulse of Greek philosophy. While they deserve congratulations for bringing

Presocratics "down to earth," and placing human life and practical concerns on the agenda, they also must be criticized for abandoning philosophy itself. The thinker first to respond to the Sophistic challenge was also the first native-born Athenian to appear in our narrative: Socrates.

Socrates

Cicero, the Roman orator and philosopher of the first century (CE), declared that Socrates "was the first to call philosophy down from the heavens and set her in the cities of men, and bring her also into their homes, and compel her to ask questions about life and morality and things good and evil" (*Tusculuan Disputations*, 5.4.10–11). This description goes to the heart of Socrates' dialectical response to the Sophists, and captures his unique contribution to the history of philosophy. Like Protagoras he brought the Presocratic project down to earth by putting human and practical concerns on the table. But unlike the Sophists he retained the traditional task of the philosopher, namely to find the Truth. Specifically, he sought the Truth, not about Being, but about the values according to which human beings shape their lives.

We know only a few facts about Socrates. He was born in 469 in Athens, the son of a stonemason. He got married late in life to Xanthippe and had three children with her. He was thickly built, very strong, and had a snub nose. Having been convicted on the charges of impiety and of corrupting the youth, he was executed by vote of his own citizens in 399. (We will discuss these charges shortly.) Beyond this, however, little is certain, for apparently by choice, and possibly for philosophical reasons, Socrates wrote nothing. What this means, of course, is that we have no first-hand knowledge of his actual views. Even if "Socrates" is a legendary name in the annals of western culture, everything one claims to know about his contribution is based on conjecture. The overwhelming source of his legend are the dialogues of Plato, in many of which "Socrates" is the main character. The name is in scare-quotes because, as will be discussed at the beginning of chapter 3, in Plato's dialogues it is impossible to tell whether the character is meant to reflect the historical figure or is more of a device to represent Plato's own views. We do not know where "Socrates" ends and Plato begins.

The other sources are Xenophon (428–354), who associated with Socrates in his youth, and wrote *The Apology of Socrates*, *Memorabilia*, and the *Symposium*, all of which recount events in his life. The comic poet Aristophanes wrote a play, *The Clouds*, which was performed in 423, and features a caricature of Socrates. Aeschines, who apparently was one of Socrates' most devoted attendants, wrote several Socratic dialogues (of which only fragments remain), which were taken at the time to be representative of the historical figure. Finally, Aristotle in several of his works mentions Socrates.

One can play the detective, and from these disparate strands of evidence try to weave together an accurate portrait of the historical figure. Not least because of the overwhelming impact of Plato's "Socrates," this is very hard to do. In this section, only a small bit will be asserted about the philosopher who lived from 469 to 399. As usual it will take its bearings from Socrates' contribution to the dialectical conversation that is Greek philosophy.

We begin with a statement from Aristotle:

> In the time of Socrates, this <concern with essence and definition> grew, but investigation into nature stopped, and philosophers turned to the study of practical virtue and of politics.[10]

From a historical perspective, this statement is vague, for it speaks only of the "time of Socrates," and makes no reference to the various connections and patterns of influence that might have held between thinkers of the fifth century. It does not, for example, support the contention offered in this chapter, namely that Protagoras provided the impetus for putting human being on the intellectual agenda during this period. Three key points can, however, be elicited from Aristotle's remark, and they prove to be decisive in characterizing the historical Socrates:

1. Like other thinkers of this time, he turned away from "the investigation into nature." This phrase is Aristotle's way of describing the Presocratics, who were, as he puts it, *phusiologoi*, ones who give a *logos*, a theoretical account, of *phusis*, of nature or what is.

2. Socrates turned towards human things, the values and guiding principles of a good life. The all-important word Aristotle uses here is *aretê*. Typically this is translated as "virtue," but often (for reasons to be discussed in chapter 4) it is better rendered as "excellence."

According to Aristotle, Socrates was concerned with what constitutes an excellent human life.

Note Aristotle's addition of the phrase "politics." As suggested above in the brief mention of Pericles, in investigating *aretê* the Greeks naturally would think about politics. For them, with only rare exceptions, the good life, indeed the only genuinely human life, was one spent in a political community. Their question was, how should we, as citizens, live our lives?

3. During the time of Socrates, Aristotle claims, "the concern for essence and definition grew." In another context, he remarks that Socrates was the first to seek definitions of the "moral virtues" (*Metaphysics*, 1078b20). This is critical. Essential to the character of the historical Socrates was his commitment to asking a specific, and deceptively simple, kind of question: "what is it?" (*ti esti*), or, to use a variant, "what is X itself?" If an answer to this question can be provided, the "essence" of X has been articulated, and a definition of X has been attained.

A definition of a general term X must cover all the particular instances of X. If X is "hat," and its definition is "a covering for the head," then that definition should apply to all individual or particular hats. If we can identify a covering for the head that is not a hat, or a hat that does not cover the head, then the definition would fail. Definitions, in short, must be universal. This is why the "itself" is important in the formulation of the Socratic question. It is not looking for examples of X, nor for a partial description or a particular feature, but for a complete articulation of what it itself, its essence, is. (See Benson 2000 for a thorough discussion of this issue.)

As Aristotle puts it, the kinds of X with which Socrates was concerned were moral virtues like justice, courage, moderation, and wisdom (the four "cardinal" virtues of the Ancient Greeks). His paradigmatic question, then, took the form of, for example, "what is justice itself?" With these notions in place, we can now sketch what will be termed the "Socratic picture," the conceptual framework implicit in the asking of the "what is it" question. (See figure 2.1.) In it, "X itself" is depicted as distinct from, yet somehow responsible for the being and the intelligibility of the particular items which are named as instances of "X."

Equally important as the kind of question Socrates asked, was the way he pursued it. Simply put, he talked to other people, who then

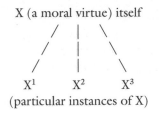

X (a moral virtue) itself

X¹   X²   X³
(particular instances of X)

Figure 2.1 The Socratic Picture

became his discussion-partners, or "interlocutors." Socrates asked them his question, they offered an answer, and he then critically and occasionally ruthlessly examined it. Typically this examination led to the refutation of the interlocutor. This often occurred when Socrates presented a counterexample to the definition proposed. For example: one interlocutor (according to Plato) defines justice as "giving back what one owes." Socrates responds: what if someone borrowed a knife from a friend, who then goes mad and becomes homicidal? Would it be just to return the knife to him? The answer is "no," and so the proposed definition fails.

Another Socratic strategy is to elicit a contradiction from the interlocutors' assertions. For example: an interlocutor defines piety as "that which is loved by the gods." But Odysseus is loved by Athena and hated by Poseidon. Therefore, Odysseus is both pious and impious, and this is a contradiction.[11]

Through a series of questions the conversation with Socrates would end in an impasse – in what the Greeks would call an *aporia* – with no definitive answer achieved. Socrates' method of examination and refutation is termed the *elenchos*. (See Vlastos 1983 for a thorough description.)

To grasp the extraordinary significance of Socrates in the history of philosophy, it is important first to understand how strange, how radical, and how potentially upsetting the "what is it" question really is. To begin, consider this feature of questions in general: none of them is innocent, for all are loaded with presuppositions. Consider what happens when I ask you, "who won the game last night?" First, I presuppose there was a game last night, and that it had a winner. Next, I assume you might know the answer, which is why I'm asking you. Furthermore, I assume two things about myself: I am ignorant of the answer, but I do want to find it out. Every question operates this way. Built into it is a set of answers to prior questions.

A typical Socratic question such as "What is justice itself?" is no exception. In asking for a universal definition Socrates presupposes that there actually is some sort of universal justice, such an essence, and that it can be articulated. In other words, he assumes (without argument) the scheme sketched above in figure 2.1. And this is a weighty assumption indeed. As such, it is entirely possible, and perhaps quite reasonable, to disagree with it. It is easy to imagine someone bombarded with Socrates' question who responds, "hey, wait a minute. That's a really bad question, and I'll have no part of it. There is no such thing as universal or absolute justice. Justice is in the eyes of the beholder, and so you're being ridiculous by asking me what it is." Protagoras and Gorgias, for example, might respond this way. After all, they are Sophists, relativists, who reject from the outset the Socratic Picture presupposed by the "what is X itself" question. They deny that the intensive pronoun "itself" is appropriate, for, according to the Sophists, nothing actually is "in itself." Instead, because human being is the measure of all things, all things depend on, are for, somebody or some community. There is no justice itself, only particular forms of justice which are upheld and variously defined by a wide variety of cities. Justice, in short, is in the eyes of the beholder.

The Sophistic response to the Socratic Picture would to be to chop off its head, leaving only the particulars at the bottom (figure 2.2). There are any number of conceptions of, for example, justice. But they are neither linked by a common thread nor grounded in a universal conception.

The "what is it" question not only presupposes a highly controversial philosophical scheme – specifically, it affirms the reality and intelligibility of "X itself" – it might suggest why Socrates was executed. His form of questioning was inherently subversive of the existing political order. This is because Socrates demanded that his interlocutor critically examine, and so disengage himself from, the particular form of justice

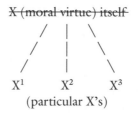

$$X \text{ (moral virtue) itself}$$
$$X^1 \qquad X^2 \qquad X^3$$
(particular X's)

Figure 2.2 The Sophistic Picture

with which he is presently allied. Squarely to face the question "what is justice itself" means to consider seriously the possibility that one's own city is not just.

If the definition of a hat is "covering for the head," and I have a visor which covers only my forehead, but I've always believed it to be a hat, then I will be disheartened to discover I've been wrong. Similarly, if I learn that Sue, who calls her motorcycle helmet a hat – a statement I've always taken to be ridiculous – is actually right, then again my sense of what a hat is will be shaken. Of course, it does not much matter how one defines a hat. But it matters enormously what justice itself is. What we take to be the answer to this question forms our conception of what makes for a good city, for a good life. In turn, this conception governs the decisions we make at virtually every moment of the day.

Consider what happens, for example, to Bob when he is drafted into the army to fight in the latest war his city has declared. Having bumped into Socrates the week before, and having failed the test of the *elenchos*, he now realizes that he does not know what justice itself is. Therefore, he reasons, he does not know whether the particular war his city is now waging (X^1 in figure 2.1) is just or not. Not knowing this, he does not know whether he should serve in the army or not. What might he do? Perhaps his newly realized ignorance will paralyze him. Not knowing what to do, he may just stay home in bed. Or perhaps, convinced that justice itself is not knowable, he may further convince himself that no single course of action is more or less just than any other. There is no reason, he then concludes, not to become a traitor and fight for the other side, or a deserter who refuses to fight at all. In short, Socratic questioning opens the door to all sorts of possibilities, and thereby potentially subverts the established political order. Can a city maintain itself if men like Bob fail to become loyal citizen-soldiers?

To reiterate: the Socratic *elenchos* was famous for ending in failure. This should not be surprising: definitions of any kind are hard to come by. Is a hat really a "covering of the head?" If so, does this mean that a motorcycle helmet, which does in fact cover the head, is a hat? What about a wig? What about a veil? If "hat" is hard to work with, imagine the difficulties with "justice itself" or "the good itself." The Socratic question is monumentally difficult to answer, and as a result perplexity, or *aporia*, is the regular outcome of the *elenchos*. Indeed, it is possible that *aporia* was not only the anticipated, but perhaps even the desired outcome of the *elenchos*. Perhaps Socrates thought there was something salutary about being at a loss. If so, this is another sense in which he was a subversive. His interlocutor may well have begun the conversation by confidently believing he knew what justice itself is. In fact, most people, however unreflectively, do think this. After all, they obey the laws of their city and do so because they think they should. People live their lives on the basis of believing they know what is right, just, good, to do. When they go to dinner in the evening, they do so because they think it is good to do so. When the city asks them to go to war, they, by and large, march forward. But what happens when the interlocutor is plunged into perplexity? If he does not know what justice is, he does not know whether this particular war his city is waging is just, or whether he should go or not. Perhaps he will refuse.

Socratic questioning is thus politically dangerous. This may well have been a reason why Socrates was executed by the Athenian democracy. (There were, of course, specific historical forces at work in Athens in the year 399, notably the traumatic aftermath of the Peloponnesian War, which ended in 404. For an account of how these may have affected the trial see Stone 1988. For a thorough treatment of Socrates see Brickhouse & Smith 2002.)

To summarize: it is likely (even if not provable) that the Socrates who lived from 469–399 had these two characteristics: he asked the "what is it" question, and he used the *elenchos* to refute his interlocutors and drive them into *aporia*. It is tempting to speculate about a third characteristic, namely the fact that Socrates chose not to write. This section will close, and the transition to chapter 3 will begin, by giving into this temptation. We will take a brief look at a passage from Plato's dialogue the *Phaedrus*, in which "Socrates" (and again I use scare quotes to indicate this is Plato's version) explains why he did not write. Whether this argument actually applies or not to the historical figure cannot be determined. But it may, and it certainly will be useful as a transition to Plato himself. In any case, the following paraphrases the story "Socrates" tells in order to offer his critique of writing in the *Phaedrus* (274b–277a).[12]

When writing was invented, it was advertised as being a fabulous new technology. Its inventor boasted that it would make people wiser by improving their memories. No longer would people have to rely on their own, highly fallible mental powers to store and then retrieve their data. Instead, they could write it all down, and then call it back up whenever they needed it. The far more reliable mechanism of writing would replace the precarious workings of the human mind.

In response, "Socrates" offered four criticisms:

1) Writing does not strengthen, it actually weakens our memories. It habituates its user to rely on a system of external symbols, and therefore the internal power of memory begins to atrophy. This point seems clearly substantiated by the experience of preliterate cultures, where, for example, the minstrel or bard was capable of memorizing enormously long epic poems, and even by the experience of children who, before they can read and write, are capable of learning by heart any number of stories and songs. Indeed, this phrase "learn by heart" captures quite well "Socrates'" point. When we use our memories we activate what is inside of us. When we enlist the services of the technology of writing, we subordinate ourselves to something external, and thereby irrevocably weaken what is in us, what really belongs to us, what keeps us alive.

2) Writing makes us dumber. It does not offer real wisdom, but only "the appearance of wisdom" (275a). Anything can be written down: notes on a lecture, a reminder about Sue's birthday, the Gettysburg Address, or the date of the Spanish Armada. Because writing is so powerful and anything can be written down, there is no way to dis-criminate between what is really worth writing down and remembering, and what is not. By contrast, because it is so limited, memory is necessarily selective. We cannot remember everything, but only things that really matter. Writing is incapable of distinguishing between what is worth saving, and what is not. Even if a written work appears im-pressive, it is only thoughtless preservation rather than careful reflection.

3) Once something is written, it takes on a life of its own. "Socrates" uses a metaphor here. The writer is the parent, and the writing is a child. Once written, the writing is like an orphan. It circulates among readers without being able to protect itself. It is "bandied about, alike among those who understand and those who have no interest in it" (275e). If, for example, this book gets into the wrong hands, someone might selectively misquote it and end up asserting (falsely) that its author is a defender of Sophistry. Indeed, someone need only quote the last seven words of the previous sentence out of context in order

to give this impression. The author, the father of the work, will not be able to correct this (mis)reading. Writing, in other words, is necessarily and inevitably subject to misinterpretation.

4) Writing cannot refuse itself to anyone. As "Socrates" puts it, writing says "only one and the same thing" (275d) to any and all. He uses a simile to clarify this point. Writing, he says, is like a painting. A painting stands still and "preserves a solemn silence" (275d) when someone looks at it. It is unable to answer any questions the viewer might have, and it has nothing to say about who will view it and who not. As a result, just as the third complaint had it, it is often terribly misunderstood. In fact, some people should not read certain writings. But writing itself can do nothing to stop them from doing so. It is open for inspection by all.

"Socrates" summarizes these criticisms by comparing writing, quite unfavorably, with speaking. Speaking is "the legitimate brother of the bastard" (276a) form of language, namely writing. Speaking is more basic, alive, and ultimately better than writing on all four of the counts listed above.

When we speak we use words written "with intelligence in the mind of the learner, which is able to defend itself and knows to whom it should speak and before whom to be silent" (276a). The preposition "in" is crucial. Speaking is the "living and breathing" dimension of language. When we speak to another human being we do not rely on an external symbolic system, and therefore we do not weaken what is "in" us.

Speaking, unlike writing, is able to be choosey. For example, any lecture whatsoever and in its entirety can easily be transcribed. By contrast, only a very few lectures, and only a few portions of any given lecture, are going to be counted as worth talking about.

Speaking can protect itself from being misinterpreted. If I am talking to you, and it seems that you do not understand what I'm getting at, I can correct you before it's too late. I can ask you, "does what I'm saying make sense?" and then check to see if it really does. Furthermore, in speaking I can always size up my audience and adjust the speech accordingly. If I am talking with a group of children, I will speak differently than I would when addressing a group of senior citizens. Writing cannot make these sorts of distinctions. As such it is but a faint imitation of a more authentic form of human communication: speaking to one another.

Speaking can refuse itself. If I decide that you are an inappropriate audience for what I have to say, I can just clam up and move on.

Whether these were the historical Socrates' actual reasons for not writing cannot be determined. But they at least conform with the picture of him sketched throughout this chapter. He was a "gadfly" (an image from *The Apology of Socrates*, written by Plato) who incessantly bugged people with his "what is it" question. He demanded that his interlocutors reflect on their own beliefs and values, and have the courage to be self-critical. He pushed them towards the universal, the "X itself," and thus away from the particulars. And all of this took place through the medium of a personal conversation, a human interaction. Perhaps Socrates did not write because his purpose was not to teach in an abstract or theoretical sense, but to transform his interlocutor. For him the issue was *aretê* and the values by which we live. His concern was with his fellow Athenians, for whom a plunge into *aporia* would be, he thought, philosophically therapeutic.

Whatever the status of these speculations about Socrates' decision not to write, one point is certain. Plato himself wrote a critique of writing in his work, the *Phaedrus*. Unless he was utterly oblivious to the implications of what he himself had written, Plato must have believed that his own form of writing could circumvent the very criticisms he had raised against it. He must therefore have conceived of his own work as able (1) to enhance rather than diminish the reader's internal faculties; (2) to discriminate, to make value judgments about what is written; (3) to protect itself from misreadings; (4) to discriminate among its readers, and even to refuse to address some readers. In sum, Plato must have tried to make his writing more like speaking. He did so by writing dialogues, or dramas, in which he himself does not appear. The characters in his dialogues – and typically, but not always, "Socrates" is the hero – speak to each other. There is never a moment in which the author turns to his audience and announces, "the following are my views." As a result, readers must always be on the alert. They must elicit the Platonic view from the dramatic context in which it is embedded. Plato is thus inherently elusive, and readers must be actively engaged in the quest for his views.

To put this point in slightly different terms, there are always two dialogues at work in Plato's writing. The first is between "Socrates" and his interlocutor. The second is between the reader and Plato. Because the questions at issue are not merely theoretical, but instead ask how we should live our lives, passivity is not tolerated. The demand is for an active engagement with the text and a philosophical form of reading. In the next chapter we will gain a better understanding of what this really means.[13]

Notes

1 This is not to say that the Greeks themselves were silent on this subject. The poets, beginning with Homer and culminating in the great tragedians of the fifth century, certainly made the human drama their central concern. But the philosophers, driven as they were by their theoretical quest for Being, were by and large silent.

2 Translations of Protagoras are my own. The Greek text is Diels.

3 Although Plato does attribute something like it to Protagoras in his dialogue the *Theaetetus*.

4 The quote comes from Thucydides, as translated by Woodruff 1993, p. 42.

5 In fairness, Fish does not actually use the word "postmodernism." He does, however, make the sorts of moves described in this section. See, for example, his comments about Protagoras and Isocrates on pp. 480–2.

6 My Greek text is MacDowell 1982. References are to paragraphs of the *Encomium*.

7 This lengthy translation (and the next two) belongs to MacDowell 1982, but I substitute "fallible" for his "slippery."

8 The view of the history of science implicit in Gorgias' *Encomium of Helen* foreshadows that of Thomas Kuhn, whose thinking Fish describes as "rhetorical through and through" and for whom (according to Fish), "the force of scientific argument is only that of persuasion" (1989, pp. 486–7). (I should note that Fish's view of Kuhn is controversial.)

9 This notion of the "destruction" of the self is often associated with the twentieth-century thinker Michel Foucault.

10 *Parts of Animals*, 640a30. I follow the translation of Irwin & Fine 1996, who place the phrase "with essence and definition" in brackets to indicate it is an interpolation.

11 The first example comes from Book I of Plato's *Republic*. The second from the *Euthyphro*.

12 All quotations are from Fowler 1982.

13 See Griswold 1988 for a thorough study of the philosophical significance of the dialogue form.

3

Plato

Preliminaries

As a young man Plato (429–347) must have spent a great deal of time in Socrates' company, and he no doubt witnessed many an *elenchos*. After all, he wrote numerous dialogues in which "Socrates" is depicted as asking the "what is it" question about the virtues, interrogating an interlocutor, and then driving him into *aporia*. Plato almost surely attended Socrates' trial: he wrote *The Apology of Socrates* in which he presents his own elaborate version of the philosopher's defense.

All of this suggests the obvious: the historical figure made a tremendous impression on the young Plato. But in reading the dialogues it is impossible to determine exactly where this influence is being exerted and where an independent Plato, who uses a character called "Socrates" to express his own views, begins to emerge. For Plato was an overpowering thinker and writer, and even if he was influenced by someone else he was constitutionally incapable of becoming a disciple. Still, many scholars have played the detective and tried to determine precisely where in the dialogues the views of the historical

Socrates are being recorded, and where Plato breaks away. They have divided the Platonic corpus into chronological periods and argued that "early" dialogues such as the *Apology*, *Crito*, *Laches*, *Lysis*, *Charmides*, and *Euthyphro* largely reflect Socrates' views, while in his "middle" works, like the *Phaedo* and *Republic*, the author articulates his own, independently conceived, philosophical positions. On this chronological account, in his "late" period, when he wrote the *Sophist*, *Statesman*, *Laws*, and *Parmenides* (dialogues in which "Socrates" is either absent or not prominent), Plato was engaged in a mode of self-criticism that propelled him even beyond his own previous philosophical positions. (Gregory Vlastos is perhaps the most well-known representative of this view; see Vlastos 1991.)

The chronological interpretation is widely held and seems plausible enough. Nonetheless it is highly speculative. Unlike many modern authors, Plato wrote no autobiography and offered no commentary on his own writings.[1] Scholars therefore have no independent basis to assess their theories of Plato's evolution. (See Howland 1991 and Tigerstedt 1977 for elaborations of this sort of critique.) Furthermore, the chronological thesis can only be substantiated by means of an interpretation of the entire corpus (some 25 dialogues and 7 letters). It is impossible, therefore, in a short book like this to assess it adequately. Consequently, this chapter will ignore chronology entirely. Instead, it will comment on passages from several dialogues – principally the *Phaedo*, *Meno*, *Republic*, *Symposium*, and *Theaetetus* – and will make no reference whatsoever to their author's development. Hereafter scare-quotes will no longer be placed around "Socrates" and all instances of this name will refer only to the character appearing in Plato's dialogues. The question of the degree to which he resembles the historical figure will not be pursued.

As usual, the strategy deployed in this chapter will be dialectical. The chief task ahead of us is to understand how Plato critically responded to his predecessors – the Presocratics and, more important, the Sophists – and how he pushed the conversation forward with the assertion of his own positive views.

A danger lurks in what follows, one broached at the end of chapter 2. Plato did not write theoretical treatises, in which a single thesis on a specific topic is methodically defended. Instead he expressed himself through masterfully crafted dialogues between two or more speakers. In none of these does the author speak in his own voice. Of course, it is likely that more often than not Socrates does represent Plato's views. But precisely because Socrates is a character appearing in a dialogue, rather than one delivering a monologue consisting of a set of verifiable propositions or articulating a theory, even this cannot be determined with certainty. A speaker in a dialogue appears in specific dramatic circumstances: he addresses interlocutors at a particular time and place. At any given moment, then, what he says may be a response tailored to the particularity of the interlocutor. So, for example, in the *Republic* Socrates is speaking mainly to two young, politically ambitious men, Glaucon and Adeimantus. What he says may be influenced by this fact. In other words, if Socrates were talking to an old man uninterested in politics, he may have spoken quite differently. In short, it is always possible that the context of Socrates' remarks helps to shape them and that, as a result, extracting a given statement from its context, and simply attributing it to Plato, runs the risk of distorting it. (See Strauss 1964 for an elaboration of this idea.)

In this chapter, only a few passages from the dialogues will be discussed in detail, and it will be impossible to establish either the full context in which each appears or to determine the extent to which it influences what Socrates says. Despite the fact that Socrates is not simply Plato's "mouthpiece" (see Press 2000 for a discussion of this term), the two will often be conflated in what follows below. Readers are encouraged to return to the dialogues, read them in full with an eye towards context, and see if in fact it is legitimate to attribute Socrates' remarks to their author, or whether Plato has his character tailor his remarks to the specific demands of the occasion.

Plato's Critique of the Presocratics

The *Phaedo* is Plato's depiction of the last day of Socrates' life. After having been convicted by the Athenian jury, he was sentenced to death. Because of a law forbidding executions during a religious festival, he was forced to spend several weeks in prison. During this period he had numerous opportunities to escape. His friend Crito, a wealthy businessman, could easily have bribed the guards and arranged for him to be transported to another city. But, for reasons he outlines in the *Crito*, and which articulate a classic argument against civil disobedience, Socrates chose not to break the law, but instead to face execution by hemlock.

While in jail he was regularly visited by his friends. On the day of his execution, they were distraught. In response to their discomfort and grief Socrates makes a startling claim. He is not afraid to die. Indeed, his emotional demeanor as well as his philosophical views seem to suggest that he almost welcomes death. Why? Because, he explains, the soul is immortal. "Soul" translates the Greek *psuchê*, which in turn is the root of our words "psyche" and "psychology." Its original (and primary) meaning in Greek is not "soul" in the modern, or Christian, sense, but "life-force" or "animating principle." In general, the *psuchê* is the aspect of the human being that cannot be reduced to or identified with the body. It is what is responsible for thinking, reasoning, and talking rationally (in other words, for *logos*), and for what loves and is self-conscious in doing so. In the *Phaedo* Socrates seems to argue for its immortality. (I say "seems" because these arguments are an excellent example of the role context may play in interpreting a dialogue. Surrounded by young men who are upset by his impending demise, Socrates may well be motivated by the desire to comfort them. If so, then perhaps his arguments for the immortality of the soul should be taken with a grain of salt. See Ahrensdorf 1995 for an example of this sort of interpretation.)

In making his arguments Socrates is vigorously challenged by his interlocutors, Cebes and Simmias, both of whom are students of Philolaus, the Pythagorean. While they are sympathetic to the claim that the soul is immaterial and immortal, they want to hear this thesis adequately defended, and not merely asserted. In other words, they genuinely desire to understand the nature of the soul, and are unwilling merely to carry around with them unsupported beliefs. Not surprisingly, Socrates admires their "elenchic" spirit: in questioning him they are doing precisely what he himself is famous for, and so he welcomes, and even seems to enjoy, the opportunity to argue with them in his last hours.

The strongest challenge to the assertion of the soul's immortality comes from Simmias.

> Someone could make the same argument about harmony, lyre, and strings, namely that a harmony in a well tuned lyre is invisible and without a body and altogether beautiful and divine, but that the lyre itself and the strings are bodies and have the form of bodies and are compounded and earthly and akin to what is mortal . . . And indeed, Socrates, I think you yourself must have this in mind, that we especially believe the soul to be something of this sort. (85e–86b)[2]

Simmias agrees that the soul is nonmaterial and so is not to be strictly identified with the body. He denies, however, that it is ontologically independent of or separate from the body. He presents his objection imagistically: the soul, he says, is like the harmony produced by the strings of a well-tuned lyre. It is beautiful and not exactly a body, but it is produced by, and so dependent on, the strings of the instrument. If they were to be destroyed, so would it.

Simmias' "harmony thesis" is powerful and plausible, and it can readily be translated into contemporary terms. Many, if not most, people today believe that the soul, or what is now called "mental activity" or "consciousness," is a byproduct of the brain, which of course is a chunk of matter. This view, often termed "epiphenomenalism," is widely held by philosophers as well as practicing neuroscientists. They take for granted the notion that consciousness, while itself not quite material, is inextricably bound to, because it is produced by, something material. (See Crick 1994 for an example.) On this account, whether in its ancient guise as "the harmony thesis" or in its modern formulation, when the body or the brain dies, so too does the "soul."

Socrates presents a series of arguments against Simmias' harmony thesis. The first (91e–92d, and then 94b–95a) addresses what he calls "recollection," a crucial set of ideas which we will discuss later in this chapter. The second (92e–93b), which I paraphrase, is this:

1: A harmony is directed by, and does not direct, its components.
2: If the soul were a harmony, then it would not direct the body.
3: But the soul does direct the body.
Conclusion: the soul is not a harmony.

The third argument (93b–94b) runs as follows:

1: It is possible for a lyre to be more or less harmonized (in tune). Harmony is a quantitative relation.
2: Quantitative relations are not susceptible to qualitative distinctions. No harmony is better than another, just more or less.
3: Souls are subject to qualitative distinctions. It is possible for one soul, one person, to be better than another. Some souls are wicked, others exhibit virtue.
Conclusion: the soul is not a harmony.

Socrates defends the same general point in both arguments: "harmony" (or "epiphenomenalism") cannot account for an essential phenomenon. Simply put, we do not take ourselves to be, compre-hend ourselves as, a material clump. When you put this book down in order to get a drink of water, it will appear that you do so by saying to yourself, "I'm thirsty; I think I'll go get a drink." Then you will (somehow) "tell" your body to move. You will get up from the chair, walk to the kitchen, and pour yourself some water. Whatever is "in" you that did the telling is the "soul." It "directed" and was not "directed by" your body. In other words, if you had decided it was better for you to resist the pull of thirst, you would have stayed in your chair. Your experience informs you that you are a "self" who has desires and beliefs, who acts intentionally for what you take to be good reasons, and who orders your body around.

In a similar vein, you make value judgments. By your lights, Sue is a marvelous person, far superior to the deceitful low-life named Bob. According to Simmias' harmony thesis, however, Bob is not genuinely worse than Sue. Instead, he only has a different set of material parts. Perhaps the neuronal architecture and the resulting connections of that part of Bob's brain responsible for emotional sympathy (the amygdala) are different from Sue's. This is a quantitative distinction between Bob and Sue, not a qualitative or evaluative one. But value judgments are the guiding principles of daily and social life, and qualitative distinctions are essential in the ordinary language we use to describe them. According to Socrates, "harmony" cannot account for these dimensions of ordinary experience.

Because it conceives of the body (the brain) as the ultimate cause of the soul and all its mental activity, the "harmony" or "epiphenomenalist" thesis is closely (although complexly) related to "materialism," the doctrine that everything is made of matter. As such, it harks back to the Presocratics, especially Democritus. Recall that, at least as Aris-totle reports his views, the atomist believes that the mind consists of and can be reduced to "primary and indivisible bodies [whose] power of producing movement is due to the smallness of their parts, and their shape" (*De Anima*, 405a713). For this reason, it is easy to imagine Democritus popping into a neuroscience laboratory and becoming enthralled by the research being done in cognitive neurobiology, the study of the cellular foundations of cognitive mechanisms such as memory and emotion. In this sense, then, Socrates' arguments against Simmias represent a critique of both the Presocratics as well as con-temporary materialists.

Socrates' two little arguments against Simmias rely on what is sometimes called "folk psychology," which is the way people ordinarily understand themselves and one another. The neuroscientist hopes to replace this with a rigorous scientific theory in which notions like the self, intention, desire, belief, acting for good reasons, and value judgment would be supplanted by precise explanations of neural activity localized to different brain structures.[3] As we will see shortly, the real question raised by this debate – indeed, by the works of Plato and Aristotle in general – is how much philosophical weight, how much epistemic value, should be attributed to what ordinary "folk" think of themselves and their lives. For the neuroscientist the answer is "next to nothing."

Sophisticated epiphenomenalists, harmony-theorists, and materialists of all stripes will hardly be silenced by Socrates' arguments. They will acknowledge that of course human beings take themselves to have selves, beliefs, desires, and values. Their purpose, they may well assert, is not to negate these phenomena, but to explain them by precisely identifying their causes. The epiphenomenalist will agree that ordinary people believe that the mind "directs" the body. But their reductionist program insists that a specific location in the brain in which this belief originated can be identified. So too with social values. A staunch believer in natural selection may well argue that our brains (specifically our frontal lobes) evolved in such a way as to produce these values in order to enhance the prospect of human survival.

The "harmony thesis" is undeniably powerful, and so far from simply dismissing it Socrates refuses to end the conversation with the arguments outlined above. To speak anachronistically, because he understands the profound challenge presented by neuroscience to his own conception of what it means to be a human being, he is not satisfied with the brief arguments he offered, and so he pushes the conversation forward. To do so he tells a little story about his own life (96a–100b). In itself, this is an interesting move. How could an autobiographical sketch possibly serve as an argument against Simmias' thesis? On the one hand, it surely cannot, for it is merely anecdotal. On the other hand, in telling his story about himself, Socrates makes an important point: we are self-conscious, reflective beings, and a significant dimension of who we are is manifested in just this capacity to give an articulate account of ourselves. We evaluate and knit together our past experiences into a coherent narrative, and thereby try to make sense of our lives. The Socratic autobiography, in both its form and content, thus presents a phenomenon that thinkers like Simmias or Democritus, for whom the ultimate cause of being human is material, cannot fully explain.[4]

One additional point: recall that, as mentioned at the end of chapter 2, Platonic writing is designed not simply to offer a theory, but to engage the reader in active reflection on the most crucial of human questions. The Socratic autobiography, indeed the dialogue form in general, is one way in which Plato accomplishes this, for it depicts its subject-matter – which we can now describe as "the life of the soul" – in those terms most faithful to it, namely dramatic.

In any case, the story Socrates tells is this: when he was young he was fascinated by the Presocratics and enthusiastically studied "natural science." He did so, he reports, because "it seemed wonderful to me to know the causes of each thing, why each thing comes to be, why it perishes, and why it exists" (96a). He was, in short, initially gripped by the prospect of understanding the natural world. He gave up this line of inquiry not because he did not admire it, but because, he says, "I seemed to myself to be naturally unsuited [*aphuês*] for this kind of investigation" (96c). There is a bit of wordplay here: *aphuês* is an adjective (whose prefix is the alpha-privative) derived from *phusis*. In essence, then, Socrates is saying, "I did not have the nature to study nature." The first sense of "nature" refers to human nature; the second, which is the Presocratic sense, refers to the world of beings outside of and independent of human being.

The young Socrates, like the rest of us, was driven by a set of likes and dislikes. He was, for whatever reason, neither interested in nor moved by the kinds of theoretical investigations undertaken by the Presocratics. Furthermore, he was disoriented by them. "I was made quite blind," he tells Simmias and Cebes, "about those things which I and others thought that I clearly knew before" (96c). Studying nature disrupted his ordinary conception of the world. Given what we have discussed about the Presocratics in chapter 1, this should come as no surprise. If, for example, Democritus was right, then there are no "souls" and the world is composed not of unified beings like rabbits and dogs, but only of atoms moving through the void. If Pythagoras was right, then nothing perceived by the senses or articulated in ordinary language is what it seems to be. Instead, the Truth about reality is revealed only through its numerical structure. "Natural science," whether Presocratic or modern, demotes the appearances, the doxic, the uniquely human, into secondary status, and obliterates the soul by reducing it to the body. Recall Democritus' dictum: "There are two kinds of judgment, one legitimate" – namely, a purely scientific view of things – "and one bastard," namely, an ordinary one based upon sense perception and natural language. Socrates, compelled by human questions, refuses to abandon the latter for the former.

After his disenchantment with natural science, Socrates' flagging interest in natural science was reignited by a chance encounter:

> Once I heard someone reading, as he said, from a book of Anaxagoras, and saying that Mind organizes and is the cause of everything. I was delighted with this cause. (97b–c)

Anaxagoras, as discussed in chapter 1, was an "elementalist" like Democritus and Empedocles. What distinguished his theory was its reliance on "Mind Itself by Itself" as the primary cause of the universe. It is anything but clear what exact role in cosmic development he intended "Mind" to play in his system. What is clear, however, is why this simple word attracted Socrates so intensely:

> I thought if [Anaxagoras' theory] was right, and the organizing mind organized everything and arranged each thing, each thing would be in the best possible condition. So, if someone wanted to discover the cause of anything, in what way it comes into being or perishes or is, it would be necessary to discover this, namely in what way it is best for it to be or to do or suffer anything. On the basis of this argument, it is appropriate for a human being, when investigating anything, to investigate nothing other than what is excellent and best. (97c–d)

Socrates hoped that Anaxagoras' theory of "Mind" would address the question with which he was most concerned: namely, "what is best?" If Mind directs the universe, he thought, everything must be what it is for a good reason. After all, that is the way Mind – or at least the human mind – seems to work. A "mindful" act is thoughtful, intentional, and purposive. Believing he had finally found a theory able to account for value and meaning, Socrates eagerly picked up Anaxagoras' book. It let him down.

> This wonderful hope was taken away from me as I went on reading and saw that the man did not make use of Mind in attributing the causes for the organization of things, but instead counted as causes air,

ether, water and many other strange entities. That seemed to me like someone who said that whatever Socrates does he does because of his mind, and then in attempting to articulate the causes of each of the things I do would say that, first of all, I am sitting here because my body consists of bones and tendons. (98b–c)[5]

To his dismay, Socrates discovered that despite his invocation of the altogether promising notion of Mind, Anaxagoras was in fact a typical elementalist and so was really a materialist. If you asked him, "Why is Socrates sitting in prison?," he would give a strictly physiological explanation in terms of the mechanical workings of the body's bones and tendons. The better answer, one that would genuinely take into account the activity of "mind," would have been this:

Since it seemed best to the Athenians to condemn me, it seemed best to me to sit here, and it seemed more just to remain and endure the punishment which they had ordered. For, by the dog, I think these tendons and bones would long ago have been in Megara or Boeotia had they been carried there by the belief that it was better to do so, and if I had not thought it was more just and noble to endure whatever penalty the city ordered rather than to escape and run away. (98e–99a)

From Socrates' perspective the best answer to "why are you sitting here?" is found not in the mechanical workings of nerves, muscles, bones, and tendons, but in the value judgments made in the "souls" of independent human beings. But what, finally, is the source and measure of these values? How can they be explained? These are the sort of questions Socrates cares about. Because the Presocratics did not address them, he had "no natural aptitude" for their form of inquiry. He turned away from "natural science" to what he describes as a "second best" way:

It seemed to me necessary to take refuge in speeches [*logoi*] and to investigate the truth of beings in them. (99e)

Instead of inquiring about, and so looking directly at, beings in the manner of the Presocratics, Socrates concerned himself with what human beings say about beings, with *logos*. This description should immediately provoke a question: is Socrates a Sophist? After all, Protagoras and Gorgias also turned away from nature and Being, and towards the world of human discourse. But Socrates is no Sophist, he is no relativist, and one word in the citation above indicates why: even if he abandoned the Presocratic quest for the "truth" about Being, he nonetheless is adamant that truth is his goal. What he wants to understand, namely the grounds of our value judgments and the practical life of our souls, is quite different from his materialist predecessors, but like them he is committed to the possibility of an objective Truth. The next section will elaborate.

Plato's Critique of the Sophists

Several of Plato's dialogues – the *Protagoras, Gorgias, Euthydemus*, and *Hippias* – are named after famous Sophists. Others, including the *Meno, Symposium, Phaedrus, Theaetetus*, and *Republic*, feature extensive arguments between Socrates and interlocutors who either are or have been influenced by the Sophists. One dialogue is simply titled the *Sophist*. The sheer bulk of these works suggests the obvious: Plato was determined to refute his relativist competitors. Indeed, they were his opponents *par excellence*.

In this section we will examine several of Socrates' strategies for arguing against them. Doing so will not only help us understand the negative pole of his dialectical response to the Sophists, it will also gradually lead us to the positive teachings that emerged from this critique.

The fact that Plato returned to the struggle against the Sophists time and again shows that he did not dismiss them lightly. In the last part of this section we will examine why exactly their relativism posed such a great challenge to him and preoccupied, or perhaps even obsessed him, throughout his life. This set of reflections will help us answer the question broached at the end of chapter 2 – why did Plato write dialogues?

a) The "self-reference" argument

In the dialogue titled *Theaetetus* Socrates spends a great deal of time arguing against Protagorean relativism. Specifically, he struggles to refute the famous dictum, "human being is the measure of all things, of the existence of things that are and the non-existence of things that are not" (152a). Below is a sample of his reasoning.

If neither [Protagoras] himself, nor the majority of people, believe that human being is the measure – as indeed they do not believe it – is it not necessary that the "truth" which he wrote is true to no one? (170e)

Then would he not be conceding that his own opinion is false if he grants that the opinion of those who think he is in error is true. (171a)

These passages contain (in condensed form) the kind of argument that came to be known as the "turning around" or "turning of the tables."[6] In such an argument, which is also called the "argument from self-reference," the opponent's thesis is turned around so that it refers to itself. Protagoras has asserted that "human being is the measure of all things." Socrates objects by pointing out the strange consequences that follow if we assume this assertion is true, and then force it to apply to itself. If so, then if someone disagrees with the statement, it becomes, by its own terms, false. Since human beings are the measure of all things, then it only takes a single person who considers (who "measures") that statement to be false, to make it false. In effect, if Protagoras is right, then he is right only for himself, and no more right than the person who disagrees with him. As a result, the Sophist can make no legitimate claim to being "wise" or able to teach others.

Why is Protagoras wise and worthy of justly becoming the teacher of others and being well paid for it, and why are we ignorant and obligated to go study with him, if each person is himself the measure of his own wisdom? (161d)

To reformulate this argument in stark terms, consider the statement, "it is true that all truth is relative." If it is true, then it too is relative, and hence is no more true than the statement, "it is false that all truth is relative." Neither is true in any objective sense. (See Mendelson 2002, pp. 12–15, for a Sophistic rebuttal of this strategy.) Since Protagoras does present himself as a teacher who is wiser than his students – after all, he charges a hefty fee for his instruction – he implicitly claims that his teaching is true and his students are more ignorant than he. As a result, his thesis refutes itself when Socrates turns the tables on it. (See Burnyeat 1976 for a thorough review of this kind of argument.)

b) The *reductio ad absurdum*

Closely related to the self-reference argument is the *reductio ad absurdum*. This sort of argument is one in which a statement or thesis is disproved by first assuming it and then demonstrating that in conjunction with other premises it generates a contradiction or some other unacceptable form of absurdity.

Socrates uses a *reductio* against a teacher of rhetoric named Thrasymachus in Book I of the *Republic*. The question under consideration here is, "what is justice itself?" (331c). Thrasymachus answers: "I say that justice is nothing other than the advantage of the stronger" (338c). By "stronger" he means the politically stronger, or the ruling body of a regime (338d). So, in a democracy, the majority of the people (the *demos*) are stronger; what they say goes. If the citizens vote to allow and protect freedom of speech, then it is just to speak freely. By contrast, in a tyranny, a single man is strongest and in charge. Even if he operates entirely for his own self-interest and forbids anyone to criticize him, it nonetheless is just to obey his orders. The nature of the regime and its conception of justice varies in these two cases, but neither is objectively superior to the other. Clearly, then, Thrasymachus is some sort of "regime relativist" (or "conventionalist"). For him, there is no absolutely true conception of "justice itself," but only particular conceptions of justice relative to the various cities upholding them.

In response Socrates offers this argument (339b–e). It begins by assuming Thrasymachus' definition:

1) Justice is the advantage of the stronger.
2) It is just to obey the rulers.
3) Therefore, it is just to obey all laws.
4) Rulers sometimes make mistakes; they make incorrect laws, ones disadvantageous to themselves.
5) Therefore, sometimes it is just to do what is disadvantageous to the ruler.
6) Conclusion: Because (5) contradicts (1), justice is not the advantage of the stronger.

Because he is a Sophistic relativist, Thrasymachus readily agrees to the first three premises. To reiterate, he believes that a wide variety of conceptions of justice are binding in the various cities that uphold them. Beyond the laws of the city, then, there is no court of higher appeal. As a result, it is just for citizens under any regime to obey the laws made by the ruling power.

Premise (4) seems to be a matter of common sense. People make mistakes, and rulers are people. When the ruler does make a mistake, he crafts a law disadvantageous to himself. For example, a tyrant might impose a very high tax on his subjects, thinking it to be to his advantage to increase his wealth. He finds out, however, that by doing so he has pushed his people too far. Facing desperate poverty, they summon the courage to rebel, and then they overthrow the tyrant. The severe tax increase backfired. It was a mistake, for it ultimately worked to the tyrant's disadvantage. Thrasymachus, however, has already agreed to premise (3): it is just for citizens to obey all laws. Hence, as (5) puts it, occasionally it is just to obey laws disadvantageous to the ruler. The initial definition – justice is the advantage of the stronger – has thus been contradicted. The *reductio* is complete.

One way Thrasymachus could have escaped from Socrates' refutation would have been to disagree with premise (4). He could have said that rulers never make mistakes because, according to his definition, whatever seems to them to be just is just. Saying this, however, would have been absurd, for surely it seems possible, in fact inevitable, for rulers to make mistakes. This seemingly trivial point is actually quite significant. According to Socrates, a decisive objection to Sophistry is that it implies the impossibility of error. If there is no objective truth, as the relativist maintains, then there also can be no error. (Because he preserves the possibility of error, then, Thrasymachus is not a full-blooded or consistent Sophist. Socrates takes advantage of precisely this inconsistency.)

This line of thought is developed throughout the *Theaetetus* (especially 152c). If Protagoras is right, Socrates argues, then "each individual would be self-sufficient in wisdom" (169d). Nobody would ever be wrong. (Aristotle makes this same point in *Metaphysics*, 1007b20 ff.) But surely this defies common sense, for "everybody would agree that some men are wiser and some more ignorant than others" (171d). To drive this point specifically against the Sophistic thesis that "human being is the measure of all things," Socrates adds the following:

> It is necessary to agree that one man is wiser than another, and that such a wise man is measure, but that it is in no way necessary for me, who is ignorant, to become a measure. (179b)

In other words, according to Socrates – and, as he believes, to any sensible person – it is absurd to count all human beings as equal measures of the Truth. When it comes to medicine, for example, the trained physician, and not the guy on the street, is the measure. So, if a woman detected a lump in her breast, and a sonogram was taken in order to determine whether it was a tumor or a cyst, she certainly would not care how the janitor who cleaned the floors of the hospital interpreted the picture. She would await the verdict of the expert radiologist. In ordinary life, basic distinctions are made between those who know and those who do not. The former, not the latter, are the measures of what should be. Sophistic relativism denies this, and by Socrates' lights, is therefore absurd.

(This use of medicine in particular, and technical knowledge in general, as an example to refute the relativist is a common strategy deployed by Socrates. See Roochnik 1996 for a thorough discussion of it. Also, as the word "interpret" in the above is meant to indicate, this argument suggests how Plato would argue against the post-modernist. For a thinker like Derrida, the whole world is a "text" subject to any number of interpretations, and resolvable by none. See Searle 1993 for a good example of a Platonic-style argument against this position.)

Another *reductio* Socrates deploys against Protagoras is also found in the *Theaetetus*. This one is directed not at relativism *per se*, but at what Socrates takes to be the basic presupposition lying behind Sophistic relativism: Heraclitus' doctrine of the "flux." This he formulates as follows:

> Nothing is one itself by itself, and you could not correctly attribute any single quality to anything, but if you call it large, it will also appear small, and if heavy, also light, and so on with all such qualities, since nothing whatever is one or of one sort. Instead, everything that we say "is" we describe incorrectly, for it actually comes from movement and change and mixture. For nothing ever is, but it always becomes. (152d)

As we know from chapter 1, because he affirms the "flux," Heraclitus denies any form of stability. In turn, if nothing is stable, then no value could be objective or absolute. Instead, values are relative to those holding them. Recall that Heraclitus expresses his view symbolically: People value gold, but "mules," he tells us, "would choose garbage rather than gold." Since individuals and groups are always changing, so too are values. In the eighteenth century, slavery was widely considered to be morally defensible as a social good. Today it is almost universally denounced as immoral. For the ethical relativist, slavery is neither good in-itself nor bad in-itself. Instead, it depends. It was good for those living centuries ago, it is bad today. Values, like all else, change.

This is the sense in which Heraclitean flux lies at the heart of Sophistic relativism. Therefore, if it can be reduced to absurdity, so too can Sophistry. Socrates suggests as much in the following passage from the *Theaetetus*.

> Nothing is one, itself by itself, but instead always comes to be in relationship to something. And so "being" should be completely abolished, not withstanding the fact that we often and even just now have been forced by habit and ignorance to use the word. But as the argument of the wise men have it, we shouldn't, nor should we acquiesce in using "something" or "somebody's" or "mine" or "this" or "that" nor any other word that brings things to a halt. (157b; see 182d as well)

If the doctrine of flux were true, then ordinary language, whose words imply the presence of stable objects, would become meaningless. Of all the words mentioned in the passage, most striking is "mine." If Heraclitus is right, then there is no stable "self" that endures through the passage of time. As Socrates puts it, "And neither shall I, furthermore, ever again become the same as I am" (160a). Heraclitean flux, and therefore Sophistic relativism, leads to the absurd conclusion that there is no "I." After all, I am going through changes all the time, and each time I do, I am different. With no stable self, no "I," no one can be held responsible for any of their actions. If "I" robbed a bank yesterday, and you accuse me of a crime, "I" can simply respond that "I" did not, could not, do it. There is no stable self to be held morally responsible.

This may sound ridiculous, but recall that a thesis just like this was offered in Gorgias' *Encomium of Helen*. In this extraordinary "defense speech" the Sophist argues that Helen was not responsible for her actions. She was, instead, the "victim" of persuasion, of *logos*, the "powerful master" which, in constructing the beliefs that frame our worldview, shapes our lives. Helen was not right or wrong, good or bad, wise or ignorant. Instead, like everybody else, she was the product of the various social and linguistic forces working upon her. Indeed, for Gorgias there is no "Helen," if with that name we mean to refer to a stable self capable of being knowledgeable and then either rightly or wrongly exerting rational control over her life. "Helen" is a construct. And so is everybody else.

Again, this notion of the destruction of the "self" is an essential component of contemporary postmodernism. A revealing passage comes from Nietzsche.

> For just as the popular mind separates the lightning from its flash and takes the latter for an action, for the operation of a subject called lightning, so popular morality also separates strength from expressions of strength, as if there were a neutral substratum behind the strong man, which was free to express strength or not to do so. But there is no such substratum; there is no "being" behind doing, effecting, becoming; "the doer" is merely a fiction added to the deed – the deed is everything. (Nietzsche 1989, p. 45)

Nietzsche, the grandfather of postmodernism, is, as discussed in chapter 1, also the direct descendant of Heraclitus. Plato thinks he can defeat both of them with a *reductio ad absurdum*. As we saw in the previous section's discussion of the *Phaedo*, Plato is committed to doing justice to "the life of the soul," to the capacity for making value judgments, having a stable self. If Nietzsche–Heraclitus–Protagoras–Gorgias are right, then there is no self able to take moral responsibility. (See Griswold 1999 on this.) Like Simmias' "harmony thesis" or epiphenomenalism, this position would annihilate the meaning of ordinary experience, for in everyday life we depend on words like "mine" and "I" and phrases like "it was my fault" to make sense of ourselves. As we saw in the *Phaedo*, Socrates' principal concern is with the meaning and Truth of "the life of the soul." His philosophical project emerges from ordinary experience and language, and one of its goals is to preserve their integrity and worth. Precisely these would be destroyed, Socrates argues, by the Sophistic onslaught. No wonder, then, that Plato is so determined to defeat it.

c) "What is it?"

A third elenchic strategy Plato deploys in his attack on Sophistic relativism takes us back to the historical Socrates who was famous for asking his opponents the "what is it?" question, and then pressing them hard to answer it. As was discussed in chapter 2, this question presupposes a conceptual background – which was called the "Socratic Picture" – which in turn represents a worldview diametrically opposed to Sophistry. An excellent example of how Socrates uses this approach comes from the *Meno*. The dialogue opens with Meno asking the following:

> Can you tell me, Socrates, whether virtue [*aretê*] is teachable? Or is it not teachable but the result of practice? Or is it neither a result of practice nor something learnable, but it belongs to human beings by nature or in some other way? (70a)

The question, is virtue teachable?, was much discussed during the late fifth and early fourth centuries. Such at least is the impression we get from a short work titled the *Dissoi Logoi*, or "Contrasting Arguments," a sophistic training manual written around 400. In it a series of "hot" topics – among them, the proposition that "virtue can neither be taught nor learned" (Sprague 1990, p. 289) – were outlined, and then arguments on behalf of both "pro" and "con" were presented. Presumably the manual was designed to prepare fledgling Sophists to enter such debates on either side. Not surprisingly, scholars have attributed authorship of it to a student of Protagoras, one of whose surviving fragments is "on every issue, there are two arguments [*logoi*] opposed to each other." (See Mendelson 2002 for an extensive discussion of the Protagorean origins of what came to be known as "antilogic.")

Among these topics, the question, is virtue teachable?, is particularly striking, for how it is answered goes a long way towards articulating not only a conception of moral education, but also the basic character of a community. If, for example, it is agreed that virtue can be taught, then an enormous premium would be placed on the person who could teach it. Recall that "virtue" translates the word *aretê* and can also be rendered "excellence." If someone can teach others how to lead an excellent life, he would be in great demand. Indeed, such a person would be analogous to an expert physician. When it comes to questions about the health of the body, we defer to the well-trained doctor and willingly subordinate our judgments and speculations to his. If virtue can be taught, then perhaps there is a "physician of the soul" to whom similar deference ought to be shown in matters concerning virtue. Such an expert should, for example, be assigned the task of constructing a curriculum for the schools in order properly to train the children. Like that of a medical school, such a moral curriculum would be tightly structured. Its goal would be to ensure that all students are well behaved and to foster the emergence of an elite group which would, in turn, supply the next generation of leadership. The community in which such moral education would play a central role would be a meritocracy in which the best and the brightest would be rewarded and placed in charge. (Plato's *Republic*, a dialogue to be discussed below, seems to promote just such a community.)

On the other hand, if a community agrees that virtue cannot be taught, but instead people possess it "by nature," then an entirely different sort of regime would follow. For example, in a traditional aristocracy, lineage and family position, rather than education and training, are counted as necessary conditions of virtue. For very different reasons a democracy, whose basic conviction is that all human beings are by nature morally equal and therefore deserve freedom and respect, also would reject the possibility of a "virtue expert." In a democracy no such authority figure would be tolerated, and all citizens would be counted equally as potential teachers of virtue. (This is a view articulated by Anytus, a character who appears in the *Meno*.)

The question, is virtue teachable?, became prominent because just these sorts of political questions were much debated around 400. The *Dissoi Logoi* manual was designed to train would-be Sophists to enter the fray and, if needed, argue on behalf of either side. Thus, when Meno, who is associated with the famous rhetorician Gorgias (70b, 71c–d), opens the dialogue by asking this question of Socrates, he probably has hopes of adding new arguments to his arsenal.

The Philosopher, however, refuses to cooperate with the Sophist. Instead of answering Meno's question, Socrates raises this objection: "If I do not know what something is, how could I know what sort of thing it is?" (71b). How would it be possible, he asks, to know whether Meno was rich or good-looking if one did not know who Meno was? Socrates' point can be generalized: the "what is it" question must precede the "what is it like" question. In other words, before knowing what qualities something has, one must know what it is. Therefore, before determining whether virtue is teachable or not, a prior question must be answered: what is virtue itself? As he often does, Socrates wrests control of the conversation away from Meno, and demands that his own question be given priority.

Meno first responds to Socrates' question by giving a series of examples. The virtue of a man, he says, "consists of being able to conduct the affairs of the city"; the virtue of a woman, he continues (betraying the fundamental sexism at the heart of Athenian life) is "to manage the home well," and so on (71e). Socrates is displeased with this answer and replies with stinging irony: "I seem to be in great luck, Meno; while seeking one virtue, I have found you to have a whole swarm of virtues" (72a). But a swarm of examples, however impressive, does not constitute a real answer. The goal of the Socratic inquiry is to discover what virtue itself really is; in other words, to define it. According to Socrates, giving examples is against what might be called the "rules" of the "what is it game." This is because an example is something like a quality. How can we know if Y is an example of X unless we know what X itself is?

Socrates reiterates this basic principle in the following passage:

> Even if they [the virtues Meno has mentioned] are many and various, they all have the one same form [*eidos*] on account of which they are virtues, and it would be a fine thing for the person attempting to answer the question to look at this and to make clear what virtue really is. (72c)

The key word here, and it will remain so for the remainder of this chapter (indeed, for the remainder of this book), is "Form." The "what is it" question seeks the "one" that unifies the "many." All the examples of X are so because there is a single X itself, a Form of X, that they have a share in and so is (somehow) responsible for the many different X's being X. Figure 3.1, a version of which was used in chapter 2 in the discussion of the historical Socrates, is meant to illustrate.

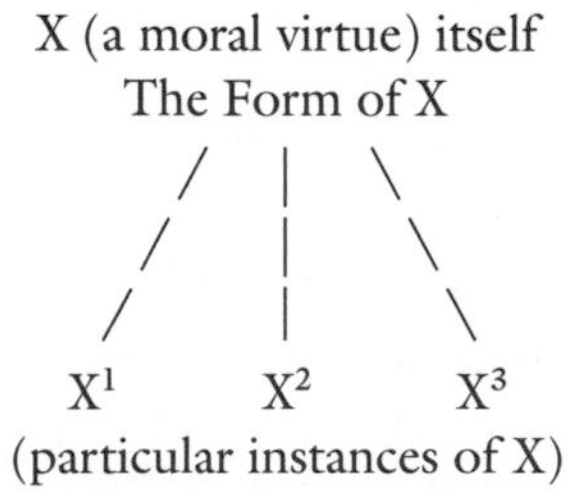

$$
\begin{array}{c}
\text{X (a moral virtue) itself}\\
\text{The Form of X}\\
\diagup \quad | \quad \diagdown\\
\diagup \quad\; | \quad\;\; \diagdown\\
\diagup \quad\;\; | \quad\;\;\; \diagdown\\
X^1 \qquad X^2 \qquad X^3\\
\text{(particular instances of X)}
\end{array}
$$

Figure 3.1

Seeking virtue itself means looking for an articulation of the Form. The Greek word is *eidos*, which is related to the verb "to see." Literally, then, it means "the look of a thing" or "that which is seen." To understand why this bit of etymology is useful, consider this example: there is a small brown car in the driveway, a large red car passing by on the street, and a toy car made of plastic on the floor. The one word "car" is used to name each of the three objects. How do we know how to use this one word to name all three objects? Why do we call the small plastic item on the floor a "car," when in fact it is so different from the objects in the driveway and the street? Because even if it is far smaller, it looks like, it has the same shape as, a car. This shape, this Form, is what allows us to recognize it, and articulate what it has in common with the other two objects.

The lines in figure 3.1 that represent the relationship of the particular X's to the "Form of X" are most in need of philosophical explanation. How does the Form "make" the particular items X^1, X^2, and X^3 into an X? This is an immensely difficult question; indeed, for Plato it is perhaps the most pressing of all. In a later section we will address it more directly. For the moment, suffice it to say that in asking Meno, "what is virtue itself?," Socrates asks for an articulation of the Form that somehow binds together the particulars into a unity.

Socrates' demand that Meno answer his question rather than provide a list of examples is neither neutral nor benign. It is an attack on the Sophistic worldview held by his interlocutor. To reiterate, this is because the question itself presupposes the conceptual scheme above, and because that scheme gives priority to the notion of the Form of X it is diametrically opposed to the Sophistic worldview. As a result, Meno need only attempt to answer the question, and he has already refuted himself. To reinvoke the game metaphor, Socrates demands that Meno play his "what is it" game. Once Meno begins to do so, he is committed to playing by the rules. And these rules stipulate that there should be an attempt to answer the question. But Meno, as a card-carrying Sophist, should deny this point. For if he agrees to it, then he agrees that he and Socrates will together search for a Form of virtue. Doing so betrays his own relativism, since the Sophist is convinced that there are only particulars, and no overarching Form exists to unify them.

The difference between Socrates and the Meno, between the Philosopher and the Sophist, is more than just a disagreement about abstract or theoretical matters. In fact, these are two fundamentally different types of human beings. Socrates explains this in the *Republic* when he discusses a certain kind of person, whom he calls a "lover of sights":

> The lovers of hearing and the lovers of sights, on the one hand . . . surely delight in beautiful sounds and colors and shapes all that craft makes from such things, but their thought is unable to see and delight in the nature of the beautiful itself. (476b)[7]

Such a person "holds that there are beautiful things but doesn't hold that there is beauty itself" (476c). The "lover of sights" simply has no taste for unity, for universality, for Philosophy. (A contemporary thinker who fits this description is Richard Rorty: see Rorty 1980 and 1982.) By contrast, the person who does "see and delight" in the possibility of Form is the Philosopher:

> And what about the man who . . . believes that there is something beautiful itself and is able to catch sight both of it and of what particip-ates in it, and doesn't believe that what participates is it itself, nor that it itself is what participates – is he . . . living in a dream or is he awake? (476d)

"Participate" is the word Socrates uses to describe the arrow in figure 3.1 which was meant to symbolize the relationship between the Form of X and the particular X's. (We will discuss this below.)

To reiterate the central theme of this section: an interlocutor who agrees to cooperate with Socrates in his inquiry, to pursue questions like "what is virtue itself," has implicitly (and sometimes unwittingly) joined Socrates' camp. This is quite similar to what happened to Thrasymachus, the teacher of rhetoric who appeared in Book I of the *Republic*. He is a Sophist, and so he professes to hold a version of relativism. Under the pressure of the Socrates' argument, however, he betrays his own convictions. When he agrees with Socrates' seemingly innocuous assertion, "rulers make mistakes," he implicitly affirms the possibility of some sort of objective, nonrelative, standard by which the mistake can be measured. As such, he has contradicted himself. Thrasymachus is a relativist, but an inconsistent one.

Similarly, at this juncture of the *Meno*, Meno abandons his own sophistic convictions by agreeing to play according to the rules of Socrates' game by trying to answer "what is virtue itself?" Later in the dialogue, after having gone on some significant detours, Socrates will ask the question again: "shall we try together to find out what virtue is?" Meno responds:

> Of course. But Socrates, I would be delighted to examine and hear your answer to the question I asked you at first, namely, whether it is necessary to pursue virtue as something teachable, or as something which is by nature, or is something human beings attain in some other way? (86c–d)

Meno is sufficiently stubborn – or from the Philosopher's perspective sufficiently obtuse – to have failed to grasp the import of Socratic questioning. Or, to shift metaphors, the "what is it" question is bait, and while Meno was initially tempted to nibble on it he finally manages to resist. He thereby eludes Socrates' grasp.

Socrates may seem like a bully who tries to force his interlocutors to play his game by his rules, and who brooks no dissent. To put this point in more technical terms, one might accuse the Philosopher of "begging the question." This is the name of a standard fallacy in which the conclusion one purports to defend is actually presupposed at the outset of the argument. For example, suppose I want to defend the statement, "God exists," and I do so by means of this argument: The Bible says that God exists; the Bible was written by God and so must be true; therefore, God exists because it says so in the Bible. In this rather silly case, I have clearly begged the question by assuming God's existence before having proven it. In a far more subtle sense, Socrates' insistence on the priority of the "what is it" question might also be question-begging. After all, the question itself presupposes the "Socratic Picture" and it is precisely this picture that should be debated, and not merely assumed.

It is important to realize that the "begging the question" problem works in reverse as well. For a Sophist such as Gorgias (or his associate Meno), there are no overarching Forms to act as standards by which the Truth of a *logos* can be measured. Instead, what measures the value of a *logos* is its effectiveness in creating a *doxa*, a belief or opinion. In other words, Persuasion replaces Truth as the goal of *logos*.

To put this point into political terms, the objective of the Sophistic game is to win votes. If two people are arguing in front of a jury or the Assembly, the winner is determined by the audience or the crowd, not by the intrinsic Truth of the argument. The Philosopher, by contrast, is willing to stick to his guns regardless of whether the crowd showers him with approval or not. So, if the sophist were to demand of the Philosopher to play by his rules, that is to debate him before a crowd and let them decide the winner, he too would be insisting that his opponent adopt his own conceptual scheme. He too would beg the question.

A second possible objection against Socrates' procedure is this: the Philosopher asserts that one cannot know what X is like, or identify an example of X, without knowing what X itself is. But is this true? Consider Bob. He regularly robs helpless children of their lunch money, and then smacks them hard across their faces to make them cry. Does Sue really need to know what virtue itself is in order to know that Bob is a menace who should be stopped from hurting innocent children? If you were walking down the street and you saw Bob smacking a kid, would you intervene, or would you wait until you could define virtue itself before taking action? Socrates might seem to be recommending the latter.

d) "The old quarrel": Philosophy v. Sophistry[8]

The preceding remarks suggest one possible answer to a question posed at the end of chapter 2: why did Plato write dialogues? Perhaps he did so precisely because he recognized the enormous gap separating the Philosopher from the Sophist, as well as the game-like structure the dispute between them takes. Perhaps he recognized that in order for these two radically different kinds of thinkers to debate one another, the real question at issue – are there Forms with which to measure the Truth, or only particulars about which there can be Persuasion? – must be begged. The Philosopher can refute the Sophist but *only* *if* the latter agrees to play by the rules of the former. If, however, someone like Meno does manage to stick to his guns, and simply refuses to answer Socrates' question, then in an important sense he cannot be refuted by the *elenchos*. In short, perhaps Plato recognized the *limits* of philosophical refutation. Reason, philosophical *logos*, cannot bridge the gap between "the lover of the sight of Truth" and the "lover of sights." Perhaps Plato wrote dialogues, in which the conflict between the two is dramatically depicted and the argumentative strategies are revealed, precisely because a definitive theoretical resolution to the debate was not forthcoming.

Recall the remarks made at the outset of this section: throughout his career Plato returned, almost obsessively, to the challenge posed by the Sophists. Perhaps he did so because he had two realizations. First, this debate is immensely important for both theoretical and practical reasons. Sophistic relativism is a powerful intellectual option, one as alive and well and attractive today (in the guise of the post-modernists) as it was 2,400 years ago. Second, it is an "old quarrel" that does not go away because it cannot go away. The one side cannot engage the other in an argument without begging the question.

The above does not imply that Plato was neutral on the question. He was a Philosopher from head to toe, and he did think there were good reasons to buy into the "Socratic Picture" and to join in the search for Forms. He may not have been completely optimistic about presenting definitive reasons for why this was so. This may be why many of his dialogues end in "impasse" or *aporia*. The Sophist keeps popping up, because his position has a kind of invulnerability to it. But Plato remained steadfast in his opposition to the Sophist, and throughout his dialogues marshaled arguments which, even if not utterly definitive, were designed to provide good reasons to favor Philosophy over Sophistry. We turn next to one of these: the notion of "recollection," a theme prominent in the *Meno* and the *Phaedo*.

Recollection

a) The *Phaedo*

It is not enough to silence the Sophist by the self-reference argument, or to defeat him by the *reductio ad absurdum*, or to corner him with the "what is it" question. In each case, the Sophist, if sufficiently wily, can protect himself. He can say, "so what if my argument fails to refer coherently to itself? Self-reference is a rational standard used by philosophers, but it interests me not at all!" So too might he reply similarly to the *reductio*. Finally, as discussed above, perhaps Socrates begs the question by demanding that "what is X" precede "what is X like" or "what is an example of X?" In short, all of the Socratic arguments examined thus far have been negative, and even on this score may not have been entirely convincing. What the Philosopher needs is a strong, positive defense of the thesis that there are Forms, and not just a world of particulars, that objective Truth is available and supersedes mere Persuasion, that moral relativism is false.

An important example of such an argument comes from the *Phaedo*. Recall that this dialogue depicts the final hours of Socrates' life and recounts his attempts to prove the immortality of the soul. One such proof is based on the notion of "recollection." It goes like this: When we measure two things, say two sticks, we might well determine that they are equal in length. A quick bit of reflection would reveal, however, that in a variety of ways such equality is in fact not perfectly exact. If I am measuring the two sticks with a cheap ruler, they may look equal according to its rather crude measurements. If, however, I switch to another, more precise ruler the outcome may differ. The first may read each stick as being 6.9 inches long and hence equal in length; by contrast, according to the second, one stick measures at 6.91 inches and the other at 6.92 inches. Even if the two sticks differ by as little as 0.0001 inches, a difference undetectable by the naked eye, they are unequal nonetheless. The conclusion Socrates draws is that no two sensible objects can ever achieve perfect or absolute equality.

There are other ways in which sensible equality – that is, the kind measurable by the senses – falls short of perfection. Assume, against all likelihood, that two sticks are precisely equal in length. By next week, however, one may have changed slightly. Perhaps it was cold outside and it shrank. Even if the sticks are equal today, they will be unequal in the future. They are not, therefore, perfectly equal. (Recall here a point made early in chapter 1: there is a conviction, some would say a prejudice, at work throughout the history of Greek philosophy: what endures is "more real" than, is ontologically superior to, what is transient.) Or consider this: perhaps the two sticks are equal in length, but unequal in width. In this regard, they are both equal and unequal, and so again cannot be counted as perfectly equal. Or this: because they are equal to my rather weak eyes, but unequal according to you who have eagle-sharp vision, their equality, or lack of it, depends on who is doing the measuring. In sum, there are a variety of ways in which sensible equality falls short of perfect equality.

Socrates completes this line of thought with the following remark:

> Look at it this way: do not equal sticks and stones sometimes, while remaining the same, appear equal to one, but not to another? (74b)

There is an ambiguity in Plato's Greek here. The words translated above as "to one, but not to another" are indefinite pronouns in the dative case. As a result, they can be translated as being either masculine or neuter. Each of the following is thus a potentially legitimate translation of the Greek phrase:

1. "Appear equal to one person, but not to another."
2. "Appear equal to one thing, but not to another thing."
3. "Appear equal in one way, but not in another way."

Each translation corresponds to one of the ways discussed above in which sensible equality is not perfect. It is thus possible that Plato intended the passage to be ambiguous. Indeed, he may well have used the ambiguity of the pronouns to signal the indefinite number of ways in which sensible equality is imperfect. The translation "equal to one, but not to another" preserves the ambiguity of Plato's Greek.

This little grammar lesson is not important in itself. But it does help to highlight Socrates' central point here: because sensible equality lapses into inequality, it suffers "some inferiority" (74d). It is therefore essentially different from "equality itself" (74e), which simply IS equal and so never "appears unequal" (74b). As Socrates puts it, "equal things [like the two sticks] and the Equal itself are therefore not the same" (74c). Nonetheless, the Equal itself, which is perfectly Equal and participates not at all in inequality, must be invoked in order to determine (or simply to say) that the two sticks are equal, however imperfectly, in length. As such, the measurement made possible by the Equal itself, the sensible equality discovered by means of it, "is inferior" (74e). Socrates summarizes and extends this thought:

> Whenever someone seeing something realizes that "what I now am seeing wants to be like some other being, but it is lacking and is unable to be like that one, and is inferior," he, in realizing this, must have foreknowledge of that to which he says the thing is alike but falling short of. (74e)

A reflective person "realizes" that the equality in length exhibited by two sticks falls short of the Equal itself. This is just one instance of a much more comprehensive, and quintessentially philosophical, realization: the sensible world itself is imperfect. (See Nehamas 1975.) It falls short of those Forms making the world intelligible and our experience possible. Because we can measure two sticks and declare, however imprecisely, "they are equal," sensible objects become comprehensible. But this intelligibility is dependent upon a set of objective realities that are superior to the particular, sensible items in the world with which we are most familiar.

Socrates' language in the passage above is somewhat odd. The two equal sticks, he says, "want to be like" the Equal itself. But sticks surely exhibit no such desire. Perhaps, then, what Socrates means is that because sensible things are made intelligible by higher realities – by Forms like the Equal itself – when someone compares the two, she "realizes" the dependence of the sensible on the Form. While equal sticks do not really desire anything, when they are seen from the perspective of the Form, their "inferiority" shows itself so strongly that it is as if they were striving to be more perfect than they are. This realization, that the ordinary world of equal sticks and stones falls short, is central to Platonism. Our lives are shot through with imperfection, but even in the simple act of measuring the length of two sticks, an inkling of perfection shines through. We have, through thought alone, access to the Equal itself, even though we can never touch it with our hands or see it with our eyes. Unlike the equality of sticks and stones, the Equal Itself is not "equal to one, but not to another"; it is not in the eyes of the beholder. Realizing this is the origin of philosophy.

Because the Equal itself is not available through the senses, we must have, Socrates says, "foreknowledge" of it. We must know it before we become aware of the equality of the two sticks. To use language made famous by the German philosopher, Immanuel Kant, the Equal itself must be *a priori*, prior to experience. Socrates puts the point thus:

> We must then possess knowledge of equality before that time when we first saw the equal objects and realized that all these objects strive to be like the Equal but fall short . . . Therefore before we began to see or hear or otherwise perceive, we must have possessed knowledge of what the Equal itself is if we were about to refer our sense perceptions of equal objects to it, and realized that all of them were eager to be like it, but were inferior. (74e–75b)[9]

Socrates builds on this thought. Since there are sensory experiences from the moment of birth, our access to the nonsensible "Equal itself" must have its source before we were born. Therefore, the argument seems to go, the human soul exists before it is incarnated: "our soul must exist before we are born" (76e). As such, Socrates argues, it is immortal.[10] As his interlocutors quickly point out (77b–c), this argument, even if successful in proving that the soul existed before the human being was actually born, fails. After all, there is nothing to stop the soul from perishing after the body has died. The most striking, and positive, result of the recollection argument is thus not the conclusion that the soul is immortal. Instead, it is the positive argument on behalf of the Forms. When one "realizes" that the sensible world is both intelligible but also deficient, that two sticks are both equal and unequal but the Equal itself is perfect and abiding, one must invoke the Form. With this argument the goal of the Philosopher is set – namely, to hunt down the Forms – and the legitimacy of Socratic inquiry, based as it is on the "what is X itself question," is secured.[11]

Two comments before proceeding. Even if he is a critic of the Presocratics, Plato's response to his predecessors is dialectical, for he does not simply negate them, but instead retains two general features of their thinking. First, like all who follow in the path established by the Milesians, he seems to be an ontological dualist. The Forms, changeless and perfect, abide in the category of Being, while sensible particulars are in the process of Becoming. By conceiving the Forms to be superior to the particulars, Plato follows in the tradition that has privileged Being over Becoming. Second, almost like a fifth-century "elementalist," Plato offers a reconciliation of Heraclitus and Parmenides. The Forms retain the Parmenidean attributes of Being, while sensible entities are Heraclitean in their flux.

b) The *Meno*

Recollection is also a major theme in the *Meno*. Meno, you recall, is an associate of Gorgias, the great Sophist of the fifth century. His principal task in the dialogue is to resist Socrates' invitation to pursue the question, "what is virtue?" The Philosopher repeatedly tries to lure Meno into joining forces with him, but he steadfastly resists. Indeed, after a while Meno becomes frustrated and annoyed with Socrates' insistence that he play by the rules of the philosophical game, and so he goes on the attack himself. He tries to undermine the very possibility of Socratic inquiry by presenting what has since become known as "Meno's paradox."

> In what way, Socrates, will you seek this [virtue itself] when you do not at all know what it is? For what sort of thing among those you do not know will you propose as an object for your search? Even if you should encounter it, how would you know that this is the thing which you did not know? (80d)

Socrates reformulates:

> It is impossible for a human being to seek either what he knows or what he does not know. For he cannot seek that which he knows – after all, he knows it, and there is no need for a search – nor for what he does not know, for he does not know what it is he is seeking. (80e)

Meno here argues against the possibility of inquiry and so of learning itself, or at least the kind of learning that would accrue to someone who, not knowing what some X is, successfully finds out. To appreciate the considerable force of his argument, imagine this scenario: I ask you, "what is a Gox-2B?" You do not know the answer. (How could you, since I just made up the phrase "Gox-2B," and as far as I know it means nothing.) Because of your ignorance, when I tell you that a Gox-2B is a new type of laser, you cannot possibly know whether this is true or not. You could trust me, of course, but this is not the same thing as actually knowing the right answer.

This, then, is the first half of Meno's paradox: if someone does not know what X is, she cannot learn what it is. The movement from ignorance, which can be conceived as a zero state of knowledge, to positive knowledge is impossible. In a parallel fashion, if you already know what a Gox-2B is, then you cannot learn what it is: learning, after all, is a kind of progress, and if you already are in the positive state, you cannot progress to it. Since (the argument assumes) one must either know or be ignorant of what X is, it is impossible to learn what X is.

As we discussed in chapter 1, a "paradox" runs contrary (*para*) to ordinary *doxa* or common sense. Since most of us think learning is possible, Meno's argument surely qualifies. Still, the central thrust of Meno's paradox has great force: moving from complete ignorance to a positive state of knowledge – from, we might say, 0 to 1 – may well be impossible. If one knows absolutely nothing, then one would have no resources whatsoever with which to learn anything at all. Socrates seems to agree with this idea, for as we will see shortly, in his response to Meno he grants this point. Nonetheless, even if he agrees that progress from 0 to 1 is impossible, Socrates maintains that learning can still take place. In order to explain how this could be, he must redefine what learning is. He begins by claiming that human beings are never at the zero state and, as in the *Phaedo*, he invokes recollection here.[12] From the moment of birth human beings already know what X, and Y, and Z are: knowledge is innate and *a priori* or, as Socrates puts it, "Since the soul is immortal and has been born many times, and has seen all things here and in the underworld, there is nothing which it has not learned" (81c). Presumably, at birth such knowledge was forgotten. Throughout the rest of our lives, then, we do not learn new bits of knowledge. Instead, we are busy recollecting old ones.

The recollection thesis, as implausible as it may initially sound to the modern ear, has one attractive feature, which can be illustrated by performing the following thought experiment. Try to remember the children who sat next to you when you were in third grade. Can you recall their faces or names? Probably not, or at least not at first. So try harder. Dig deeper into the recesses of your memory. Perhaps a blurry image of a girl is beginning to form in your mind, and a name flutters on the tip of your tongue. You cannot quite reach it, but you can feel its presence. Suddenly, for no discernible reason, it pops into view: it was Sue, who had blonde hair and used to wear red sneakers. This knowledge was "in" you even when you could not recall, and so were unaware of, it.

The process of retrieving such a stored bit of memory required concentration and inquiry, albeit inquiry into oneself, and when it was completed progress had been made. But such progress was not a moving from 0 to 1. You were already in state 1, but you just did not realize it. Despite the fact that you only "moved" from 1 to 1, the experience felt much like moving from 0 to 1. You were forced to look within yourself and to work hard; in other words, you did exactly what is required for someone to learn. For this reason, even if it itself seems implausible, the recollection thesis, unlike Meno's argument, has the great advantage of not generating paradoxical results. In other words, if one assumes it is true, then the phenomenon, the experience, of active learning is preserved as a meaningful activity. This is what Socrates means when he says about recollection that it

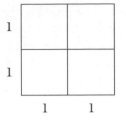

1
1
1   1

Figure 3.2

makes people "energetic and keen on the search" (81d). According to the recollection thesis we should rigorously pursue our inquiries, even if learning is not what we think it is, namely moving from 0 to 1.

In the *Meno*, Socrates tries to demonstrate the truth of recollection by means of an experiment. Meno is accompanied by a slave boy who speaks Greek, but is otherwise completely uneducated. Socrates has a lengthy conversation with him, at the conclusion of which he claims the boy knows something about geometry. Socrates, however, also claims that he has taught him nothing, at least if one means by "teach" bring someone from the zero state to the positive state, from 0 to 1. Instead, Socrates maintains that he has only asked questions, and these in turn sparked the boy to recollection. The answers the boy ends up with, the little bit of geometry he can identify, came from within, and not from an external source.

The first step of this experiment has Socrates drawing a square in the sand and asking the boy if he recognizes the figure. The boy says yes. Socrates then asks, "A square then is a figure in which all these four sides are equal?" (82c). The boy agrees. Next (figure 3.2) Socrates draws two bisecting lines and so cuts the square into four smaller squares. Each is treated as a unit; in other words, as having a side with length 1.

What the boy can now see clearly is how to compute the area of square whose side has a length of 2. Socrates asks him, "If then this side were two feet, and this other side two feet, how many feet would the whole be?" (82c). Because he sees and can simply count the four squares right before him, the boy can give the correct answer.

Next, Socrates poses a problem for the boy to solve: What is the length of a side of a square whose area is double that of the figure in the sand, or 8. The reader knows in advance that the boy is in trouble. Because the area is computed by squaring the length of the side, the answer to the question is the square root of 8, which is an

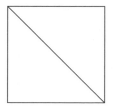

Figure 3.3

irrational number. Unaware of the difficulty awaiting him, the boy confidently pushes forward: "Obviously Socrates, it will be twice the length" (82e) of the original square, or 4. This is a wrong, but not an unreasonable, answer. It might well seem intuitive to someone who is bright but has never studied geometry simply to double the length of the side in order to generate double the area. Socrates can show the boy his error by again drawing in the sand (figure 3.3).

By counting the internal squares, the boy sees that the square with length 4 has an area of 16. So, he tries again, this time answering 3. Again, the boy is thinking quite reasonably. If 2 is too small, and 4 is too big, then the answer should be in-between, or 3. Of course, all Socrates has to do to show him he is wrong is have him again count the visible square units and see that the area is 9.

The boy is genuinely stumped. 4 is too big, 3 is too little, and because he is unaware of fractions, and certainly irrational numbers, he knows nothing in-between. His response is excitedly to declare, "By Zeus, Socrates, I do not know" (84a).

Socrates then shows the boy a kind of geometric trick. He bisects a square by drawing a line from corner to corner (figure 3.4). The

Figure 3.4

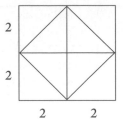

Figure 3.5

resulting two triangles, as the boy can see, each have an area one-half the original area of the square.

Equipped with this illuminating geometric figure in front of him, the boy is prepared to see the last of the drawings. Socrates bisects each of the four squares comprising the larger square whose area is 16. The resulting 4 triangles each has an area one-half of 4, or 2 (figure 3.5). The four triangles together comprise a square within a square, which has an area of 4 times 2, or 8.

Socrates concludes his "lesson" by saying, "Clever men call this [the bisecting line] the diagonal, so that if diagonal is its name, you say that the double figure [with area 8] would be based on the diagonal" (85b). He then triumphantly turns to Meno and engages him in this little bit of conversation:

Socrates: What does it seem like to you, Meno? Has the boy answered with any opinion not his own?
Meno: No, they were his own.
Socrates: And yet, as we said a short time ago, he did not know?
Meno: What you say is true.
Socrates: So these opinions were in him, were they not?
Meno: Yes.
Socrates: Therefore, the man who does not know has within himself true opinions about the things that he does not know . . . And he will know it without having been taught but only questioned, and he himself will grasp the knowledge from with himself.
Meno: Yes.
Socrates: And is not grasping knowledge from within oneself recollection?
Meno: Of course. (85c–d)

The implications of Socrates' experiment with the slave boy, and the claim he makes that it validates his recollection thesis, are controversial.

Did Socrates really do no more than ask innocent questions, or did he ask him leading ones that in effect transmitted information to the boy? Remember that the boy knows how to speak Greek, can recognize a figure in the sand as a square, and (perhaps most significantly) he knows how to count and even to add. How would Socrates explain these intellectual capacities? Finally, what are we to make of the drawings Socrates uses to illustrate his "lesson?" Perhaps they too communicated positive bits of information, and were not as innocent as he makes them seem.

These questions cannot be resolved here. In fact, Socrates himself seems to acknowledge the inconclusiveness of his experiment by saying,

> On the one hand, I do not insist that my argument is right in all other respects, but I would contend at all costs both in word and deed as far as I could that we will be better men, braver and less idle, if we believe that one must search for the things one does not know rather than if we believe that it is not possible to find out what we do not know and that we must not look for it. (86c)

Socrates admits his demonstration of the recollection thesis is open to objection. Surely there are other ways of explaining how the boy came to his "understanding," if it is that, of the square within the square. Nevertheless, Socrates holds fast to recollection. He does so because he thinks that believing it, even if it cannot be conclusively proven, makes people better. Those who accept recollection are poised to look within, to think hard, and to drive themselves forward on the path of inquiry. Those who join forces with Meno are stopped dead in their tracks.

The recollection thesis may well seem preposterous to the modern reader. Who among us could actually hold the view that the soul had a prenatal existence? I close this section with a suggestion: this seemingly antiquated notion of recollection and the *a priori* is alive and well today, albeit in a much-altered guise. I am referring to the basic concept of genetics, namely the transmission of "information" through the code built into the structure of DNA molecules. In a significant sense, a human being "knows" everything before he or she is born or even conceived. The basic blueprint required to develop a functioning brain is already present in the chromosomes of the father and mother. The information – a word in the middle of which is Plato's word "form" – is already there, *a priori*, just as Socrates says it is. Both modern genetics and Plato agree that it is impossible to go from 0 to 1. Because of the presence of DNA in our ancestors, no human being is ever at 0.[13] For the geneticist the prior knowledge is built into a material thing, namely a DNA molecule. For Plato it is found in the human soul, which has access to the Forms. While the former option is vastly more palatable to a modern sensibility, the latter should not be dismissed. Meno may be right that moving from 0 to 1 is impossible, but he is surely wrong that learning is impossible. Without something like recollection, human beings would be lost and philosophy would be impossible. But as those reading this book can testify, we are not lost and philosophy is surely not impossible.

The Divided Line and the Form of the Good

a) The divided line

It is hardly accidental that Socrates uses a geometric problem to demonstrate the truth of his recollection thesis in the *Meno*. For Plato, mathematics is the crucial stepping-stone towards, the all-important clue about, our knowledge of the Forms. To elaborate, we will turn next to a few passages from Books VI and VII of the *Republic*, one of Plato's longest and most complex dialogues. First, a bit of background.

The *Republic* begins with a set of questions concerning justice. As mentioned above, in Book I Socrates confronts a Sophist named Thrasymachus. One of his most notorious statements is "that injustice is profitable" while justice is harmful and but "a very high-minded simplicity" (348c). In other words, according to Thrasymachus, justice is for suckers, while injustice should be practiced by those who want to get ahead in the world. Socrates does manage to defeat the Sophist, or at least to silence him. At the beginning of Book II, however, two of his young interlocutors, Glaucon and Adeimantus, object that regardless of how seemingly effective Socrates' refutation was, it was not entirely convincing. What is needed, they insist, is a far more thorough explanation of why one ought to be just. "Socrates," they ask, "do you want to seem to have persuaded us, or truly to persuade us, that it is in every way better to be just than unjust?" (357b). To get what they want, Glaucon and Adeimantus beg Socrates "to seek out what each [justice and injustice] is" (368c). As in the *Phaedo*, where he met but welcomed stiff resistance from Simmias and Cebes, he is glad to oblige. After all, nothing could be better than talking with young men eager to pursue the "what is it question." Socrates agrees to do a better job than he did in Book I, and to explain fully what justice itself is and what affect it has on the human soul.

Socrates' task is enormous and so it occupies him for all of the subsequent nine books of the *Republic*. In Book II, he begins by devising a plan to make the project a little "easier" (368e). He proposes to construct a perfectly just "city in speech." Because a city is a large entity whose structure is readily visible, building a city in speech will make it easier to see justice itself or justice as it appears in an individual. This then becomes the task of Books II–VII. Without going into any of the vast number of details (some of which we will examine below), only one feature of the just city, its most prominent as well as most controversial, will be mentioned here: philosophers are its rulers, its kings and queens.

In Book VII of the *Republic*, Socrates sketches what he takes to be the proper education for these rulers. It is thoroughly mathematical, and it begins with arithmetic, which Socrates describes as follows:

> The lowly business of distinguishing the one, the two, and the three. I mean by this, succinctly, number and calculation. Or isn't it the case with them that every kind of art and knowledge is compelled to participate in them? (522c)

Recall that "number" translates the Greek word *arithmos*, the origin of our word "arithmetic." It plays such a central role in the education of the philosopher-rulers of the *Republic* because of its unique ability to "draw the soul from becoming to being" (521d). Socrates illustrates what he means with the following example. Some perceptions, he says, "summon the intellect" (523b), while others do not. An example of the latter would be seeing a single finger. When I see it, I do so without effort or problem. It is a stable, simple perception; a finger, no more or less. By contrast, when I see three fingers – "the smallest, the second, and the middle" (523c) – a certain destabilizing complexity, paradigmatic of the nature of becoming itself, enters the picture. The second finger looks bigger than the smallest, and smaller than the middle. The second finger, as I look at it, "goes over to its opposite." It is both bigger and smaller, smaller and bigger. This sort of perception "summons the intellect" precisely because it is at odds with itself, and perception itself is powerless to stabilize it. But human beings have an easy and natural way to remedy the self-contradictory nature of such perceptions: order and then measure the fingers. The smallest finger (the pinky) is counted and is, say, 2 inches; the second is 3 inches, and the third (the middle) is 4 inches. The second finger is no longer in the confused state of being both larger and smaller. It is now known to be simply 3 inches long, and its position in the sequence is clearly demarcated.

This little bit of counting, this little flirtation with *arithmos*, is on the one hand "lowly." It is an intellectual act ordinary human beings typically perform effortlessly and without need of reflection. But, much like the measuring of the two sticks Socrates describes in the *Phaedo*, the seemingly innocuous act of counting conceals something extra-ordinary. When the fingers are counted as 1, 2 and 3, and then measured as 2 inches, 3 inches, and 4 inches, numbers are invoked. These numbers are not identical to the fingers. Indeed, they surpass the fingers: the very same numbers can be used to count three toes or apples or oranges. The numbers are stable, intelligible, available to all human intellects, and applicable to all sensible items. They cannot be touched with the hands nor seen with the eyes. They are universal and objective. Regardless of whether one uses the Greek word *treis*, or the English "three," the number being named is the same everywhere and for all. When it is added to 2 the sum always equals 5.

In short, numbers have all the attributes of Being that were discussed throughout chapter 1 (especially in the discussion of Pythagoras). Without them, the sensible world would be chaotic: the middle finger would oscillate between being bigger (than the smallest) and smaller (than the biggest). Without them, there would be no art, no science, no intelligibility at all. Numbers are ontologically superior to the sensible items whose count they make possible. This is what Socrates means when he says that the study of arithmetic will draw the soul away from Becoming and towards Being.

To explain more fully we must take a step backwards in the *Republic*, to the end of Book VI and a famously dense passage that has come to be known as "the divided line." As he did in the *Meno*, Socrates here sketches a figure in the sand, this time a line with four segments (figure 3.6). On the left side of the line are various objects, and on the right are the modes of cognition human beings use to apprehend them.

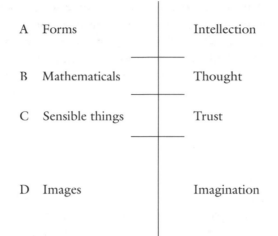

A	Forms		Intellection
B	Mathematicals		Thought
C	Sensible things		Trust
D	Images		Imagination

Figure 3.6 Socrates' divided line

The best way to understand the divided line is to begin at the bottom. Images (D) are images of real things (C). So, for example, if there is a powerful lamp on my desk, and I place my hand between it and the desk, a shadow of my hand will appear on the surface of the desk. The shadow is but an image of my hand and as such is not quite real. Its reality depends on my hand: if I remove it, the shadow disappears. This relationship is not symmetrical, since my hand in no way depends on the shadow. Instead, it is the original object responsible for the appearance of the image. This is why "sensible things," like my hand, are "higher" than their images. The latter are always images *of* originals to which they are ontologically inferior.[14]

As Klein (1975, pp. 115–24) has shown, the relationship between image and original works its way through, and so is the key to understanding, the entire divided line. This is most apparent in the relationship between segments B and C, between mathematical and sensible objects. To explain, let us return to the three fingers. Upon simply perceiving a finger I am in segment C, the realm of "sensible things." On the cognitive side, I am operating by means of "trust," a word Socrates uses to label the most familiar mode of human inter-action with the sensible world. When a single object, like the finger, is placed before me, I see it clearly and trust what I see. When I am given a ring, and asked to put it on, I will not make a mistake by, for example, trying to place it on my elbow. The world of sensible things, however, is not always so trustworthy, for some sense perceptions "go over to their opposites." Sometimes the sensible world, far from being obvious, becomes a self-contradictory mess, or as Socrates calls it, a "barbaric bog" (533d). In the case of the fingers, it is when my second finger looks to be both larger and smaller. To stabilize these kinds of perceptions, I measure the fingers. By my doing so, by my "summoning of the intellect," the movement of perceptions over to their opposites is replaced by the clarity and fixity of numbers. Measuring and counting move me upwards on the divided line, from C to B.

Upon reflection, even if it is "lowly," this little bit of arithmetic actually has earth-shaking consequences. When I invoke numbers to do my counting, I implicitly transform my three fingers from originals into images. The numbers are pure and invariant, immune to change, indifferent to what sensible item they count, and able to count them all. For this reason, they are "more real" than the things they are counting. The sensible world, formerly the one I trusted best, has been transformed into an image of a higher reality. Mathematics turns the soul from Becoming to Being because it demonstrates that the world of sensible things we trust and normally call our own, isn't all it's cracked up to be.

The divided line makes plain a basic tendency of human thought. After having moved from C to B, from the sensible world to the mathematical/intelligible one, the human mind experiences a powerful force, a great temptation, to move back down again. This force is expressed best in the work of what Socrates calls the "so called arts" (511c). The word in Greek is *technai*, which is the root of our words "technology" and "technical." In his astonishing prefiguration of modern physics and the technology to which it gave birth, Plato conceives of technical knowledge as applied mathematics. In other words, the sensible world is manipulable through the knowledge available in mathematics. Counting and measurement are only the most obvious examples.

This characteristic of the line is depicted through its most salient visual (and geometrical) feature: B and C are equal in length. This is especially striking because the few directions Socrates gives for drawing it at 509d are, with this one exception, ambiguous. It is not immediately apparent, for example, even whether the line should be vertical or horizontal. Only some remarks Socrates makes later, at 511a and 511d, suggest it is vertical. (See Smith 1996 for a thorough discussion.)

Far more perplexing is the question which segment, A or D, is the larger. While my version above shows segment D longer than A, there is no way of proving this is correct. By sharp contrast, what can be proven is that given the directions Socrates offers for constructing the line, B and C are exactly equal. (See Klein 1975, p. 119, for a proof of this point.) This equality symbolizes the unique fit between the sensible and the mathematical realms. The book of nature, as the Pythagoreans intuited and as modern physics so thoroughly elaborated, is written in the language of mathematics.

This is the sense in which the divided line depicts a fundamental tendency of human thought, namely to move downward from B to C. Because the fit is so perfect, because mathematical knowledge is so amazingly useful in the sensible world, it is always tempting to submit to the force of "intellectual gravity," to apply mathematical knowledge to the sensible realm where it works so well, and to engage in technical manipulation of the world. The curriculum of Book VII of the *Republic*, however, is designed to prepare the philosopher-rulers to resist this temptation. They would not be allowed to treat the study of mathematics

> after the fashion of private men, but to stay with it until they come to the contemplation of the nature of numbers with intellection itself, not practicing it for the sake of buying and selling, like merchants or tradesmen, but for war and for ease of turning the soul itself around from becoming to truth and being. (525c)

In other words, despite the extraordinary power and usefulness of mathematics, and the lure of applying it through technology, the rulers would be forced to defy intellectual gravity. They would move upwards to "the nature of numbers" themselves, as a prelude to their study of the Forms.

Far and away the most difficult item to understand on the divided line, and perhaps in Plato's work as a whole, is the relationship between Forms and mathematical objects, between segments A and B. It is, for example, unclear exactly how the study of the latter prepares one to apprehend the former. Or to reformulate, the relationship between pure numbers – the one, the two, and the three – and an entity like "justice itself" remains obscure. Indeed, because Plato's text is so remarkably sparse at this juncture, figuring out exactly what is going on in this passage is impossible. Still, even if complete explanation is not forthcoming, a few comments are in order.

To reiterate, mathematical objects have all the features of Being long associated with Ancient Greek Philosophy. They are enduring and fully intelligible, universal and objective. For this reason, studying arithmetic turns the soul around, away from the flux of sensible becoming, to the stability of Forms. At the core of Platonism, then, is a transference of those qualities that belong to mathematical objects to objects like "justice itself." Just as the arithmetical sentence "3 + 2 = 5" is objectively and universally true, so too would be the definition of the Form of justice. Indeed, one seeks the Form of justice – one pursues the "what is it" question; indeed, one pursues philosophy itself – precisely because one has been instructed or inspired by the great lesson of mathematics. It should not be surprising, then, that in Plato's Academy, the school in Athens he founded, students were required to study geometry before anything else. (See Mueller 1992 for a discussion of mathematical studies in the Academy.)

To put this point one final way: Plato's great reliance on mathematics is another way in which he combats Sophistry. Regardless of whether an audience is persuaded that 3 + 2 = 5, it simply is the case; it is objectively, perfectly, true. Just this conception of Truth, especially concerning those values pertaining to the issue of human excellence or *areté*, guides Platonic philosophy in general.

b) The Form of the Good

At the very top of the divided line, and so at the pinnacle of reality itself, lies what Socrates calls "The Form of the Good" (505a), or sometimes simply "the Good."[15] To determine precisely what he means is, once again, beyond our reach. We can, however, note that he attributes the following characteristics to it:

1. The Form of the Good is "the greatest study" (505a).
2. By "availing oneself of it . . . just things and the rest become useful and beneficial" (505a). It is the source of all value.
3. It is what "every soul pursues" and that for the sake of which human beings do everything they do (505e).
4. It is "the cause of knowledge and truth" (508e).
5. It is the cause of being (509b).
6. "The good isn't being but is still beyond being, exceeding it in dignity" (509b).

This is a handful. The Good is the Form of Forms and is the source of value, knowledge, Being, and Truth. Yet it is somehow beyond them all. This line of thought should remind the reader of a Presocratic like Xenophanes. For him, the *archê*, the source and first principle of all reality, is God, and is radically different from all those beings that constitute the world of becoming. The Platonic *archê* (see 510b), the Good, plays somewhat of an analogous role.

To make all this a bit more comprehensible, Socrates offers Glaucon a comparison (508a–e). The Good, he says, is like the sun. The sun is the cause of both of life and of light – which are analogous to Being and Truth – but it itself is neither alive nor can it be directly seen. As painful experience teaches, if one stares into the sun, one goes blind. Without protective glasses, the best one can hope for is an occasional glimpse of the sun, and an awareness of it through its reflections and what it makes visible. I know the sun is shining when I see a tree cast a shadow, or when I see the ocean sparkling, or when I am aware of the brightness of the sky and how clearly a mountain rises in the distance. I know the sun is there, even if I cannot see it, and in this sense, know it directly.

Socrates suggests that our knowledge of the Good is like this. We know that human experience is saturated in value; all we do is because we think it to be good. We know the world is intelligible; this, after all, is the great lesson of arithmetic. We know there is Being. And so we conclude there must be an *archê*, a cause, a principle of order making all else possible. This is the Form of the Good, the ultimate object of philosophical inquiry.

To summarize this chapter so far: Plato, emerging at the beginning of the fourth century, was undoubtedly inspired by Socrates, specifically by his "what is it" question, his relentless commitment to the *elenchos*, and by his search for the ground of human excellence. As such, Plato became a critic of the Presocratic materialists who, by his lights, had reduced the entirety of the universe, including the human soul, to nothing more than matter in motion. Even more so was he opposed to the Sophistic relativist, for whom Truth was a delusion. Indeed, the Sophists were his competitors *par excellence* precisely because they, like himself, were concerned with human life and *logos*. In his dialogues, Plato has Socrates deploy a variety of argumentative strategies against them, including the self-reference argument, the *reductio ad absurdum*, and the "what is it" question. While these arguments pack some punch, ultimately they are negative: even if they succeed in showing that Sophistic relativism cannot be maintained, they fail to demonstrate that there actually is objective Truth when it comes to human values. To this end, Socrates offers a variety of arguments on behalf of the Forms. In the *Meno* and the *Phaedo*, he defends the recollection thesis, and his argument substantially relies on mathematics. Not only does mathematics provide a theoretical basis on which to ground one's confidence in the accessibility of objective Truth, but it is also inspiring. As the apparently "lowly" act of counting reveals, utter perfection, in the guise of numbers, regularly intrudes into our messy lives, and so can inspire us to think about the greatest matters that shape experience of the world, namely our values. The search for the Truth about these values, a Truth which resides in the Forms, is Platonic philosophy.

We turn next to a very different kind of argument on behalf of the Forms: a psychological one. We turn to the *Symposium*, the dialogue in which Plato offers his thoughts on Love (or Eros). We will find out that the Forms are what all human beings ultimately do love, even if they rarely are aware of this being so.

Eros

According to Presocratic materialism, what ordinary human beings typically take for granted and care about so deeply – namely, the life of a soul, guided by its value judgments, that both loves and hates, and can direct the body – is really just an illusion. At least for thinkers like Democritus, Empedocles, and Anaxagoras – ancient philosophers who are stunningly modern in their outlook – reality, even psychological reality, is at bottom no more than matter in motion.

In the *Symposium*, the dialogue to which we turn next, Plato offers precisely the kind of *logos* he finds missing in the Presocratics, namely an account of what human life is like from a psychological perspective, the perspective of a soul. In this dialogue, Socrates attends a "symposium," a drinking party (which was a regular feature of Athenian social life). At this particular gathering, however, the guests promise to refrain from drinking (a promise they eventually break). Instead, they decide to entertain themselves not with alcohol, but with discussion. They agree each to give a speech on Eros. This word was used in chapter 1 during the discussion of Hesiod. Its original meaning was "sexual desire," and for Hesiod "Eros" was one of the primordial gods. (Recall that the mechanism by which the Hesiodic world comes into being is sexual reproduction. Thus, in order for the "theogony" to take place, Eros must be present at the beginning.) But "Eros" can have a far broader sense, and often it can usefully be translated simply as "love." For reasons that will become apparent as we proceed, in what follows the two words will be used interchangeably.

Preceding Socrates were five speakers – Phaedrus, Pausanias, Eryximachus, Aristophanes, and Agathon – each of whom offered his own eulogy to Eros. Even though these speeches cumulatively make a significant contribution to the dialogue, Socrates' speech dwarfs them all. Not surprisingly, he begins by interrogating the previous speaker, the tragic poet Agathon.[16]

Agathon expressed a rather conventional Greek view, namely that Eros should be praised as a god. Eros, he said, was the most beautiful and beauty loving of all the gods. By examining this assertion, Socrates elicits the following four characteristics of Eros, which can be paraphrased as follows:

First, Eros (says Socrates) is always "of something." Assume some person P loves. If so, then P loves or desires some X. (The addition of "desires" will be explained shortly.) Eros must have an object. In this regard it is like consciousness. When sensing or thinking, it is impossible not to sense or think of something; similarly, when loving, it is impossible not to love something. To use a technical term, Eros is *intentional*. To verify this, one needs only to perform the same sort of experiment readers were asked to perform when discussing Parmenides in chapter 1: try to think without thinking of something. It seems impossible. Next, try to love without being directed toward, without loving some object; try simply loving. It is again impossible. To love is to love something.

The second characteristic of Eros is that the something, the X, loved by P *is not* possessed by P. When I am hungry and desire food, it is because my stomach lacks food. When my stomach is totally full, I feel no hunger. If I am weak or sick, then I desire to be strong or well. The general statement "If P loves X, then P does not possess X" thus seems to hold. Eros is *negative*.

This statement above, however, cannot quite stand as formulated, for there is an obvious counterexample to it. If I now possess health, I may still desire to be healthy. Socrates explains this by saying if P loves X, and P possesses X, then P desires to possess X in the future.

Since this third statement contradicts the second (because it allows P to love and to possess X), we should amend the second: If P loves X, then P does not possess X permanently and completely. If I am healthy and still desire health, it is because health requires continual maintenance to be preserved.

These few remarks (which occur from 199c to 201c) decisively shape Socrates' later discussion, for they disclose the third characteristic of Eros: It is essentially *temporal*. Human beings are caught in the flow of time. We are incomplete, or finite, and aware of our incompleteness.[17] We are continually lacking and so we are continually loving. We love and want what we lack, and our lives are spent in perpetual striving to overcome incompleteness (or finitude). Aristophanes, the famous comic poet and an earlier speaker, had touched upon this theme earlier when he had said, "The desire and the pursuit of the whole is called Eros" (192e). For Aristophanes, however, wholeness was found only in sexual union with a well-matched partner (accompanied by a healthy dose of religious piety). In other words, Aristophanes, like most comedians, retained the ordinary meaning of "Eros." Socrates does not. For him, Aristophanes' was an insufficient account of Eros because, as we will see, human beings can never be fully satisfied, can never achieve the completeness we crave, through intercourse with other human beings.

The first three characteristics all rest on the fourth, which is simply assumed throughout Socrates' discussion. Eros is a desire, a going after its object. It is a motive force, for it impels the one loving to pursue, to move toward, an object. The Greek word for desire is *epithumia*. Let us, therefore, describe Eros as "epithumotic."[18]

Armed with these four characterizations of Eros, Socrates refutes Agathon, who had said that Eros was the most beautiful and beauty-loving of the gods. Since Eros is of what it lacks, if it is the love of beauty it lacks, it cannot itself have beauty. Indeed, it is clearly implied by Socrates' analysis that if Eros loves beauty, then it cannot be a god, for the gods lack nothing. Agathon quickly admits that his own account cannot be sustained. Socrates then dispenses with him and tells a story.

He had once, he says, been instructed in erotic matters by a priestess named Diotima. She had put him through an interrogation in much the same way that Socrates himself had examined Agathon. Socrates too had once believed that Eros was a god, both beautiful and beauty loving. When he learned that Eros could not be such he was at a loss.

If Eros was not good and beautiful, he asked, was it then ugly and bad? If Eros was not an immortal god, was it then mortal? Diotima rebuked him sharply for thinking only in these extreme terms. Socrates, she says, had ignored the possibility of the "in-between." Eros is in-between a human and a god, the mortal and the immortal. It is a *daimon*, a spirit (201e–202e).

Diotima devotes the rest of her speech to articulating the structure of this *daimon*, this "spiritual" force that shapes human lives. She is most concerned with explaining the objects of Eros. This makes sense: if Eros is intentional, then it is precisely the capacity to enter into relationships with objects. Therefore, to explain the structure of Eros means explaining the nature and order of its objects.

The first statement Diotima makes is that Eros has as its object "beautiful things" (204d). Quickly, and without argument, she substitutes "the good" for the "beautiful" (204e). (This substitution is not quite as arbitrary as it sounds: the Greek word for beautiful, *kalos*, often has moral overtones.) If P loves, P loves and desires to possess X. If P loves and desires X, it is because X is felt or believed to be good (to be positive, attractive, beautiful). P expects that attainment of X will result in a state of affairs better than the one not including X. This can be reformulated: the object of P's Eros is the attainment of "happiness" (*eudaimonia*: 204e), that state of affairs achieved when good or beautiful things are possessed. It is, therefore, what we all want.

All this may sound quite "idealistic." But in fact it is not. From the criminal to the thoroughly decent man next door, all action is directed toward some goal thought to bring advantage. Human beings go after what they take to be to their benefit, what they take to be good. In other words, Diotima has added a fifth characteristic to the list: Desire is *purposive or teleological*. Human beings are moved by a desire for an object, for a goal (*telos*) they believe or judge to be good. This process of judging is rarely made articulate. The criminal rarely bothers to attempt to articulate why he believes (incorrectly) that his crimes are good. But he does believe, however inarticulately, that what he does is for his own good. If he did not, he would not do it. Diotima's point is that, in principle, every action propelled by desire could be made articulate. If P desires to move toward X, it is because P "thinks," however inarticulately, that X is somehow good. If P did not think X were good, P would go elsewhere. In sum, "what everyone loves is really nothing other than the good" (206a).

The next stage of Diotima's analysis begins with a crucial transition. If P loves X, X is thought or felt to be good and so P desires X to be his own in order to be happy. Furthermore, P desires X always to be his own (206a). The desire for what is good is the desire for the permanent possession of what is good. Soon this is reformulated even more dramatically: Eros is Eros of immortality (207a), in the form of the immortal possession of the good.

At first, this statement may seem incredible. Does it make any sense to say that we want to be immortal? If it does, it is because of the earlier discussion Socrates had with Agathon. There it was agreed that Eros is epithumotic and necessarily contains within it a negative moment: we desire what we do not have. Eros is teleological: we desire and move towards what is good. Eros is essentially temporal: we desire good things whose possession extends into the future. Ultimately, what we do not have is immortality. Immortality, therefore, is the ultimate object of desire. It is what we all want whether we say, admit, know it or not.

Think of it this way: If you ever got totally what you wanted, you would cease to desire. Since desire is a necessary condition of life, if you ever got totally what you wanted you would cease to be alive as a human being. This can mean one of two things: Either you would be dead or you would become immortal. Rarely do human beings want to die. Therefore, insofar as you desire to get totally what you want, you desire immortality.

Perhaps Diotima's position can be made more clear by considering a possible objection to it. Assume a woman desires some object (Y) even though, or just because, it is an object only to be temporarily possessed. She might desire to scale a mountain even though she knows she must return to the plains. She might argue that mountain-climbing is made even more attractive just because she must return to the plains. Diotima's response could take the following form: Assume Y is an object that fulfills a desire. If the woman desires to possess Y on a temporary basis, there must be some reason why she does not desire Y on a permanent basis. There must be some desirable object Z that supplements, replaces, or conditions the desirability of Y. But Y has been assumed to be fulfilling and so it should not require any supplementation. Therefore, either Y is not fulfilling, in which case some other object Z is more desirable, or Y must be desired as a permanent possession. (If the latter option is chosen, then the same analysis would be applied to Z.)

The mountain-climber might say, "You're crazy. Immortality is the furthest thing from my mind. I want to climb a mountain, but I do not want this as a permanent possession; part of the thrill of the mountaintop is that I know I must return to the plains." If she says this, she actually denies that what she wants is to climb a mountain. The mountaintop (call it Y) only seems to be the object of her desire; in reality, she desires to have a complex feeling that includes both the thrill of the mountaintop and the security of the plains (call it Z). What she wants is the complex object $Y + Z$ (call it Q). This, not Y, is what she wants. If she argues that she wants Q only temporarily, some other object, R, will arise, and then we will have to say that she really wants $Q + R$, or S. And if she thinks about it she will have to admit that, finally, it is S that she wants . . . and wants as a permanent possession.

An opponent might object: "What if there is no termination point; what if we desire an indefinite array of objects, none of which we desire permanently?" On this account, we love the seeking of pleasures and goods and neither permanence nor total satisfaction. For the opponent, the fact that the objects of desires neither are orderly nor terminate is not a problem but a delight. Again, however, the opponent cannot explain why any object is not in itself totally fulfilling. Why is there a need to return to the plains at all? Why not perish on mountaintops? Human beings are restless and never quite satisfied; we move on. We do so, not because all objects are equally unfulfilling, but because we seek an object that is completely fulfilling. If this weren't the case (if this weren't a belief implicitly operative in us), then there would be no motive force to keep us going from one object to the next.

It is our temporality, our being in and of time, that makes Diotima's account compelling. It is the awareness of our temporality that shapes and pushes forth our actions. Only because we are aware of the flow of time in which we are caught do we move, strive to achieve, push ourselves forward.

I wake up and realize that this morning feels much the same as yesterday's. Soon this morning will disappear and become tomorrow. I am caught in a flow that cannot be stopped, cannot be reversed, and even my youngest child will soon age. I look back at yesterday's morning and realize it is gone, vanished; only a memory, usually dim, remains. And I understand that this very morning will soon be an equally dim yesterday. I imagine my dying and realize that just before its moment this very morning will be as insubstantial as yesterday's morning is now. I imagine my father, so very old, and understand that the way he looks back at his past is no different from mine. We are all caught. This is a very common feeling. We think about dying and the flowing away of our lives. Often it is easy to feel swept away in the current of time and sympathize with the famous lines of Macbeth:

> To-morrow, and to-morrow, and to-morrow,
> Creeps in this petty pace from day to day,
> To the last syllable of recorded time;
> And all our yesterdays have lighted fools
> The way to dusty death. Out, out, brief candle! Life's but a walking
> shadow, a poor player
> That struts and frets his hour upon the stage
> And then is heard no more; it is a tale
> Told by an idiot, full of sound and fury
> Signifying nothing.

If Diotima is wrong, then Macbeth is right. If there is no way to get out of time, then time is but a succession of "syllables" pacing toward their end. Diotima tells us that we desire life to be more than a petty path of yesterdays leading to dusty death. Macbeth has lost that desire; and he is a madman. We desire to escape, to stand outside, the flow of time. When Diotima says this she is not being overly idealistic or mystical. She is being realistic about ordinary human experience. We want to jump out of time. Only by understanding this desire can we hope to understand, and affirm, who we are.

There is, of course a big problem. How can we, ever aging, "jump out of time?" What sense could this phrase possibly make? How can we gain access to or make contact with that which is not finite? At this point a metaphor takes command of the passage: Human beings are pregnant. Our lives are spent in giving birth to what will remain when we are gone. The parent's child, the family legacy, the fame earned on the basketball court, the poet's poem, all represent the human urge to overcome finitude. As Aristophanes had put it, even in sexual embrace the soul desires something else that it cannot articulate, but only intuit, namely wholeness (192d). Diotima supplies the articulation that the comedian leaves out. She is willing to explain how it is that finite beings desire and attempt to give birth to that which is immortal.

It is here that Diotima launches into what has become known as the "ascent passage" (210a–212a). Here she supplies her own analysis of desire, of Eros, as a hierarchical structure. She couches her lesson in language of religion, as she asks us to imagine a young man becoming "initiated" in, and then ascending through the various stages of, the "mysteries" of Eros. The first two stages are these:

Stages 1–2: A lover who goes about this matter correctly must begin in his youth to devote himself to beautiful bodies. First, if the leader leads aright, he should love one body and beget beautiful speeches there;[19] then he should realize that the beauty of any one body is brother to the beauty of any other and that if he is to pursue beauty of form he'd be very foolish not to think that the beauty of all bodies is one and the same. When he grasps this, he must become a lover of all beautiful bodies, and he must think that wild gaping after just one body is a small thing and despise it. (210a–b)

Eros begins with the love of a single body. What is surprising is that this first stage, this first and most familiar desire, soon slackens and its object is counted as "something small." Why? Is Diotima a prude who finds bodies distasteful? No. After the very first stage of loving individuals, "beautiful speeches" are generated. Human Eros, Diotima rightly explains, does not remain mute. We speak to our beloveds, call them "beautiful," tell why we love. Bodies, in and of themselves, simply do not satisfy for very long. For whatever reason, the urge is soon felt "to give birth" to *logos* which supplements, and soon comes to overwhelm, touch.

Our hypothetical initiate has felt the urge to speak. He generates a beautiful speech. As a result, he comes to realize that the individual body beside him is not totally satisfying. And so he moves to stage 2, love of all beautiful bodies. It is not obvious what Diotima means here. Does she allude to a bisexual Don Juan? Probably not. More likely she indicates that the production of *logos* leads to the realization that the extension of the word "beautiful" outstrips any single body. What comes to the fore here is what she calls "the beautiful in form." Because of our use of language we come to realize that what we love when we love even a single body is not what it seems to be.

The initiate says to his beloved, "I love you because you are beautiful." This is a speech produced by Eros. The speech triggers a realization: The word "beautiful" he has used does not exclusively refer to the body lying beside him, but to all bodies that can be described as "beautiful." There is a movement implied by the use of language – a quintessentially Platonic movement – away from particularity (this beautiful body right here) to universality (to the "beauty" shared by all beautiful bodies). Language forces us to realize that what we want is not an individual; we want more.

This first transition of the ascent passage, from stage 1 to 2, is paradigmatic of the entire erotic journey. Because we talk, the objects of our Eros change. *Logos* functions like a lens through which we see the objects we love. When there is a disparity between what we are saying and what we are loving, then a need is felt to move on. A single beautiful body simply is not satisfying to one who speaks, for speaking refers to the beautiful in form. By speaking the initiate realizes (sees) that the single body does not fully satisfy and in this sense must be counted as "a small thing." The initiate goes forward.

(*Before proceeding, a warning*: It is obviously not necessary that every person who loves come to this realization. It is possible for someone to spend an entire life loving only particular bodies. What Diotima wishes to explain is the structure of the process that is engendered by dissatisfaction at the various stages of the ascent. Once the initiate comes to realize the discrepancy between the *logos* used to comment upon his beloved at a particular stage and that beloved itself, he feels a lack and is driven forward, upward. He is driven to harmonize his *logos* and his Eros. It is not necessary, however, than any single initiate must undergo this experience. Diotima's objective is not to explain what happens to everybody, only to those whose desires are powerful enough to make them feel dissatisfaction and then want more.)

> *Stage 3*: After this he must think that the beauty of people's souls is more valuable than the beauty of their bodies, so that if someone is decent in his soul, even though he is scarcely blooming in his body, our lover must be content to love and care for him and to seek to give birth to such ideas as will make young men better. (210b–c)

Here there is another realization, namely that the object of Eros is not bodily at all. A body is necessarily particularized and the initiate's love is now for the beautiful in form, for the universal. Therefore, he must redirect his Eros to the soul, which he takes to be the locus of universality. The soul, not the body, is the origin of *logos*, and it was the generation of "beautiful speeches" that sparked the initial drive toward universality. Our initiate now realizes that genuine satisfaction comes through talking. As a result, he can be attracted by someone (like Socrates) whose body is ugly but whose soul is beautiful. This realization pushes the initiative forward again.

> *Stage 4*: The result is that our lover will be forced to gaze at the beauty of activities and laws, and to see that all this is akin to itself, with the result that he think that the beauty of bodies is a thing of no importance. (210c)

Stage 4 is the love of "activities and laws." This phrase probably refers to all public activity directed towards the *polis*, the city as a whole. In other words, this stage is really about love of politics. Here Eros is not concerned with individuals at all, for the city is not simply an aggregate of particular bodies. It is a unified entity capable on its own of commanding the loyalty and passions of its citizens. The political person loves, not individuals, but the "soul" of the city, its principles, ideals, history. These are disclosed through *logos*, which is (or at least used to be before TV came to dominate politics) the medium of political life.

The process of wanting more, sparked by our talking, takes us beyond individual bodies to souls. Again, this is not idealism or prudishness; it is a description of what happens to people with powerful desires. They want something more than individuals. They want to be talked about. They want their words to reach far. They want to be recognized by the city, and not just by their individual beloveds. Such recognition can take many forms; one might desire fame, political power, literary influence, the good feeling of deeds applauded as well done. Diotima does not spell any of this out. But her basic point, that because of *logos* the objects of Eros progress upward, is clear.

Diotima is virtually silent about both the fourth ("the political") and what comes next, the fifth stage of the ascent.

> *Stage 5*: After laws he must move on to various kinds of knowledge. The result is that he will see the beauty of knowledges. (210c)

Politics (stage 4) and a love for the particular kinds of knowledge (stage 5) are briefly mentioned and then soon left behind. We are not told why. An obvious inference is that it is because neither is fully satisfying, and the ascent passage presents the structural development of a soul in search of genuine satisfaction. But why are these two human activities unsatisfying? First, to politics.

In concrete political terms, the city, especially a contentiously democratic one like Athens, always suffers from factionalism. It is riddled with disagreement and can never become either fully harmonious or just. This is due precisely to the erotic nature of human beings. There are always individuals who seek "to have more" than their fair share. There is among some of the citizens a desire for power. This is simply a specific application of Diotima's general teaching: Eros is the desire for completeness, for total satisfaction. And one variant of such a desire is political. As Socrates puts it in the *Republic*, "Eros has from old been called a tyrant" (573b6). Eros drives, it pushes; those with the strongest desires desire all. Political Eros, therefore, issues in the desire for complete rule, for tyranny.

The city is a conglomerate of competing desires and speeches. Each politician speaks to the public (or, in a system less democratic than the Athenian, to his competitor), but only to advocate a specific political program. The goal is not realization of a universally just city, but the fulfillment of a particular desire. Eros cannot be controlled, these speeches cannot be purged of their particularity, and so the city cannot be made either fully just or secure. Political *logos*, therefore, is necessarily unsatisfying, for the city is a cauldron of competition. If a politician's goal is total satisfaction, he has gone into the wrong business.

This point can be reformulated: Earlier we saw that Eros seeks that which is immortal and so nonhuman. Since the city is strictly a human affair, Eros cannot be satisfied through politics. Upon realizing this, the initiate must again metamorphose the object of his Eros. He turns to the various forms of knowledge. Presumably what is available here is intellectual satisfaction. Imagine the following scenario. For years our hypothetical initiate was driven by pursuit of his career in politics. But he finally became frustrated. Politics, he learned, always requires compromise and capitulation and less than perfect solutions to its problems. The political man is forever pitted against others of his kind. His *logos* must, therefore, continually take into account what these others will say. Politics finally becomes ugly and after a while our initiate realizes that he desires something clean, something complete. In response he turns away from the city and toward any one of the particular sciences such as history, mathematics, or biology. Here he engages an object free from the hurries of human interference. The object doesn't vary, doesn't tantalize. The *logos* his science affords him need not direct itself to other human *logoi* that aim to thwart it. There is no need to compromise. He studies and learning pleases him.

But soon even this experience becomes unsatisfying. We wish Diotima had said more about why. It must be because, like politics, any of the sciences is partial and Eros desires completeness. The problem is specifying the exact nature of their incompleteness. Perhaps this is a result of the fact that the sciences proceed on the basis of unproven assumptions (axioms), or categorical distinctions that are not made explicit. Perhaps the individual sciences are unable to give a full account of their foundations and what exactly it is that makes them sciences. Perhaps it is because they cannot give an account of their own goodness. In any case, they are partial, they "cut off" a portion of reality and study it. Biology, for example, studies only one small subject: living beings. Mathematics is only concerned with abstract magnitudes. Our initiate, a man driven by Eros, wants more. He wants a logos of all things. He turns toward philosophy, the love of wisdom. The initiate turns away from, for example, biology, mathematics, or history, and toward "the great sea of the beautiful" where "he gives birth to many beautiful and magnificent speeches and thoughts in unstinting philosophy."

What is the object to which the initiate finally turns? Ultimately it is the Form of Beauty itself.

> *Stage 6*: You see, the man who has thus far been educated in matters of Love, who has beheld beautiful things in the right order and correctly, is coming now to the goal of Loving: all of sudden he will catch sight of something wonderfully beautiful in its nature . . . First, it always is and neither comes to be nor passes away, neither waxes nor wanes. Second, it is not beautiful this way and ugly that way, nor beautiful at one time and ugly at another; nor is it beautiful here but ugly there, as it would if it were beautiful for some people and ugly for others. Nor will the beautiful appear to him in the guise of a face or hands or anything else that belongs to the body. It will not appear to him as one idea or one kind of knowledge. It is not anywhere in another thing, as in an animal, or in earth, or in heaven, or in anything else, but itself by itself, it is always one in Form. (211a–b)

The words Diotima uses should now be familiar. The Form of beauty "always is": it is eternal. It is not beautiful "for some people and ugly for others": it is utterly objective, and allows no speck of relativism to infect it. "It is not anywhere on earth": it is thoroughly intelligible, and not material. It is "itself by itself": it is ontologically independent, or absolute.

Philosophy attempts to articulate the vision of beauty itself and thereby to satisfy the highest human desire. Only beauty itself, understood as an object of human Eros, can produce a satisfying *logos*. Diotima describes philosophy as "unstinting." Unlike all others, philosophical *logos* does not run out. At every other stage of the ascent frustration had to occur. At stage one, for example, there was a discrepancy between the speech that expresses the love the initiate had for his beloved, and his beloved. His speech used the word "beautiful," a word that would describe all beautiful objects. But the object of his Eros at that stage was a particular body: His speech and what it was he was talking about did not harmonize. Only at the highest stage of the ascent, in philosophy, is there a harmony between the *logos* and its object. Because its object is complete, perfect, singularly formed, philosophical discourse addresses that which is commensurate with its need for total satisfaction. According to Diotima, philosophy is the highest human activity, for it and only it has as its object that which is unchanging, immortal; that toward which Eros can direct all its energy without fear of its object failing to satisfy.

To summarize: Diotima is a kind of inverse Freudian. By her lights, latent within sexual attraction is the love of wisdom, of beauty itself. Don Juan, we might say, is a repressed philosopher. What we really love when we love (when we speak about what we love) is nothing particular. We really want to articulate what is permanent and un-changing within our experience. Diotima exhorts us to know ourselves and thus to acknowledge the desire for immortality. We are what we love and this, if understood properly, is wisdom. Therefore, only philosophy, the love of wisdom, adequately expresses the restless urgings of an Eros that speaks.

The Political Implications of the Forms

In the "ascent passage" of the *Symposium*, Diotima describes the philosopher as someone who has moved beyond the particular and altogether human concerns of the city in order to catch a glimpse of

"Beauty itself by itself." In the *Phaedo* and the *Meno*, Socrates argues on behalf of "recollection" and the attempt to gain access to those universal Forms making ordinary experience possible. When drawing the "divided line" in the *Republic*, he articulates the all-important role mathematics plays as the means by which we turn from Becoming to Being, from sensible things to the Forms. Clearly, then, the Forms define Plato's philosophical enterprise by providing it with its ultimate goal and greatest hope.

It would be a terrible mistake, however, to conclude from this that Plato is some sort of "otherworldly" thinker who is indifferent to human life here on earth. As we will see in this section, Plato is not out simply to solve conceptual puzzles or construct abstract theories. In fact, he never loses sight of the human and political implications of his ideas. Strangely enough, he will have Socrates argue that philosophers, even though they gaze beyond the particulars and upwards at the Forms, are best suited to rule a city. As we will learn, only the person who cares least about governing "the ship of state" is able to govern it well. We turn again to the *Republic*.

As discussed above, in this dialogue Socrates and his young interlocutors become "city planners." They build a city in speech that they claim is just. Its key feature is to place the rule in the hands of philosophers. This is not explicitly stated until Book V (473c), but even earlier in Book IV the basic principle of the just city is made clear: those who have knowledge should govern the city (428a–429a).

This proposal is dangerous. When someone has knowledge, he or she becomes authoritative. So, to use the sort of example Socrates himself is fond of, if you were to break your arm, you would not hesitate to rush to the hospital and demand to see a trained surgeon. You would then gratefully submit to her expert judgment about how to treat your arm. Years of training in medical school have molded the surgeon into an authority in the field. The analogous expertise gained by the philosopher-rulers of Plato's *Republic* would presumably be knowledge of the Form of the Good. But, to press the analogy one step further, would not a city governed by such masterful rulers become uncomfortably authoritarian? Just as you would not ask your friends how to fix your broken arm, nor put the question up for a free and open debate, so too the putatively just city Socrates constructs will not tolerate dissent or encourage discussion. It will be repressive. Such, at least, has been the verdict of many a reader of the *Republic*. In the twentieth century, the most notable spokesman of this highly critical view was Karl Popper, whose book *The Open Society and Its Enemies* (Popper 1950) identified Plato as one of the chief enemies of the liberal, democratic state.

Support for Popper's position can undoubtedly be extracted from the *Republic*. For instance, censorship is practiced in the city Socrates builds. Because the rulers are counted as being wise, they are taken to know what kinds of poetry, music, and cultural activity are beneficial for the citizens, and what are not. Thus, in Books II and III of the dialogue, Socrates offers an extensive list of myths to be censored. To cite two representative examples: in the *Theogony*, Hesiod tells a story about the intergenerational strife that plagued the earliest gods, specifically Uranus and his son Cronus. To make the story short, Uranus tried to suppress the next generation of gods, fearing that they would usurp his power. Cronus managed to escape his father's grasp, and he then plotted revenge. Eventually he fought and defeated (in fact, he castrated) his own father. About stories like this, Socrates says, "not even if they were true would I suppose they should so easily be told to thoughtless young things; best would to keep quiet" (378a). Because the gods function as mythic role models, such a tale may seem to legitimize rebellion against authority as such. Socrates thus recommends banning it.

A second kind of story Socrates censors is any that depicts death negatively (386a–387c). After all, if the citizens think death is horrible, then they would fear it and thus be less willing to perform the ultimate act of citizenship, namely to sacrifice their lives for the good of the city and their fellow citizens.

Socrates invests such authority in his hypothetical rulers that he even allows them to lie to their subjects. In Book III, he recommends their telling a "noble lie" (414c). Citizens will be told that "the rearing and education" they had received were really "like dreams." Instead of being raised by their parents, "they were under the earth within, being fashioned and reared" (414d). The land on which they live, the city itself, is their true mother, and all citizens are siblings. Therefore, "as though the land they are in were a mother and nurse, they must plan for and defend it, if anyone attacks, and they must think of the other citizens as brothers and born of the earth" (414e). The clear intention of the noble lie is to inculcate the virtue of "patriotism" – which is derived from the Greek *patêr*, "father" – in the citizens. They must identify their own interests with that of the city as a whole.

The lie has a second part:

> "All of you in the city are certainly brothers," we shall say to them in telling the tale, "but the god, in fashioning those of you who are competent to rule, mixed gold in at their birth; this is why they are most honored; in auxiliaries, silver; and iron and bronze in the farmers and the other craftsmen." (415a)

In order to create a city in which citizens are content with their political status and so feel no resentment or need to compete for positions of authority, Socrates tells them they have one of three metals in their soul. If it is gold, they are meant to be rulers; if silver, they will be auxiliaries, who assist but are subordinate to those above them; if bronze (or iron), they are workers who should keep their noses to the grindstone and obey orders. The tasks citizens are given to perform, and the stratum of the city to occupy, is fixed with the rigidity of metal. There is thus no reason for citizens to complain, protest, or rebel. They should simply work as hard as they can at their assigned tasks.

The noble lie tells much about the principal objective of Socrates' political strategy. His goal in constructing the city in speech is to make it maximally stable. Towards this end his putatively just city requires, above all else, cooperation and harmony among the citizens, each class of whom should be prepared "to do its own work in the city" (434c) and be willing to sacrifice for the good of the whole. Indeed, the very definition of justice itself is formulated in these terms: "justice," Socrates says, "is doing one's own work and not meddling with what isn't one's own" (433b). Its opposite, injustice, would be the condition of factionalism, where there is conflict between citizens and competition over the distribution of power and rule.[20]

Clearly, these political proposals express a comprehensive critique of Socrates' own city of Athens, which had a proud history of being democratic, free, and egalitarian. In the city sketched in the *Republic*, "power" (*kratia*) certainly does not belong to the people (*demos*): it belongs to the ruling elite, those few who are wise. Socrates expresses his harshly critical view of contemporary politics in a little story he tells, the allegory of the ship of state.

> Though the shipowner surpasses everyone on board in height and strength, he is rather deaf and likewise somewhat shortsighted, and his knowledge of seamanship is pretty much on the same level. The sailors

are quarreling with one another about the piloting, each supposing he ought to pilot, although he has never learned the art [*techné*] . . . And they [the sailors] are always crowded around the shipowner himself, begging and doing everything so that he'll turn the rudder over to them. And sometimes if they fail at persuasion and other men succeed at it, they either kill the others or throw them off the ship . . . They don't know that for the true pilot it is necessary to pay careful attention to year, seasons, heaven, stars, winds and everything that's proper to the art, if he is really going to be skilled at ruling a ship. (488a–d)

The city is a ship, its citizens are sailors, and its pilot controls the rudder. (The Greek for "captain" or "pilot" is *kubernêtês*, which is the root of our word "governor.") The essential flaw of democracy, as this allegory would have it, is that it allows citizens to compete against their fellows for leadership. As a result, the sailors, preoccupied as they are by their quest to defeat their opponents, keep their eye trained on the rudder and the other sailors. When one sailor does win the battle and becomes the pilot – perhaps by enlisting the services of a Sophist to help him persuade his fellows to grant him rule – he is shockingly ignorant of how to sail the ship well. After all, in order to navigate properly what needs to be studied is not the art of persuasion, nor the group dynamics of sailors on a ship, but "the art of seamanship."

The full force of this criticism can be felt when Socrates mentions the "true pilot." This is the man who has studied the sky, the stars, the winds, and "everything that's proper to his *techné*." He has spent his life gazing upwards, away from his fellow sailors and to the heavens, for only by looking there can one gain genuine knowledge of how to navigate a ship. But the true pilot pays a big price for his intellectual seriousness: by looking upwards he does not pay much attention to what is in front of his nose, namely the other sailors, many of whom are competing furiously for control of the rudder. As a result, he is singularly inept at persuading the others that because of his expertise he should guide the ship. The allegory of the ship of state thus presents a dire picture of democratic politics: the only man capable of knowledgeably guiding the ship will never be chosen (elected) to do so, for his expertise lies not in the art of gaining power, but in navigation. The *polis* is doomed to be governed by *doxa*, not knowledge, and it will sail badly.

The only way to rectify the sad dilemma of politics is somehow to install the true pilot – or the philosopher – at the helm. But, as we have just seen, such a person would much prefer to gaze at the stars than to bother with his fellow sailors, and in fact is not very good at working with other human beings. Socrates tells a second allegory in order to address this problem:

> See human beings as though they were in an underground cave-like dwelling with its entrance, a long one, open to the light across the whole width of the cave. They are in it from childhood with their legs and necks in bonds so that they are fixed, seeing only in front of them, unable because of the bond to turn their heads all the way around. Their light is from a fire burning far above and behind them. Between the fire and the prisoners there is a road above, along which see a wall, built like the partitions puppet-handlers set in front of the human beings and over which they show the puppets . . . Then also see along this wall human beings carrying all sorts of artifacts, which project above the wall, and statues of men and other animals wrought from stone, wood, and every kind of material . . . (514a–c)

This bizarre image is meant to reflect "our nature in its education" (514a). Human beings, according to the allegory, spend their lives looking at images which they mistakenly think to be real. Their light comes from a fire, rather than the sun, and their world is obscure. Ordinary human beings are, in short, ignorant. Eventually, however, "a man is released and suddenly compelled to stand up . . . to turn his neck around, to walk and look up toward the light" (515c). As this man turns around and moves upwards, he progressively "realizes" that what he had thought was real is actually no more than an image. He sees the fire and the puppets, and understands that he had spent his life staring at shadows rather than true beings. When he actually reaches the surface, he beholds "the things in heaven." Instead of shadows, he sees "the light of the stars and the moon," and finally, when his eyes have become accustomed to such brightness, he can glimpse "the sun and sunlight" (516b).

The allegory of the cave reiterates themes already familiar to us. Its key notion is the distinction between original and image, between what really is and what only seems to be, which was central to the "divided-line" passage. Philosophical progress is measured precisely by the degree to which one moves away from the latter and towards the former; away, in other words, from *doxa* and towards the Truth. Accomplishing this requires philosophers to "turn around," to entirely transform their orientation to the world. Instead of particular things or bodies being counted as most real, the philosopher "realizes" (a word crucial in the *Phaedo*) that entities making such things possible and intelligible – first numbers and then Forms – are ontologically superior. As in the ascent passage of the *Symposium*, where the "initiate" transcends the city, so too in the allegory of the cave the philosopher finally makes it above ground where he can bathe in the light of the sun, the analogue to the Form of the Good.

The last chapter of the cave allegory, however, includes a significant addition to the ascent passage of the *Symposium*, and it shows how Socrates proposes to remedy the city by investing the "true pilot" with the power to rule. After having left the cave, the philosopher naturally would prefer to stay in the sunlight rather than return to the darkness. He is not, however, to be permitted to do so. "Our job as founders," Socrates says to his interlocutor Glaucon,

> . . . is to compel the best natures to go to the study which we were saying before is the greatest, to see the good and to go up that ascent; and, when they have gone up and seen sufficiently, not to permit them what is now permitted.
>
> *Glaucon*: What's that?
> *Socrates*: To remain there and not be willing to go down again among those prisoners or share their labors and honors . . .
> *Glaucon*: What? Are we to do them an injustice, and make them live a worse life when a better is possible for them?
> *Socrates*: My friend, you have forgotten that it's not the concern of law that any one class in the city fare exceptionally well, but it contrives to bring this about in the city as a whole, harmonizing the citizens by persuasion and compulsion, making them share with one another the benefit that each is able to bring to the commonwealth. (519c–e)[21]

The "city in speech" Socrates sketches in the *Republic* is one in which philosophers are forced to rule. As such, it violates one of the central tenets of a democracy, namely its protection of the individual's free pursuit of happiness. In Book VIII, Socrates spells out his critique of democracy in literal (nonallegorical) terms, and far more detail. By his reckoning, it suffers the following weaknesses.

1. Because it allows great freedom, citizens in a democracy are not required to be politically active. As Socrates puts it, there is no "compulsion to rule in this city" (557e), even for those who are most competent to do so. Too often in a democracy the best and the

brightest will disregard politics in favor of pursuing their private interests, and the city will be deprived of those most capable of ruling it. It will thus be governed not by those who know best how to rule, but by those who want most to be in charge. In allegorical terms, the true pilot is allowed to continue gazing at the stars, and the philosopher having left the cave is not "compelled" to return.

2. The citizens do not "care at all from what kinds of practices a man goes to political action, but honors him if only he says he's well disposed towards the multitude" (558c). In other words, regardless of what sort of man he really is, a politician who tells the citizens what they want to hear will win the day. In running for office he may, for example, promise to lower taxes and to improve healthcare. What matters is not whether he understands the complexities of the issue, or has the courage of his convictions, but only whether he succeeds in convincing the majority of voters that he wishes them well. His goal is to get elected, not to steer the city well, and to do this he must be an expert in flattery, not true leadership.

3. Because its ethos is egalitarian, the democracy distributes "a certain equality to equals and unequals alike" (558c). Its basic principles are "one citizen, one vote" and "equality before the law." From Socrates' perspective, however, such egalitarianism obliterates critical distinctions that do exist between human beings. Simply put, some people are superior to others and thus deserve certain privileges as well as significant responsibilities. From a democratic perspective it does not matter if someone is intelligent or stupid, decent or cruel, a "true pilot" or an ambitious but ignorant sailor: everyone gets an equal vote, and thus an equal say in how the city should be governed. If, however, the goal is to run the city intelligently, this sort of egalitarianism becomes, according to Socrates, absurd.

4. The democracy, considered both as a regime and in terms of the typical characteristics of its citizens, is whimsical and hence unstable. Socrates voices this view in the following description of what he takes to be a paradigmatic democratic citizen:

> He also lives along day by day, gratifying the desire that occurs to him, at one time drinking and listening to the flute, at another downing water and reducing; now practising gymnastic, and again idling and neglecting everything; and sometimes he engages in politics and, jumping up, says and does whatever chances to come to him; and if he

ever admires any soldiers, he turns in that direction; and if it's money-makers, in that one. And there is neither order nor necessity in his life, but calling this life sweet, free, and blessed, he follows it throughout. (561c–d)

Having been nurtured in an environment that promotes freedom and self-expression, the democratic person is disorderly and undisciplined. Because he has never been forced to do much of anything, he is accustomed to jumping around from one activity to another, from one set of convictions to another. From a political perspective, what is most worrisome is that if a politician or a party platform happens to captivate his imagination, he can be whipped into a frenzy. "Jumping up," the impressionable citizen may passionately urge his city to go to war (even if he does not really know much about the enemy), or to institute the death penalty (even if he does not know whether this punishment actually deters capital crimes), or to place a punitively high tax on the filthy rich (even if he does not know what impact this will have on the economy as a whole). The long-term consequences of these proposals are not well thought out. They are flights of dangerous fancy. To use a metaphor that, after our discussion of the divided line, should make sense, in a democracy nothing and nobody can be counted upon.

5. Habituated by their freedom, the citizen of a democracy grows intolerant of authority of any sort and "spatters with mud those who are obedient, alleging that they are willing slaves of the rulers" (562d). This anti-authoritarianism turns the democracy into what might be termed a "youth culture." Unlike a traditional society, in which the ways of the parents are passed on to the children, and where the elders are thus automatically granted pride of place, in a freedom-loving democracy, traditions, and so age as such, have no intrinsic value. So, for example, "a father habituates himself to be like his child and fear his son" (562e). Because children have been raised to value their freedom above all else they may well question why they should be constrained even by their parents. And on the father's side, the repeated resistance he faces in trying to exert his influence may lead him to abandon his authoritative position altogether and revert to more youthful forms of irresponsible activity.

Another example: "the teacher in such a situation is frightened of the pupils and fawns on them, so the students make light of their teachers" (563a). Even (in fact, especially) the value of knowledge, and of the transmitters of knowledge, namely the teachers, is demoted in a democracy. What is paramount is not the received wisdom of the ages, but creativity and originality, presumed manifestations of the free play of the imagination.

To summarize this line of thought, Socrates says that in general the citizens of a democracy "end up . . . by paying no attention to the laws, written or unwritten, in order that they may avoid having any master at all" (563d). They are thorough anti-authoritarians. By contrast, for Socrates in the *Republic*, not least because of his philosophical reliance on the Form of the Good in Book VI, authority, especially intellectual authority, makes good sense. To him, the egalitarianism lovers of democracy hold so dear is really quite pernicious.

Sentiments such as these are obviously repugnant to modern liberal thinkers like Karl Popper. One remark that Socrates make in the *Republic* should, however, force his opponents at least to reconsider their hostility. In Book VIII he says this about democracy:

> Because, thanks to its license, it contains all species of regimes, and it is probably necessary for the man who wishes to organize a city, as we were just doing to go to a city under democracy. (557d)

The key phrase is "as we were just doing." This is a remarkable admission. Those who want to "organize a city" as Socrates and his interlocutors have just been doing – that is, engage in political philosophy by thinking through the basic problems facing the *polis* and trying to concoct the best of all possible regimes – should probably go to a democracy. Because of the extraordinary freedoms it permits, and the way in which it allows citizens to engage in private activities of all sorts, there is tremendous diversity in a democracy. It is like a "general store" of ideas, and citizens can pick and choose which ones they like. Within a democracy, then, are the intellectual resources a philosopher needs to understand the full range of human possibility. In this sense, a democracy "contains" other kinds of regimes. So, for example, Socrates critically examines (in Book VIII) the oligarchical regime, which is the rule by a wealthy few (*oligoi*). Within the democracy those who have oligarchic tendencies – namely, really rich people who think people like themselves should be in charge – are allowed to express their views. So too with the "timocracy," in which rule is invested in lovers of honor (*timê*) and victory, typically highly spirited men who have excelled in the military. The democracy is "a general store" of political conceptions because it allows divergent views of a good city to be expressed and articulated.

Even more important for the emergence of the philosopher is the freedom of speech protected by a democracy. One might argue that philosophy requires precisely this freedom to challenge all orthodoxies and to be relentlessly self-critical. (Monoson 2000 argues for this view.) To put the point in nearly paradoxical terms, only in a democracy, such as Athens, is it possible to criticize democracy as openly and philosophically as Socrates himself does in the *Republic*. In this regard, consider Socrates' description of how a philosopher lives in actual cities like Athens:

> He keeps quiet and minds his own business – as a man in a storm, when dust and rain are blown about by the wind, stands aside under a little wall. Seeing others filled full of lawlessness, he is content if somehow he himself can live his life here pure of injustice and unholy deeds, and take his leave from it graciously and cheerfully with fair hope. (496d)

Philosophers, the passage seems to suggest, require privacy in order to do their own work. This is a sentiment Socrates also expresses in the *Apology*: "a man who really fights for justice must lead a private, not a public, life" (32a). Recall that in a democracy even the best citizens are not required to be politically active. They are instead given the option to live private, rather than political, lives. It is possible therefore (as Roochnik 2003 has argued) that Plato is not quite as hostile to democracy as he may appear. This is not to suggest that the criticisms of democracy he presents in Book VIII are not meant to be taken seriously. They are. Because of its freedom, its egalitarianism, and its toleration of private pursuits, human projects of all kinds can flourish in a democracy. Most are pretty awful. But one, at least, is vital to the human spirit: philosophy itself.

To conclude: there is a tension in the *Republic* between the thoroughly antidemocratic "city in speech" Socrates builds, and the freedom of speech and thought available in a democracy that allows it to be built. In the former, philosophers are forced to rule. In the latter, they are free to imagine beautiful cities of any sort, even those radically at odds with the status quo. This tension may well keep the reader on edge. It simply is not clear exactly what Plato's views really are. This edginess, however, may be far from accidental. Rather than providing a blueprint according to which an ideal city should actually be constructed, perhaps the purpose of the *Republic* is to spark readers to philosophical reflection and self-examination. Virtually everyone reading this book, for example, lives in a democracy. It is imperative, therefore, for us to wonder what sort of regime it is, and whether a better one is possible. Doing so forces us to ask basic questions about the nature and meaning of human life. And this, rather than providing answers, may well be the ultimate goal of Plato's *Republic*. It is a dialogue taking place not only between Socrates and his interlocutors, but between its author and his readers. And like so many of the dialogues, it may well end in *aporia*.

Notes

1   Plato wrote some letters, and especially the "Seventh" does offer some self-commentary.
2   Unless noted otherwise, translations of Plato are my own. The Greek text is Burnet 1967.
3   Thanks to Rahul Desikan for some advice on these matters. Any errors in this section are, of course, mine alone.
4   This isn't entirely fair. The neuroscientist, notably its great bard, Oliver Sacks (see Sacks 1987), has much to say on this subject.
5   Interestingly, the Greek word for tendon is *neuron*.
6   In Greek it is the *peritropé*, a term which comes from Sextus Empiricus. See his *The Outlines of Pyrrhonism*, II.128 and II.185, and *Against the Logicians*, II.463.
7   All my translations of the *Republic* come from Bloom 1991. In this passage I substitute my "beautiful" for his "fair."
8   The phrase "old quarrel" is used in the *Republic* (607b) to describe the conflict between philosophy and poetry. For many reasons, however, some of which should now be apparent to the reader, Plato often identifies the Sophist with the poet. Hence, the title of this section.
9   This translation largely follows that of Grube in Cohen et al. 2000.
10 I avoid all questions about the status of the fetus.
11 Readers should be able to raise objections to this argument. In particular, they should consider whether instead of "recollecting" concepts like the "equal itself," we arrive at them by generalizing from particular instances. This would be an empiricist's rebuttal to recollection.
12 There is much dispute among scholars about whether the two conceptions of recollection are really the same.

13 The problem for both Platonic recollection and modern genetics is explaining the very beginning of this process.
14 Some of the material in this section was originally published in Roochnik 2001.
15 This is also called "the Idea of the Good." "Form" and "Idea" are synonyms for Plato here.
16 I use the translation of Nehamas & Woodruff 1989. For a thorough interpretation of all the speakers in the *Symposium*, see Rosen 1987. Much of my own commentary here was originally published in Roochnik 1990, pp. 109–20.
17 This view stands at odds with the apparent proofs of the immortality of the soul Socrates offers in the *Phaedo*. This is thus a case where the chronological interpretation of Plato may seem useful. Perhaps the *Symposium* is the earlier dialogue and its author changed his mind. Or, perhaps Socrates is addressing a different audience. In the *Phaedo* he is conversing with young men distraught at the prospect of his impending death. Perhaps they need comfort.
18 This is the source of the famous distinction between pagan "love" or Eros, and Christian love or *agapé*, which is thoroughly non-epithumotic. See Soble 1989. Also, see Hyland 1984, pp. 139–51, for an excellent discussion of Eros, one that has influenced me greatly.
19 A disastrous mistake Woodruff and Nehamas make in their translation is "ideas" instead of "speeches" for *logoi*.
20 I deviate from Bloom here, who translates the key phrase as "minding one's own business."
21 I have transformed what in fact is a narrative into a dramatic dialogue for the purpose of clarity.

4

Aristotle

Preliminaries

Aristotle is the culmination of the dialectical development of Ancient Greek Philosophy that has been chronicled in this book. He is the hero, and at times has even been the guide, of our story. One of the several senses in which this is true is that Aristotle himself is consummately dialectical in his own approach to philosophy. He regularly looks back to the past, considers carefully what his predecessors have said, and then responds critically. His response, however, is never entirely negative. Instead of simply jettisoning his predecessors' work, he retains what he takes to be positive in their thought – in, as he puts it at *On the Soul* 403b21, the "*doxai* of those who came before" – and then incorporates it into his own, much more comprehensive view. To put it metaphorically, Aristotle weaves together his own ideas with all the many strands of past Greek philosophy, and forms one monumental tapestry.[1]

No predecessor was more important to this endeavor than Plato. Born in Stagirus in 384, Aristotle arrived in Athens at the age of 17 to study at Plato's school, the Academy. He remained there until Plato died in 348, at which point he struck out on his own. Throughout his works both the debt Aristotle owes to his teacher, as well as his unique turn away from Plato's thought, can almost always be felt.

A decisive way in which Aristotle diverged from Plato was in their relationship to the Presocratics or, as Aristotle likes to call them, the *phusiologoi*, those who offered a rational account (*logos*) of nature (*phusis*). As discussed in chapter 3, Plato puts a great distance between himself and the Presocratics. Recall the "autobiographical" remarks Socrates makes in the *Phaedo*: as a young man, he abandoned "natural science," not because he did not admire it, but because, he says, "I seemed to myself to be naturally unsuited [*aphuês*] for this kind of investigation" (96c). He did not have the nature to study nature. The first "nature" refers to what belongs uniquely to human beings, and it especially concerns the loves and desires that shape the quest for *aretê* or "excellence." The second, Presocratic sense refers to the world as a totality in which a human being is but one of many homogeneous parts. Socrates pursues only the first, and so his inquiries are decidedly "practical"; that is, they address *praxis* or human activity. He abandons a more strictly "theoretical" form of inquiry in favor of, as he describes it, his "second best way": he turns away from the direct study of beings (or "ontology") to an examination of *logoi*, of what human beings have to say. For these reasons Plato writes dialogues that dramatically depict the life of the human, particularly the philosophical, soul. Little wonder, then, that they frequently end in *aporia*.

By contrast, Aristotle gives answers. He is a theoretical thinker whose written work takes the form of methodical treatises.[2] He not only studies nature – especially the nature of living beings – but he loves it. It is possible that he inherited this passion from his father, who was a physician. Whatever the reason, the study of living nature, or biology, is rarely far from Aristotle's mind. As Gotthelf and Lennox (1987, p. 5) report, "the biological writings constitute over 25% of the surviving Aristotelian corpus." They elaborate: "There are, first of all, the 'big three': *Parts of Animals, Generation of Animals, History of Animals* . . . Then there are the smaller works . . . *Progression of Animals* . . . *Motion of Animals* . . . and the essays collected as *Parva Naturalia*." There is also *On the Soul*, Aristotle's psychology, which, as we will see, is strikingly biological in its orientation. So too does the *Physics*, Aristotle's study of nature in general, take its bearings from living being.

To describe in a nutshell the sense in which Aristotle is the culmination of Ancient Greek Philosophy: he combined the Presocratic commitment to theory, to giving a *logos* of nature, with the Platonic love of the Forms and concern for the best possible human life. For Plato, the Forms were mainly of entities such as Beauty, Justice, and, most important, the Good. These are all values and knowledge of them is intrinsic to attaining *aretê*. Surely his battle against what he took to be the pernicious influence of Sophistic relativism sparked and helped to shape this side of the Platonic project. Unlike Protagoras or Gorgias, for whom there was no Truth about questions of justice or goodness, Plato argued time and again that objective knowledge, and not merely opinion, was both possible as well as necessary in living the good life.

Aristotle fully absorbed this lesson from his teacher. In his book the *Nicomachean Ethics* (named after his father), he gives an account of the "highest good" available to human beings. In the *Politics*, he addresses justice and the best possible political regime. In his *Poetics*, he explains what sort of structure an excellent, or beautiful, drama must have. In each case, the subject at hand has a form or a nature that can be comprehended. The accurate apprehension and consequent articulation of that form results in a claim for the truth about basic human values. In this sense, then, his project is Platonic. But Aristotelian forms, even if they, like their Platonic counterparts, can bear the weight of objective truth, differ significantly. As we will see in detail below, they are not ontologically separate from the particulars, nor are they restricted to qualities like justice, goodness, and beauty. They do not reside on a higher level of a "divided line" (which is why the first letter of the word "form" is no longer capitalized). Instead, they are, quite literally, "down to earth." Aristotle, then, was the first philosopher in the West both to acknowledge the distinction between Being (forms) and becoming (particulars), and also to overcome the ontological dualism this distinction brings with it.

This point can be addressed in grammatical terms. Platonic Forms are usually correlated with adjectives ("just," "beautiful," "good") or with nouns that name qualities or virtues ("Justice," "Beauty," "The Good"). For Aristotle, forms correspond to nouns that name ordinary beings in the world: "rabbit," "star," "tragedy," "human being." When the notion of a form is applied to the animal world – when, for example, Aristotle discusses the form of a rabbit – the meaning of what had been Plato's word (*eidos*) subtly, but critically, changes. It becomes "species."

Nature, according to Aristotle, is organized into clearly visible forms, kinds, or "species." (Recall that *eidos* is derived from the Greek verb "to see.") It is apparent that rabbits are not dogs, mammals are not amphibians, animals are not plants. Perhaps most important, a living being is not an inanimate one. Unlike a Platonic Form, which requires the intellect to push itself away from sensible things and climb high up on the divided line, an Aristotelian form is present, and manifests itself, in nature. It is intelligible through particular natural entities apprehensible by ordinary perception. Throughout this chapter, we will elaborate this notion, which is central to Aristotle's entire philosophical project, and which sharply distinguishes him from his most important predecessor.

The relationship between Plato and Aristotle – at once so intimate and yet so distant – has fascinated readers for centuries. On a visual level, it was famously captured in Raphael's often reproduced painting, "The School of Athens." In it, Plato and Aristotle are standing next to each other. But their stance differs. The former is depicted with his arm lifted upward and his finger raised high. This visual detail expresses the salient feature of Platonism: it aims to turn the intellect around, from becoming to Being, as Socrates says in Book VII of the *Republic*. The Platonist aspires to move upwards on the divided line, to ascend the Erotic ladder, to rise up and out of the cave in order to behold the sun. By contrast, Raphael has Aristotle extend his arm out straight and hold his hand flat as if to say, "what is of interest lies right before us, on this earth, in the world of nature."

A second, and nearly as famous, way of expressing the fundamental difference between the student and his teacher, comes from Coleridge, who said "Every man is born an Aristotelian, or a Platonist. I do not think it is possible that any one born an Aristotelian can become a Platonist; and I am sure no Platonist can ever change into an Aristotelian."[3]

To the first sentence there is a quick retort: it is wildly optimistic. Nonetheless, Coleridge captures something basic about this relationship. Despite the fact that Aristotle studied with Plato for 20 years, the difference in intellectual temperament between student and teacher is enormous. The Platonist turns away from "this" world to concentrate on the purity of the Forms, while the Aristotelian remains faithful to it. To exemplify this, consider a remark Aristotle makes in his *Parts of Animals*:

For even though some of the animals we study are unattractive to perception, still the nature that has produced them provides amazing pleasures for those who are capable of recognizing the causes and who are naturally philosophers . . . That is why we must avoid childish complaints about examining the less honorable animals; for in all natural things there is something wonderful. (645a7–20)[4]

In his biological work, Aristotle studies, to cite only one of dozens of examples, lobsters and crabs, and asks why the former have tails while the latter do not (684a1–5). It is difficult to imagine Plato poking around on the beach, getting his feet muddy, and observing carefully and with delight the creatures he finds.

To put this same point in slightly more technical terms: Plato is a rationalist, who believes knowledge is attainable through the use of reason alone, while Aristotle is an empiricist, for whom knowledge is derived from sense experience and observation.[5] This difference between rationalism and empiricism was first broached in chapter 1 in the discussion of Anaximander. According to this Presocratic the *archê* was what he called "the indefinite." Whatever the word exactly means, this much is certain: it cannot be observed by the senses, which, because they themselves are limited, can apprehend only limited objects. "The indefinite," therefore, can only be accessed by pure thought, which thereby becomes the essential means of attaining knowledge. Anaximander, then, is a rationalist. Thales, by contrast, identified water, an ordinary and observable substance, as the *archê*, and he did so (at least according to Aristotle) on the basis of empirical observations (such as, all living beings contain water).

As oversimplified as this distinction is, it nonetheless supplies a way of roughly characterizing the two greatest thinkers of antiquity. Aristotle is the thorough empiricist for whom the testimony of the senses is essential. Plato, inspired as he is by the purity of mathematics, is far more the rationalist.

For the several reasons just sketched, the first subject we will take up in this chapter is Aristotle's conception of nature. We will see the all-important role form plays in Aristotle's *Physics* (literally, "the study of natural things"), and how it differs so significantly from Platonic Forms.

There is another good reason to begin here. As has been suggested throughout this book, the best justification to study Ancient Greek Philosophy is to retrieve ideas that could prove to be valuable even today. There is no better case of this than Aristotle's conception of nature. A fear haunts many of us that nature has somehow been lost, or even destroyed, by the massive intrusions of a technology born from a specifically modern conception of physics. In their sometimes desperate quest for alternatives, people have looked far and wide: to, for example, various forms of mysticism and irrationalism, as well as to the great traditions of India and China. While the East can no doubt provide wonderful resources with which to forge radical alternatives to modern western thought, they will always be just that: radically different. One of the great virtues of Aristotle's physics is that while his conception of nature is genuinely different from our own, because it is Greek and hence stands at the beginning of western philosophy and science, it is neither entirely distant nor utterly foreign. Even if it is not modern, it is still western. Precisely because he helped to found it, Aristotle is able to present a powerful challenge to the status quo.

This chapter will have four main sections. The first will address Aristotle's conception of nature. The second will discuss his psychology, his account of the human soul that is able to perceive and understand nature. The final two sections will treat Aristotle's *Nicomachean Ethics* and his *Politics*, the works in which he most directly developed the legacy of Platonism.

Aristotle's Conception of Nature

a) "By nature"

In contemporary marketing, especially of various kinds of food, but also of paper products, cleaning fluids, cigarettes, and toothpaste, the word "natural" is regularly used to entice buyers. A natural cookie, which presumably does not contain the artificial ingredients and chemicals found in nonnatural ones, is made to seem not only nutritionally superior, but somehow morally superior as well. In addition to wondering why this word has taken on such a remarkably positive connotation in our retail economy, another more basic question needs to be raised: what exactly does it mean? Regardless of how pure its ingredients are, a cookie made in a factory and placed into a box is hardly natural. But what, then, is? Aristotle provides an answer in the opening lines of Book II of the *Physics*:

> Of beings, some are by nature, while others are by other causes. By nature are animals and their parts, plants, and the simple bodies, namely earth, fire, air, and water (for we say that these sorts of beings are by nature). All of these appear to differ from those beings that are not constituted by nature. For each of them has in itself a principle of motion and rest; some of locomotion, others of growth and decay, while others of alteration. (*Physics*, 192b8–15)[6]

This passage articulates a fundamental distinction, uses terms critical to Aristotle's entire enterprise, and discloses some basic features of his general philosophical approach. Some beings (*onta*), he says, are "by nature" or, as we might say, "natural," while others are not. Note that "animals and their parts" are first on Aristotle's list of examples. As we will see throughout this chapter, this small detail will prove to be significant.

A natural being has within itself the "principle" of motion and rest. The Greek word here is an old friend, *archê*, which for the Presocratics meant "the first principle or source of all reality." Here its meaning is more modest. When something moves, its movement has a cause or an origin. I, for example, might use my hand to push the cup across the desk. The origin of the cup's motion, then, is in me. But what moves me? I move myself and so am the origin of my own movement. The cup, by contrast, is a lifeless and unnatural thing, and so cannot move without something else moving it.

These remarks are hardly as straightforward as they might seem, but for the moment let them stand. Assume that I function as the origin of my own movement in pushing the cup across the table. This is an important clue to what "natural" means. Beings that are "by nature" move themselves. Plants move towards the sun and their roots grow downward. No external force needs to be applied for this to occur. Animals have desires and move towards what they want, namely food and water. In the most self-conscious and advanced case, namely that of human beings, there is the explicit decision to move a hand towards a cup. In each of these examples, there is self-motion of some sort.

Or consider this: most of what remains of my hair has changed from black to gray. The little bit of black still up there will gradually become gray. The origin of this development is in me. I am a living being who was born, matured, and has begun his decline. Such is the rhythm of the biological world. Remember, the first item on Aristotle's list of natural beings was animals. The sort of change exemplified by my disappearing hair thus represents for him a paradigmatic case of self-originated natural motion.

(The terms used in the previous paragraph may seem odd. We do not typically call the "change" of my hair from black to gray a "motion." The Greek word Aristotle uses, however, namely *kinêsis*, can sustain these meanings for it can encompass the English words "change," "motion," or "movement." In *On the Soul* 406a12, for example, Aristotle lists various kinds of movement (*kinêseôn*): change in place (locomotion), alteration (qualitative change), decay and growth. Also, see *Physics*, Book V.1 for a discussion of this and related words, especially *metabolê*, the origin of "metabolism," and the word whose breadth of meaning actually comes closest to our word "change.")

To clarify Aristotle's conception of nature a bit further, consider a very different kind of object going through different kinds of change: a house. A builder constructed it out of timber. Then rain fell on it, and so the wood weathered. There was a flood, and so the foundation began to deteriorate. The owner repaired the foundation, and while doing so added a room in the basement. Finally, someone else bought the house, and then decided to tear it down. All these changes undergone by the house, all these motions, originated in causes external to the house itself.

The difference between what goes on with the house and the movement of my hand as I push the cup, or the changes in the color of my hair as I age, is that the latter are natural. They emanate from a living, and hence developing, organism. This of course does not imply that I could not suffer externally caused changes. Someone could force me to dye my hair purple or chop me into pieces. While a natural being is subject to these sorts of interventions, they can be identified as motions that, precisely because they originate from the outside, are not natural. If an animal is lucky, it will grow, mature, flourish, gradually decline, and die when its natural lifespan has been traversed. To express this point visually, the basic pattern of an individual's development is symbolized in the "bell curve" that represents a "normal" distribution (figure 4.1; with approximate age numbers given for a human lifespan). We will refer to this figure more than once in this chapter.

So far, the discussion of the "natural" has exclusively cited living beings as its examples. Aristotle's own list, however, contains more,

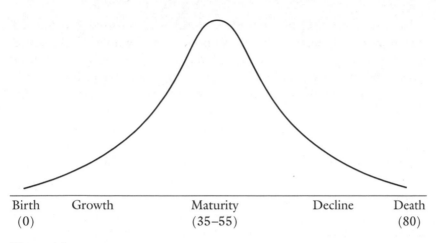

Birth	Growth	Maturity	Decline	Death
(0)		(35–55)		(80)

Figure 4.1

what he calls "the simple bodies, such as earth, fire, air and water." Like animals and plants, these lifeless bodies have a principle of motion and rest in themselves. More specifically, each of these four elements – which, like Democritus' atoms, are the building-blocks from which all material objects (on earth) are compounded – has a natural movement associated with it. If no countervailing force acts upon it, fire, for example, will move upwards (*Physics*, 192a36) towards its natural place, which is in the heavens above. The same is true of air. Water and earth, by contrast, move downwards, towards the center of the earth. (See *On the Heavens*, 269a18.) When each element has reached its natural place, it will stay there unless, once again, a countervailing force moves it.

Phrases like "natural movement" and "place" will sound strange to a modern ear. After all, we are accustomed to a modern physics, with its attendant concepts of gravity and inertia, that is far more like Democritean atomism; that is, a worldview in which the elements of matter are homogeneous and move purposelessly through an infinite space (called by Democritus "the void.")[7] The language articulating the structure of such a universe is mathematics, whose equations express the laws according to which the atoms move, and its result is a physics that empowers its possessor to predict the movement of, and therefore to manipulate, material objects. The physical world conceived by Aristotle, by contrast, is limited and qualitative, and its language is ordinary or natural; it is a language of places and qualities.

To use a new term, Aristotle's world is a "cosmos," a limited, hierarchically organized whole, and not an infinite universe. Its center is the earth; its zenith is in the perfectly circular orbit of the fixed stars. Fire on its own will naturally move upwards, water downwards. In general, the various beings of the world have their natural place in a cosmic hierarchy. On the earth, for example, are "sublunar" entities of the lowest order, while the stars are far "above," both in their place and in their very being. In fact, Aristotle's celestial bodies are made of a fifth element not found on earth, which is weightless and ontologically superior to anything "here." (See *On the Heavens*, I.1–3.)

This little sketch may – indeed, should – seem preposterous to anyone raised on the doctrines of modern physics. We take it for granted that the earth is certainly not the center of the cosmos. In fact, for us there is no cosmos at all, only an infinite universe with neither a center nor an "above." Ours is a physics of unlimited space, not of limited place, and it conceives of matter not as qualitatively differentiated, but as essentially homogenous. How, then, did Aristotle arrive at such apparently ludicrous ideas?

An important clue is given in a line from the passage cited at the beginning of this section. After offering his list of natural items, Aristotle says, "All of these *appear* to differ from those beings that are not constituted by nature. For each of them has in itself a principle of motion and rest." The key word is "appear." In Greek, the verb is *phainetai*, which itself is derived from *phainein*, "to bring to light," "to bring into sight." (Both are originally derived from a root meaning "light.") When something appears it shows itself; it makes itself visible. When it has done so it becomes a "phenomenon," another direct descendant of *phainein*, which means "that which appears to be or seems to be the case."

Aristotle's *Physics* – indeed, his entire philosophical project – takes its bearings from the phenomena. For him, a successful physical theory must explain and do justice to the phenomena, to the appearances or the way things seem. To clarify by contrast, recall comments made in chapter 1 about Parmenides. He was there described as a "paradoxical" thinker. The conclusion of his highly abstract *logos* was that Being is one, motionless, and indivisible. Regardless of the logical validity of his arguments, his view stands utterly at odds with *doxa*, with "opinion," or better "the way things seem." After all, nothing is more apparent than multiplicity and motion. All we have to do is open our eyes, and many things seem to be buzzing all around us. Parmenides, however, denies that this basic phenomenon informs us at all about the Truth (*alêtheia*). While multiplicity and motion undeniably appear to be occurring, his argument concludes that they must be taken as epistemically worthless.

While Aristotle takes this argument seriously, his basic response is really very simple: Parmenides' *logos* is radically paradoxical and this is sufficient to discredit it. The goal of Aristotelian physics, by contrast, is to "save the phenomena."[8] A good, truthful account must be faithful to the appearances. In this regard, the contrast between Aristotle and Democritus, whom we have already identified as the most "modern" of the Presocratics, is also instructive. The latter conceives of a world composed entirely of atoms – indivisible, invisible, bits of matter that have only shape, size, and velocity, quantitative features all – and the void, or empty space. As a result, Democritus is like Parmenides in being a "paradoxical" thinker who strictly separates *doxa* and Truth. Ordinary experience suggests that my pet rabbit is a real object in and of itself. As a result, if someone asked me, "what is that hopping about in your backyard?," I would quickly respond, "a rabbit." For Democritus, however, this would be the wrong answer. Only apparently is that object a being suffused with its own ontological integrity. In reality, it is no more than a conglomeration of atoms moving through the void that happened to group together and will eventually separate. In this account, my rabbit is not essentially different from the cup in my hand.

To reach this conclusion Democritus explicitly rejects the testimony of *doxa*. "There are two kinds of judgment," he declares, "one legitimate and the other bastard. All the following belong to the bastard: sight, hearing, smell, taste, touch." Ordinary sight cannot reveal the atomic structure of the cup: the atoms are, after all, invisible. Instead, Democritus, by means of inference and the construction of a theory, concludes that reality is found only in atoms and the void, neither of which can be empirically observed, neither of which are phenomena.

Aristotle could not be more different. Sense perception, the ordinary apprehension of ordinary objects, is not "bastard" at all. To the contrary, it is a reliable way of attaining the truth about the world, especially living beings in the world. For Aristotle, Democritus' theory, like Parmenides', is repugnantly paradoxical. Obviously, then, this would be the basis of his critique of modern physics as well. As powerful as it is in comprehending the mechanical workings of material objects and predicting their movements through space, by divorcing *doxa* and *alêtheia*, it robs the phenomena of all truthfulness, and ultimately of meaning.

What we are discovering is that, to use a word made famous by Husserl in the twentieth century, and mentioned in the Introduction to this book, Aristotle is a "phenomenologist." The goal of his *logos* is to give a faithful account of the phenomena or, to quote Heidegger, whose language is cumbersome but quite precise in describing the Aristotelian project, it is "to let that which shows itself be seen from itself in the very way in which it shows itself from itself" (1962, p. 58.)

With this little bit of Aristotelian methodology in hand, we can now make more sense of his notions of natural motion and place. Fire, if not forced to move otherwise, will move upwards; water downwards. However at odds with the basic tenets of modern physics, in which matter and motion are essentially homogeneous, the Aristotelian observation is, in one important sense, true. In ordinary experience – in other words, outside of the laboratory and without the use of instruments such as the telescope or microscope – fire does appear to move upwards. Anyone who has built a campfire knows this, and so begins by putting the kindling below the larger pieces of wood. One holds a match under a cigar in order to light it. Aristotle takes his bearings from, attempts to "save" and explain, a phenomenon such as this.

Another phrase from the *Physics* passage cited above is crucial in understanding, and appreciating, Aristotle's "phenomenology." Notice the comments he makes after presenting his list of natural beings such as animals, plants, and the simple bodies: "for we say that these sorts of beings are by nature." Two questions: who is the "we" doing the saying, and why does what "we say" matter at all when it comes to studying physics?

The "we" reflects Aristotle's conviction that the phenomena are largely consistent for all human beings. In other words, he is a great believer in "common sense." (Feyerabend 1978 helpfully discusses this.) It is commonsensical to believe that many beings exist and move around, and that therefore both multiplicity and motion are quite real. Such beliefs are reflected in what linguists would call "natural" language (English, Spanish, Greek, and so on.). The plural, for example, implies multiplicity, adjectives refer to qualities, and nouns name objects. What "we say," then, itself provides evidence about, and is in harmony with, the nature of reality.

Recall the all-important contrast with Democritus: when asked, "what are you now holding in your hand?," a normal person will answer, "a book." For Democritus the language used to identify the object is fundamentally misleading. For ultimately there is no "book," only atoms moving through the void. For Aristotle, by contrast, what "we say" tells us something important. As mentioned in chapter 1, Simplicius, a sixth-century (CE) Aristotelian, expresses this contrast well when he says about Democritus, he "does not make any thing out of them [atoms and the void] that is truly one." Only atoms have genuine ontological integrity. Books, cups, dogs, and rabbits do not. Such a view is radically at odds with the testimony offered by ordinary language, in this case its nouns. For Aristotle, by contrast, objects in the world (especially animals), named by the words "we" commonly use and experienced as unified beings, are quite real.

To make this point even more strongly: for Aristotle, the way we speak about things is itself a dimension of the phenomena themselves. (See Nussbaum 1986, pp. 240–57, and Owen 1975.) Therefore, if the final results of a theory radically diverge from what "we say," then there is something wrong with the theory.

In maintaining such loyalty to ordinary language, Aristotle follows Plato's lead. Recall, for example, Socrates' criticism of Heraclitus in the *Theaetetus* which we discussed in chapter 3. He deploys a *reductio ad absurdum* against his opponent's doctrine of radical flux. If the flux doctrine were correct, then those words apparently referring to stable objects would be emptied of all their truth and meaning. As Socrates puts it,

> Nothing is one, itself by itself, but instead always comes to be in relationship to something. And so "being" should be completely abolished, not withstanding the fact that we often and even just now have been forced by habit and ignorance to use the word. But as the argument of the wise men have it, we shouldn't, nor should we acquiesce in using "something" or "somebody's" or "mine" or "this" or "that" nor any other word that brings things to a halt. (157b)

If there is a single good reason to retrieve the views of Plato and Aristotle perhaps it can found right here. As different as their philosophical projects are, they are both animated by the common objective of remaining faithful to ordinary language. Their work takes its bearings from and attempts to "save" as well as enhance human experience. While neither has a bit of patience with Protagorean relativism and the dictum "human being is the measure of all things," they nonetheless share with the Sophist the demand to take full cognizance of what it means to be a human being, and as Aristotle puts it in the *Politics* (1253a11), "of the animals only human being has *logos*."

As attractive as (I hope) it may appear to be, Aristotle's phenomenological approach in his physics must of course be examined critically. Consider, for example, the basic distinction between natural and nonnatural objects with which this section opened. For Aristotle it is given to us by the phenomena and is both reflected in, as well as verified by, what "we say." There is no such thing, then, as a "natural cookie," for this bit of food was the product of an external cause. But a moment's reflection reveals just how problematic this apparently obvious distinction really is. What about a domesticated cow that has been bred in order to have certain desirable traits? Is such an animal really natural? What about a mule, the offspring of a donkey and horse that is usually sterile? It is an animal, and hence seems to be the paradigmatically natural object, but it comes into being by virtue of the intervention of human design. Is it really "by nature?"

Such difficult cases are vastly more pressing today. Is a baby conceived "in vitro" as natural as one conceived in normal sexual intercourse? Was Dolly the cloned sheep natural? What about genetically modified crops? These questions challenge Aristotle's bold assertion that the distinction between the natural and the nonnatural is apparent. As a result, they highlight a decisive feature of his thinking: his enormous *confidence* in the human capacity to attain the truth about the world. Consider, for example, this comment he makes in the *Physics*:

> It would be ridiculous to attempt to prove that nature is, for it is apparent [*phaneron*] that there many such kinds of beings. Proving what is apparent [*phanera*] by means of what is not apparent is evidence of an inability to discriminate between what is intelligible through itself, and what is not intelligible through itself. (193a2–6)

Notice the use of "apparent," which translates *phaneron* and is related to *phainetai*. It would be "ridiculous" to try to prove that there is nature, for nature stares us in the face. A rabbit is "by nature" and a house is not. Aristotle is confident that human beings, using their commonsense, ordinary perceptions, and the words that come naturally to them, can successfully make this kind of distinction. Anyone (such as a contemporary postmodernist) who denies that this is so, or calls the existence of nature itself into question, would merely be playing word games rather than arguing seriously. The fact of nature's being is, for Aristotle, phenomenologically self-evident. It is a given.

To reinforce this point, consider the following remark from the *Rhetoric*: "human beings," Aristotle writes, "are naturally disposed towards the truth, and most of the time they hit upon the truth" (1355a10). The truth comes naturally to us. Or, in a more elaborate formulation:

> The study of truth is in one sense difficult, in another easy. This is shown by the fact that whereas no one person can obtain an adequate grasp of it, we cannot all fail in the attempt; each thinker makes some statement about the natural world and as an individual contributes little or nothing to the inquiry; but a combination of all conjectures results in something considerable. Truth is like the proverbial door which no one can miss, in this sense our study will be easy; but the fact that we cannot, although having some grasp of the whole, grasp a particular part, shows its difficulty. (*Metaphysics*, 993a30–b10)

The beings of the world show themselves to us as they really are in themselves. As a result, it is "easy" to get a roughly correct sense of the way things are. No one, he says, can miss a door. At the same time, however, Aristotle understands full well that working out the details of one's "study" (which translates the Greek word *theoria*) is vastly more difficult and liable to be erroneous. Indeed, he is hardly ignorant of the fact that people make lots of mistakes. Still, even in the face of error, his basic conviction remains intact: by careful scrutiny of what appears to us, it is possible to attain the truth.

b) Form and matter

Aristotle's *Physics* Book II begins by characterizing those beings that are "by nature." A rabbit is natural, a house is not. But the house is not entirely nonnatural either. Certain changes, for example, will occur in the wood from which the house is constructed, and rather than being externally caused these will emanate from its nature. The wood in its walls, for example, will undergo some of the same transformations undergone by a fallen tree in the forest. If the roof happens to be made from grass thatch, some of which is still alive, it may begin to sprout.

These considerations suggest something important: matter is "by nature." After all, the material constituents of the house and the cup and the book, rather than these objects themselves, remain after the manufactured items disappear, and precisely this attribute of endurance would seem to belong to nature. "This, then, is one way we speak of nature: as the primary matter that underlies each of the things that has within itself a principle of motion and change" (193a28–30). Matter "underlies" various changes. The carbon atoms in an organic body endure even when the organism dies or undergoes various changes. Understanding matter, then, is obviously of great importance in the study of the physical world.

According to Aristotle, this sort of consideration led earlier thinkers – namely, the Presocratics – to become "materialists." "Those who philosophized a long time ago," Aristotle reports, "were the first to study nature and the material principle and cause" (*Parts of Animals*, 640b6–7). Some said fire, others (Thales and Anaximenes) said water or air was the nature "of that which is" (*Physics*, 193a21–2). Such *phusiologoi* identified a material element as the *archê*, as the fundament of nature itself. In doing so, they stumbled upon an important truth: matter is natural. As we saw above in the discussion of the "simple bodies," Aristotle himself is quick to endorse this notion. But he is equally quick to point out its limitations. The Presocratic or materialist account, while not wrong, is radically incomplete.

> In another way [nature is] the shape and the form, which is in accord with the rational account [*logos*]. For just as we speak of craftsmanship in what is in accordance with craft and is crafted, so also we speak of nature in what is in accordance with nature and is natural. But if something were only potentially a bed and still lacked the form of a bed, we would not yet speak of craftsmanship or of a product in accordance with craft; nor would we say the corresponding thing about anything that is constituted naturally. For what is only potentially flesh or bone does not have its nature, and is not naturally flesh or bone, until it acquires the form in accordance with the account by which we define flesh or bone and say what it is . . . Indeed, the form is nature more than the matter is. For we call something "flesh, bone, and so on," when it is actually so, more than when it is only potentially so. (193a31–b10)[9]

Without doubt matter is by nature. In keeping with his precept "no one can miss a door" – in other words, we are beings for whom the truth comes naturally – Aristotle grants that the Presocratics were smart people, and so could not possibly have been all wrong. But they were not all right either, for nature is more fundamentally revealed in "form" – Plato's famous word – than it is in matter. Note that Aristotle actually uses an example taken from craft to solidify his point about nature, and that, just as he did in the previous citation, he relies on what "we say."[10] None of "us" would call a pile of lumber in a workshop an actual "bed." Instead, it is potentially a bed, as well as potentially a desk, chair, or table. It is an indeterminate, formless, heap. The same would be true of calcium atoms: we would never describe them as actually bones, only potentially so. The atoms, the matter, have not achieved their nature until they combine with other elements and attain a form.

From these sorts of reflections, Aristotle concludes, "form is the nature more than the matter is." Few sentences in his corpus carry more weight than this one. Perhaps the best clue to its full meaning is to return, yet again, to etymology: the Greek word *eidos* is derived from the verb "to see." A form is a "look," a visible shape. Nature, for Aristotle, is most fully manifested in the way things look. We do not see carbon atoms or any of the other material elements of a rabbit. We see, instead, a whole being, a unified entity. The stuff of which the rabbit is composed is part of its nature. But this stuff could just as well make up a horse or a duck, and so cannot be identified with its nature. In order for the rabbit to be, and to be seen (and said) as what it really, or "actually," is, it must have both the requisite matter of, as well as the shape of, a rabbit. In sum, Aristotle is a "hylomorphist," according to whom natural beings are composites of matter (*hulê*) and form (*morphê*, a synonym of *eidos*).

Two words in the passage above are especially important: "potentiality" and "actuality." The former is associated with matter – the pile of lumber could be made into a bed or a table; the calcium atoms could find their way into bones – the latter with form. Even if he is a hylomorphist, for Aristotle form/actuality is ontologically superior, is more natural than, matter/potentiality. This means that what things actually are on the macroscopic level is more significant than the microscopic particles comprising their material constituents. In short, the key to a natural being for Aristotle is not what it is made of, or what it might become, but *what it is*.

The last three words should trigger a memory: they were made famous by the historical Socrates whose primary question was, "what is it?," which in turn was eventually developed by Plato into his conception of the Forms. Aristotle, superbly dialectical, accepts the centrality of Socrates' question, but fundamentally changes its scope. The primary quest for both Socrates and Plato was to discover the basis of an excellent human life. The target of the "what is it" question was thus virtues like justice and courage. As we will see later in this chapter, Aristotle will ask these sorts of questions as well. But in the *Physics* he extends the reach of the "what is it" question into his investigation of nature. Nature, in its fullest sense, is exemplified by actual and identifiable "somethings"; more specifically, by "the form in accordance with the account [*logos*]." To risk putting this point in somewhat odd terms, a natural being – a rabbit, a frog, a plant, Bob, Sue – welcomes the question, "what is it?" A natural being shows itself as what it actually is, and Aristotle's goal is, to cite Heidegger again, "to let that which shows itself be seen from itself in the very way in which it shows itself from itself." The means by which this "seeing" is accomplished is by a meticulous and patiently elaborated *logos* or "theory" (the root of which is in the Greek verb *theorein*, meaning "to look at"), one which does justice to the phenomena.

Aristotle concludes the passage above with a sentence he likes to repeat: "A man comes to be from a man, but not a bed from a bed" (193b10). This little saying does no more than reiterate the most apparent feature of biological life: it reproduces itself. But its significance for Aristotle is enormous. Indeed, it is a motto which describes the essential working of nature itself. As mentioned at the outset of this chapter, Aristotle's study of nature – arguably his entire philosophical project – takes its bearings from biology, the *logos* of living beings. And the salient feature of them is that "a man comes to be from a man": living beings pass on their form to the next generation. This simply means that parents and offspring are of the same species. With biology as his paradigm, Aristotle can confidently assert "the form is nature more than the matter."

One last point: recall that the very first debate in Greek philosophy was between Thales, who claimed water, a definite and hence readily identifiable substance, was the *archê*, and Anaximander, who argued that only the "indefinite" (*to apeiron*) could possibly function as the first-principle and source of all reality. Since matter is potentiality and hence indefinite, while form is actuality and so definite, Aristotle's "hylomorphism" can be construed as a dialectical synthesis of these two positions. Neither Presocratic was entirely wrong, but the positions of both were one-sided and so radically incomplete.

c) The four causes

Aristotle begins the first chapter of *Physics* II by saying, "Of beings, some are by nature, while others are by other causes." But what exactly is a cause? Aristotle offers this answer:

> We should consider how many and what sorts of causes there are. For our inquiry is for the sake of knowledge, and we do not believe that we know something until we grasp the reason why about each thing; and this means to grasp the primary cause. (194b16–20)

A "cause" is an explanation or an answer to the question "why?" As we will see, what Aristotle has in mind here is far broader than the modern notion of "causality," which is typically conceived as a relation between two distinct items or events, one of which is "the cause" and the other "the effect." While it will include this sense, Aristotle's "causes" correspond to different kinds of explanation, different ways of fully knowing an object, particularly a natural one. A cause for him is not a thing; it is a way of answering a question and hence understanding a thing.

Aristotle conceives of four causes, which have traditionally been given titles that, even if he himself does not use them, are helpful nevertheless:

1. The *material cause* answers the question, "what is its stuff," or "what is it made of?" Bronze, for example, is the material cause of the statue.
2. The *formal cause* answers the question, "what is it?"
3. The *efficient cause* corresponds most closely to the modern conception of causality. It answers the question, "what moved or produced it?" For example, the adviser is a cause of the action, the father of the child, the producer of the product, and the mover of the moved (194b30–2).
4. The *final cause* is something's goal, purpose, or end (*telos*). It answers the question, "what is it for" or "for the sake of what is it?" Aristotle's example is health, which is understood as the "end" of walking (194b33).

Characterizing causes as answers to questions does not reduce them to merely linguistic entities. Aristotle is hardly a "nominalist," someone who denies the real existence of universals. Instead, and as has already been emphasized, what "we say" is a dimension of the phenomena, which in turn become the window through which we can "study" or "look at" ("theorize") the nature of reality itself. It should thus not be surprising when in summarizing the four causes he says, "We may take these, then, to be the ways we speak of causes" (195a4). The way "we speak" says much about the way things really are.

To reiterate, the "efficient cause" comes closest to the modern conception of causality. For Aristotle himself, however, and for reasons already suggested, far and away the most significant of the four is "the formal." In order to fully understand X, one must understand and articulate what X is, and this means grasping its form.

The "final cause" is perhaps the most jarring to a modern ear. It is the basis of what has come to be known as Aristotle's "teleology," his *logos* of the *telos*. This word is often translated as "end," which in English, as in Greek, has various meanings. An "end" is a termination point, as in "death is the end of life." But it also connotes "completion" or "fulfillment," as in "happiness is the end of life." When something has reached this sort of "end," it has achieved its "goal" or "purpose," two other possible translations of *telos*. This is the import of Aristotle's example: for someone following the doctor's order to get some exercise, health is the end of walking.

Aristotle's "final cause" implies that to understand natural beings, one must comprehend their purposes. As he puts it, "nature produces everything for the sake of something" (*Parts of Animals*, 641b11), and "nature does nothing pointlessly" (*Politics*, 1253a8). These maxims express a guiding principle for his actual research. So, for example, in investigating anatomy, Aristotle notes that the humans are the only animal with eyelashes on both lids and, unlike most other quadrupeds, have more hair in the front than in the back. To answer the question "why," he reiterates his conviction in teleology: "out of given conditions, [nature] is always the cause of that which is the better." In this case, since the front of the body is better (or even, as he says, "nobler") than the back, the human animal has elaborate means of protecting the front (*Parts of Animals*, 658a15–25). Aristotle generalizes his conviction: "processes that are for something and are not a matter of luck are most characteristic of the products of nature; and the end for which these things are constituted or have come to be counts as something beautiful" (645a24–6). Nature is beautiful because it is orderly and purposive.[11]

Perhaps no single idea held by the Ancient Greeks proved to be more offensive to early modern philosophers such as Bacon, Spinoza, Descartes, and Galileo – all of whom were architects of what has become known as "the scientific revolution" of the seventeenth century – than Aristotle's final cause. Indeed, their rejection of teleology was decisive in the birth of the modern worldview itself. For a thinker like Spinoza (1632–77), final causality is simply false: "Nature," he says, "has no fixed aim in view . . . all things in nature proceed eternally from a certain necessity."[12] In other words, there are no final causes, only efficient ones proceeding not "for the sake of something," but because of a strict and mechanical causality. To think otherwise, as Aristotle did, is a fundamental error produced by the fact that "Men commonly suppose that all natural things act like themselves with an end in view." For Spinoza, teleology is a projection of human behavior – which (at least much of the time) is obviously purposive – onto nature itself, which is not the slightest bit like us. Final causality, therefore, is wrong-headed because it is anthropomorphizes nature.

Bacon (1561–1626) makes much the same point: "the human understanding is of its own nature prone to suppose the existence of more order and regularity in the world than it finds." Furthermore, it "is like a false mirror, which receiving rays irregularly distorts and discolors the nature of things by mingling its own nature with it."[13] To believe that nature acts for "what is best" is a prime example of such anthropomorphizing, such misleading "mingling" of the human with the nonhuman.

For Spinoza, what saved European science from Aristotelian teleology was mathematics: "The truth [that there are no final causes, only efficient ones] might have lain hidden from the human race through all eternity, had not mathematics, which deals not in the final cause, but the essence and properties of things, offered to men another standard of truth." The laws of motion, formulated in the equations of mathematics, tell the truth about nature and its structure of efficient causality, not the "fabrications" of ignorant men who think nature acts purposively and like themselves.

Aristotle is prepared to respond to these objections, because he had the Presocratics behind him. It is not just Spinoza and his colleagues who rejected teleology, it was Democritus as well. As Aristotle puts it, "Democritus, neglecting to speak about the 'for the sake of which,' attributes everything nature uses to necessity" (*Generation of Animals*, 789b2–4).[14] "Necessity" characterizes the movements and contact actions of atoms, those indivisible bits of being whose attributes or "primary qualities" (size, shape, velocity, weight) can be articulated in the equations of mathematics, and whose interactions can thus in principle be accurately predicted.

Aristotle was acutely aware of the sorts of (stunningly modern) objections that could be brought to bear against his teleological physics. In fact, in chapter 8 of *Physics* Book II he articulates the position of his potential critic:

> A puzzle now arises: why not suppose that nature acts not for something or because it is better, but of necessity? The rain does not fall in order to make the grain grow, but of necessity. For it is necessary that what has been drawn up is cooled, and that what has been cooled and become water comes down, and it is coincidental that this makes the grain grow . . . Why not suppose, then, that the same is true of the parts of natural organisms? On this view it is of necessity that, for example, the front teeth grow sharp and well adapted for biting, and the back ones broad and useful for chewing food; this result was coincidental and not what they were for . . . On this view, then, whenever all the parts came about coincidentally as though they were for something, these animals survived, since their constitution, though coming about by chance, made them suitable for survival. Other animals, however, were differently constituted and so were destroyed; indeed they are still being destroyed, as Empedocles says of the man-headed calves. (198b17–33)[15]

Aristotle's opponents – Democritus and Empedocles (whom we shall discuss shortly), as well as modern thinkers like Spinoza – take their bearings from a process like the falling of rain. This is a purposeless or mechanical event that occurs only because of the contact actions between various elements. Because of its material constituents, when water is heated it evaporates and is drawn upwards in the atmosphere, where it is then cooled. Becoming more "earth-like," or heavier, it falls to the ground. While it is true that rain is necessary for grain to grow, and in this sense causes it, it does not fall for the sake of the grain. Agriculture is just a coincidental, a lucky, byproduct of an otherwise mechanical ("efficient") set of events.

It is important to emphasize that Aristotle agrees with this causal analysis of rain. He does not attribute the water falling from the sky to any sort of purposive action or benevolent deity. (In other words, his teleology is not "global": see Nussbaum 1985, pp. 59–99, for a good discussion of this.) Where he believes his opponents have gone wrong is in their comprehensive extension of efficient causality. He seems primarily to have Empedocles in mind. Presumably, this Presocratic would explain the sharpness of our front teeth as a mere coincidence. More specifically, it was a chance event that occurred in some of our ancestors, enhanced their survival prospects, and so (in ways he could not possibly have understood) was passed on to future generations. There was no purposiveness at work in the front teeth becoming sharp, only random events that happened to work out well for the human organism. Aristotle argues against this view:

> This argument, then, and others like it, might puzzle someone. In fact, however, it is impossible for things to be like this. For these <teeth and other parts> and all natural things come to be as they do either always or usually, whereas no result of luck or chance comes to be either always or usually. For we do not regard frequent winter rain or a summer heat wave, but only summer rain or a winter heat wave, as a result of luck or coincidence. If, then, these seem either to be coincidental results or to be for something, and they cannot be coincidental or chance results, they are for something . . . We find, then, among things that come to be and are by nature, things that are for something. (198b33–199a7)

While rain can be explained as a mechanical process (heating and cooling) and by means of efficient causality, it would be a terrible mistake to extend this view of nature to the parts of animals. This is because their structure is organic and hence too orderly to be explained by "mere" chance. With only a small fraction of exceptions, generation after generation of human beings have sharp front teeth. This is a stable feature of our species, and so anyone without such teeth is readily identified as deficient. Efficient or mechanical causality, coupled with chance, cannot do justice to the beautifully purposive organization of an animal that can reproduce itself. Indeed, it is especially "evident in the case of animals other than man" that teleology is at work, since, despite their using "neither craft nor inquiry nor deliberation in producing things," their formal characteristics are "always or usually" reproduced. In fact, "if we advance little by little along the same lines, it is evident that even in plants things come to be that promote the end – leaves, for instance, grow for the protection of the fruit" (199a20–8).

Clearly, another name must be added to the list of imaginary opponents Aristotle is arguing against here: Darwin. The notion of adaptation and survival, which Aristotle attributes to Empedocles, suggests the theory of natural selection. Darwin himself says as much when he comments on this very passage from the *Physics:*

> Aristotle . . . after remarking that rain does not fall in order to make the corn grow, any more than it falls to spoil the farmer's corn when threshed out of doors, applies the same argument to organisation: and adds . . . "so what hinders the different parts [of the body] from having this merely accidental relation in nature? as the teeth, for example, grow by necessity, the front ones sharp, adapted for dividing, and the grinders flat, and serviceble for masticating the food; since they were not made for the sake of this, but it was the result of accident. And in like manner as to the other parts in which there appears to exist an adaptation to an end. Wheresoever, therefore, all things together (that is all the parts of one whole) happened like as if they were made for the sake of something, these were preserved, having been appropriately constituted by an internal spontaneity; and whatsoever things were not thus constituted perished, and still perish." We here see the principle of natural selection shadowed forth, but how little Aristotle fully comprehended this principle, is shown by his remarks on the formation of the teeth.[16]

For Darwin, Aristotle's description of the Empedoclean explanation of the front teeth is just right. It captures the sort of random variation and the principle of survival basic to the theory of natural selection. Where Aristotle goes wrong, according to Darwin, is in his rejection of this explanation, and his stubborn insistence that efficient causality and chance, coupled with the drive to survive, are not sufficient to explain organic structure, and that some measure of purposiveness must be introduced into nature itself. Or, to reformulate the same objection, because he underestimates the power of chance to generate beautifully organized animals, Aristotle wrongly invokes final causality.

Aristotle's "final" is intimately related to his "formal" cause. In the following passage he virtually equates the two:

> And since nature is two-fold, nature as matter and as form, and the form is the end, and since everything else is for the sake of the end, this cause [the formal] must be what things are for the sake of. (199a31–3)

"Form is the end." To explain, just consider again the development of an animal. After it is born, it matures: this means it grows into its form. It actualizes the potentiality available to its species (its *eidos*). When it comes to the human animal, Aristotle repeatedly identifies "rational activity" as the crucial potentiality. Because a child is more of an emotional than a rational being, he is incomplete or not fully formed. When he comes of age it is precisely because he is able to think rationally. And when the man becomes very old, and perhaps suffers from Alzheimer's, he again becomes incomplete.

Aristotle expresses and elaborates upon this view in the opening line of the *Metaphysics*: "All human beings by nature desire to know" (980a21). This famous sentence is paradigmatic of Aristotle's thought in general. (Although he translates it somewhat differently, Lear 1988 uses it in the title of his excellent book.) What is most striking and problematic about it is the "all." Surely not every single human being desires to know. Consider old Bob: he is a slacker, who prefers to drink beer when he is not sleeping. One who desires to know attempts to learn, and Bob exhibits no such tendency. Let us assume, then, that he does not "desire to know." Even so, this does not falsify Aristotle's contention. This is because he adds "by nature" as a qualification, and nature is teleological. An essential feature of the human animal is to know, and when someone actualizes this potential, he is completing his nature. It is entirely possible that a given individual like Bob may sleep and drink his life away. But in doing so, he becomes a radically deficient human being. The teleological conception of nature allows for just such judgments.

This last point suggests an important consequence of Aristotelian teleology, which can be explained by once again resketching the "bell curve" (figure 4.2). The bell curve graphically shows how Aristotle's teleological conception of nature provides the grounds for making certain kinds of normative judgments. Just as an eagle born with abnormally small and hence dysfunctional wings is an inferior member of its species, so someone who, for whatever reason, is unable to think clearly or who has a terrible memory falls short of being a complete human being. The very young or very old, or those mature adults who have suffered some sort of brain damage that has compromised their cognitive ability, fall on the lower ends of the normal distribution depicted in the curve. Unlike many contemporary thinkers, who would prefer to describe an adult with, for example, an extremely low IQ as "special," Aristotle does not shy away from

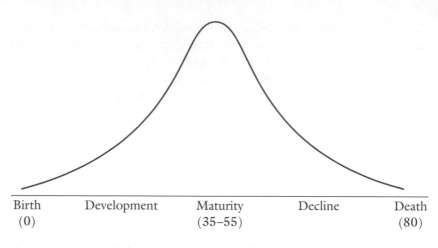

Birth   Development   Maturity   Decline   Death
(0)   (35–55)   (80)

(movement towards form) (achievement of form)   (loss of form)

Figure 4.2

what he takes to be a fact of nature: such a person is inferior. Not surprisingly, we will see the significant role this feature of Aristotelian teleology plays in his thinking about ethics and politics. Simply put, unlike many of us today, Aristotle does not believe all human beings were created equal. He is not an egalitarian.

To conclude this section: Aristotle is profoundly impressed by the orderliness of nature. In the winter (in Greece) it is almost never hot. In the summer it almost never rains. Our grandparents as well as our grandchildren have sharp front teeth. Unless there is an accident, a animal is born, grows into maturity, declines, and then dies. Of all things natural, nothing is more impressive to Aristotle than the organic structure, the development, and the reproductive capacity of animals. Every part of the animal contributes to the well-being of the whole. And the whole is more than the sum of its parts: it is well-ordered, it has a form. The parts are "merely" the material stuff of the animal. This orderliness, and its intelligibility, is a basic phenomenon: it is the way nature shows itself or appears. Because the goal of his physics is to "save the phenomena," Aristotle attributes not just efficient causality to nature, but formal and final as well. His predecessors, particularly Democritus and Empedocles, those two most modern of the ancients, failed to do this.

While the descendants of Democritus and Empedocles, namely Galileo and Darwin, are of course vastly more sophisticated in their understanding of the mechanisms of nature, and offer accounts so powerful that they might seem to have utterly overwhelmed Aristotle and rendered him philosophically useless, Aristotelian phenomenology, infused as it is with formal and final causality, nonetheless can muster a defense. It bespeaks ordinary experience and human life as it is actually lived here on earth. In our daily lives animals *are* identified by means of their visible species, the natural kinds to which they belong and which appear to be stable. Animals are macroscopic beings with ontological integrity, and some of them can even become our friends. A burning match is held underneath a cigar: fire *does* move upwards towards the heavens. For us, as members of families and as citizens, the earth *is* the center of the world, at least the one in which we live and in which we bury our dead. Unless we are in a laboratory, or examining the latest transmissions from the Hubble telescope, for us the world *is* a meaningful cosmos, not an infinite, and hence meaningless, universe. While over the millions of years of earth's history the climate in Greece has changed, in human memory it has "always or usually" been hot there in the summer. Seen from the perspective of human, rather than geological time, the sequential change of the seasons, the life of the planet itself, is orderly, stable, and beautiful. Nature makes good sense. Such, at least, is the conviction animating Aristotle with such confidence and propelling him forward in his vast theoretical inquiries.

Aristotle's Psychology

So far we have concentrated on Aristotle's conception of nature. We began here because this is where Aristotle himself begins. He is the empiricist and the biologist, who takes his bearings from ordinary experience and sense perception. He is the theoretical philosopher who walks around looking at (*theorein*) whatever presents itself to his field of vision, confident that his endeavor to understand the world will succeed. When he opens his *Metaphysics* by boldly declaring that "all human beings by nature desire to know," there is no hesitation in his voice, no doubt about his insight into the nature of the human animal, or in the power of language to communicate such insight without distortion.

Aristotle's confidence should not be confused with pride or egotism, for he is far from thinking that he alone has the ability to attain the truth. In fact, to cite again a line from the *Rhetoric*, human beings in general, he says, "have a sufficient natural capacity for the truth and indeed in most cases attain to it." The following passage helps to explain why this is so.

> Spoken words are symbols of affections in the soul, and written words are symbols of spoken ones. And just as written words are not the same for everyone, neither are spoken ones the same. However, those primary things of which these affections of the soul are signs are the same for everyone. And what these affections are likenesses of, namely real beings, are also the same. (*On Interpretation*, 16a4–8)[17]

This dense paragraph divides the relationship between the human soul, language, and the world into four components. First, and for Aristotle foremost, there are "real beings": rabbits, fire, the stars above, Bob and Sue. Second, there are "affections" of the soul. The Greek word *pathêmata*, related to our word "pathos," comes from a verb meaning "to suffer, to be affected by, to experience." *Pathêmata*, then, refers to how the soul is affected by "real beings" through, for example, sense perceptions. When I see a fire, or touch a rabbit, my perceptual apparatus, or my "soul" – and here again it is critical to remember that the Greek *psuchê* does not have the same (often Christian) connotations of our word "soul" – is affected by sensible objects.

Both "real beings" and "affections" are "the same for everyone." In other words, there is only one world out there, and all human beings largely experience it in the same way. Because we are all members of the same species, we share the same basic perceptual and cognitive faculties. We see, hear, taste, touch, smell, and ultimately think about – we are affected by – the "real beings" of the world in roughly the same way. Furthermore, these affections are "likenesses" of "real beings." This is crucial: for Aristotle our perception of things in the world is, much or even most of the time, accurate. If you see a red object, you can be confident that an actual red object is out there and caused you to see it. Our perceptions can be trusted, at least usually, to give us reliable information.

When it comes to language, the story becomes more complicated. "Spoken words" are not the same for everyone. The German "Hund" is different from the English "dog," even if what is signified by both is the same object. Spoken language is a conventional operation, and the meaning of "spoken words" is largely arbitrary (is a matter of *nomos*). If everyone agreed, then "cat" could just as easily signify what is now signified by "dog."

As various and conventionally differentiated as "spoken words" are (and "written words," the fourth component of the relationship, are even more so), they share one feature: they are "symbols of affections in the soul." In turn, because these are "likenesses of real beings," words signify what can be termed "mental content," which itself represents actual things in the world. The meaning of words, then, depends on their ability to refer to actual things. There is, in short, a direct link between what people say about the world, and the actual things in the world affecting them. This link makes it possible for language to articulate the truth about those actual things. (An extended discussion of this passage from *On Interpretation* is found in Modrak 2001.)

More needs to be said, for the passage from *On Intepretation*, even if it expresses in some detail Aristotle's confidence that *logos* connects to, and thus can reveal the nature of, beings in the world, does not yet justify it. That it requires justification should be apparent. After all, a thinker like Gorgias (himself the forerunner of contemporary "postmodernists" like Rorty, Derrida, and Fish) holds beliefs diametrically opposed to Aristotle's. For the Sophist (as discussed in chapter 2), *logos* is powerless to refer to a language-independent reality. Instead, it is restricted to *doxa*, to the way things seem to people. Since *doxa* itself is largely constructed by language, according to Gorgias *logos* ultimately only talks about or refers to itself. To put this same point in Protagorean terms, "human being is the measure of all things." Aristotle, by contrast, takes the world to be the measure of all things, and is confident that *logos* generally does a pretty good job representing, or opening a window to, it. But why believe Aristotle is right and Gorgias or Protagoras wrong? To justify his confidence Aristotle must supply an account of the *psuchê* which is responsible for sense perception and for *logos*. We turn next to *On the Soul*, one of the most complicated of all Aristotle's works.

In the first chapter of Book II, Aristotle gradually works his way towards a definition of soul. He begins by arguing that it must be a "substance" (*ousia*). Specifically, it is substance in the sense of "form" (412a20): it is the form of a natural body potentially having life. Since, as we discussed above, form is "actuality," soul is the actuality of a natural body potentially having life (412a27–8). Finally, "organic" is added to the definition (412b6).[18]

Before trying to figure out what all this means, an additional wrinkle must be added. There are two senses of "actuality," and soul is "the first actuality of a natural organic body" (412b5). Aristotle illustrates by means of an example. Imagine two people. One, representing the first sense of actuality, has knowledge of arithmetic but is not now using it. The other is actually using that knowledge, say by trying to figure out what the sum of 1,836 and 5,472 is. While the second person is performing the computation, she has activated her knowledge and thereby raised it to the second level of actuality.

Or consider an example from the *Nicomachean Ethics* (1146b34). I know eating a fourth piece of chocolate cake is bad for me, but I may still do it. If so, then I merely have, but do not use, my knowledge. If, by contrast, I manage fully to activate my knowledge of the bad effects of eating too much cake, then according to Aristotle I will not do it.

Aristotle uses an analogy to clarify these two levels of actuality. While asleep, I am alive but I am not engaged in, for example, seeing. While awake and with open eyes actively seeing things, my soul is working at a higher level of actuality. Therefore, having knowledge is to sleeping as actually using that knowledge is to waking. Equipped with this analogy we can now understand what Aristotle means by describing the soul as "the first actuality of a natural organic body." Simply being alive requires my soul to be active. Even if I am asleep or my eyes are shut, I "actually" can see. This is the first level of actuality. (It could also be conceived as a higher or second level of potentiality.) When I am actually seeing, I reach the second level of actuality. These nuances will prove to be important as Aristotle proceeds.

Aristotle offers two additional comparisons to illustrate what he means by defining the soul as the "actuality" of a natural body potentially having life. (1) If an axe were a natural body, being an axe – that is, being able actually to chop wood – would be its soul. When an axe becomes so severely rusted that it can no longer chop, it is an axe only in name (412b11–15). (2) "If the eye were a living thing, vision would be its soul" (412b18–19). An eye unable to see – say an eye in a painting or carved in stone – is an eye only in name.

The seeing eye and the chopping axe illustrate the most distinctive, and for many readers the most appealing, feature of Aristotle's conception of soul. It is not a separate thing. Instead, it is the living activity of the body. The Greek "actuality" is *energeia*, which can literally be translated as "being at work."[19] The soul, then, is the living body at work.

One way of clarifying all this, as well as specifying why the English word "soul" is so potentially misleading as a translation of *psuché*, is to note that, according to Aristotle, plants have souls. This statement should not conjure up an image of a happy plant being sung to by a melodious gardener. Instead, it means something far simpler: plants are alive. They nourish and are able to reproduce themselves. These are their biological functions; these are what Aristotle calls their "nutritive souls" at work. To explain, we turn next to Aristotle's account of nutrition.

Nutrition has three components. These are (1) what is nourished, namely the living body; (2) what it is nourished by, the food; (3) what nourishes, what he calls "the nutritive soul." When I look at a cookie sitting on the table it is something unlike me. When I have eaten the cookie, when it has become digested, it has become like me. The becoming actually alike of what is potentially like but actually unlike, the process or activity of digestion, is the work of the "nutritive soul," and it is this sort of soul plants have. This triadic scheme (presented at 416b20–1) can be represented as in figure 4.3.

To reiterate the critical point: the "nutritive soul" is not a thing. It is what does the nourishing. It is the being-at-work of a living body, which by metabolic processes transforms objects in the world that are "unlike" into ones identical to the living body itself. It is the primal expression of life, namely the ability of an organism to maintain a unified form over time by interacting with, and often incorporating, an external environment.

It might seem strange to begin a work of psychology, a subject we typically associate with the study of human functions like emotion and thinking, with a discussion of nutrition and the metabolic activity

That by which the body is nourished → The body which is nourished
(the food)

↓

That which does the nourishing
(the nutritive soul)

Figure 4.3

we share with plants. But Aristotle's doing so says much not only about his conception of soul, but about his worldview in general. As mentioned at the outset of this chapter, he is very much a naturalist and a biologist. For this reason, when he addresses human beings in *On the Soul* he conceives of them, of us, as living beings who, like plants, have to eat. Of course, we can do far more than plants, for we are also able to perceive the external world by means of our senses, and so to feel pleasure and pain, and thus to have desires. These capacities, however, we share with animals. In fact, sense perception is what differentiates an animal from a plant. In turn, what differentiates a human being from an animal is the ability to think.

These, then, are the three kinds of soul, of living activity, Aristotle identifies: the nutritive, the perceptive, and that "by which the soul has knowledge and intelligence" (429a10) or "mind." We turn next to perception.

Aristotle begins his analysis of perception (*aisthêsis*) by describing it as a kind of being affected, and thus as what he calls an "alteration" (416a33). Perception is of external objects that affect our sense organs. In the act of perception, a sense organ changes from a state of potentiality (my eye can potentially see a red object but is not seeing it now) to actuality (when the red object is placed in my field of vision, I see it). We have already mentioned the two senses of actuality Aristotle holds. There are, then, three elements in his analysis, which he illustrates by using the same example cited above: knowledge of arithmetic.[20] Imagine three people:

A: A person capable of learning arithmetic.
B: One who has learned, and thus knows, arithmetic
C: One who is actually using his knowledge of arithmetic.

Person A is called "knowledgeable" simply because she is a certain kind of being, namely the human kind able to acquire knowledge. This person does not actually know arithmetic, but she can learn it. She potentially knows it. Person B is "knowledgeable" because she has learned and so possesses knowledge of arithmetic. She is not now performing a computation. Hence, her knowledge of arithmetic is also potential, but at a level so much higher than A's that Aristotle will also call it the first degree of actuality. As long as no external factor hinders her, she is able to solve her problem and do arithmetical work whenever she wants. Person C knows arithmetic and is performing a computation right now. She has reached the second and highest level of actuality.

When A learns arithmetic (when A becomes B) she has been altered and so has changed from one contrary (not-knowing) to another (knowing). As Aristotle explains in *Metaphysics* 1048b18–35, learning is a paradigmatic case of an "incomplete change" (or *kinēsis*). This means that when it is completed it itself ceases. When A has learned arithmetic, she has become knowledgeable, and so is no longer learning.

By contrast, when B exercises the knowledge she already has (when B becomes C), she has also shifted from potentiality to actuality, but either this is not an alteration at all, or is different in kind from that involved in changing from A to B. It cannot be a true alteration because it is not a shift into a contrary state. Instead, it is a "progress into itself and into actuality" (417b6). When B becomes C she comes into her own nature (417b16).

When Aristotle applies this triadic scheme to explain perception, it becomes this:

A^1:   The male seed.
B^1:   The human being able to perceive from the moment of birth.
C^1:   The human being actually perceiving an object right now.

Because perception is an essential attribute of living animals, human beings necessarily have the ability to perceive from birth. Therefore, the change from being a "seed" to being a newborn, A^1 to B^1, is analogous to that from A to B, from not knowing arithmetic to knowing arithmetic.[21] It is not technically an "alteration" because it is a coming-into-being of a substance, but it is a change from one contrary (not being born) to another (being born). By contrast, the change from B^1 to C^1, from potentially being able to perceive an object to actually perceiving it, is analogous to that undergone by someone who knows arithmetic (B) and then uses it (C). As such, it is a "progress into itself and into actuality." When human beings perceive objects, they are not significantly changed; they come into their own nature.

It may not be immediately apparent, but this somewhat convoluted discussion goes to the heart of Aristotle's worldview and is the basis of his great confidence in the human capacity to attain the truth. It is

That by which the body is nourished → The body which is nourished
    (the food)

$$\downarrow$$

That which does the nourishing
(the nutritive soul)

That perceptible object → The organ of perception

$$\downarrow$$

That which does the perceving
(the perceptive soul)

Figure 4.4

the nature of human beings (as well as other animals) to accurately perceive objects in the external world as they are in themselves. We are able to do so without changing either them or ourselves. Perception does not alter our being; it completes it. Aristotle expresses this notion by describing the change from B^1 to C^1, the actual perception of an object, in the following way: "Just as has been said, the perceiver is potentially such as what the perceptible object actually is. So, when it is being affected it is not like [the perceptible object], but having been affected it has become like it" (418a3–6).

This characterization of the soul's capacity to become "like" its object expresses the central tenet of Aristotle's psychology. The activity of the soul, its work, just is this becoming actually like of objects actually unlike but potentially like. Or to reformulate, perceiving is like eating. This can be shown by figure 4.4, which is meant to highlight the analogical structures of the nutritive and perceptive souls.

To reiterate, like nutrition, perception is an activity of the soul by which the potentially like but actually unlike becomes actually like. Perception is of course quite different from nutrition. Unlike a cookie, the perceptible object does not itself become identical to the organ of perception. My eye does not become the red object it sees. Instead, as Aristotle puts it,

In general it is necessary to grasp about perception as a whole that each sense is receptive of the perceptible forms without the matter, like wax receives the imprint of the ring without the iron or gold . . . Similarly, each sense is affected by the thing that has color or flavor or sound, but not insofar as it is said to be that thing, but insofar as it has quality. (424a18–24)

Even if they are different in this regard, perception and nutrition are analogous in the kind of change the soul undergoes when this activity occurs. In other words, like perception, the act of nutrition is a B–C change:

A^2: The male seed.
B^2: The human being in need of nutrition from birth.
C^2: The human being eating a cookie.

Changing from B^2 to C^2 would not be a genuine alteration, even though it is a changing from a potentiality to actuality. Instead, it is "a progressing into itself." The cookie, potentially unlike, becomes like. This activity or work is the nutritive soul. In an analogy, there is similarity and difference, and so if perceiving is like eating, it is also different. Nutrition is the integration of the entire object into the body, matter as well as form, while perception is the reception of sensible forms without the matter of the object (424a). How this actually works is notoriously problematic. (Several of the essays in Nussbaum & Rorty 1992 address this question.) One critical implication of the analogy is, however, clear: both perceiving and eating represent a B–C change, a "progress into itself," which Aristotle illustrates by the example of someone actually exercising the knowledge, say arithmetic, he already possesses.

All of this complicated stuff can be translated into a single metaphor: human beings are at home in the world. If perception is like eating, and in eating the food becomes identical to the living body consuming it, then perceptible objects become (formally) identical to the perceiver. As a result, we see the world for what it really is. We can trust our sensory apparatus to provide us with reliable information, and we can therefore be confident in our capacity to attain the truth about the world.[22]

The third kind of soul, that "by which the soul has knowledge and intelligence" (429a10), and which Aristotle calls "mind" (*nous*), presents serious difficulties and has vexed scholars for centuries. (Again, consult Nussbaum & Rorty 1992 for an overview of the literature.) The most notorious puzzle associated with it occurs when Aristotle describes it as "separable" (429a11) and denies that it is "mixed with the body" (429a25). This is a problem because to this point in the discussion the decisive characterization of the soul has been as the living, and hence inseparable, activity of the body. Recall the comparison Aristotle makes: "If the eye were a living thing, vision would be its soul." Vision is the work of, and so cannot be separated from, the eye. Indeed, one of the great boasts Aristotle can make about his psychology, indeed his philosophy in general, is that it overcomes the ontological dualism inherent in both Milesian and Platonic thinking. There are not, in his account, two independent categories of Being and Becoming, Form and matter, or soul and body. They are unified. When it comes to mind, however, the story changes. Describing it, Aristotle not only says it is separate, but that it "alone is immortal and eternal" (430a23).

Fortunately, the limits of this chapter preclude discussion of the intricacies of this dilemma. Instead, I return to the central theme of this section: the three kinds of soul Aristotle treats are analogous. Thinking is like perception, which in turn is like eating. This is important because, once again, it suggests the foundation of Aristotle's enormous confidence in the human ability to apprehend "real beings" in the world. Since nutrition is the metabolic process by which something other becomes identical, and since perception is like eating insofar as the form of the perceptible object becomes identical to the sense organ apprehending it, thinking too is a process by which an intellectual object becomes identical to, and thus can be truthfully apprehended by, the intellect. We eat, perceive, and think about actual things, and in the last two cases, we can get things right.

Figure 4.5 summarizes this section by representing how the "three souls" are analogically related.

Just as perception differs from nutrition, so too does mind differ from perception. The latter is of particular external objects, while knowledge and thinking, the work of mind, are of universals, and these are "somehow in the soul itself" (417b23). Because they are analogically related, there is also similarity: perception and thinking are both a kind of affection (429a14). In sum, the soul, whether it is thinking, perceiving, or eating, is a being-at-work in which what is actually unlike (1) but potentially like becomes actually like (2). In the three diagrams in figure 4.5, this activity, by which (1) is transformed into (2), is represented by the "→" and is the work of (3), the soul.

$$\begin{array}{cc} (1) & (2) \end{array}$$

That by which the body is nourished → The body which is nourished
(the food)

↓

(3)
That which does the nourishing
(the nutritive soul)

$$\begin{array}{cc} (1) & (2) \end{array}$$

That perceptible object → The organ of perception

↓

(3)
That which does the perceiving
(the perceptive soul)

$$\begin{array}{cc} (1) & (2) \end{array}$$

The intelligible object → The mind

↓

(3)
That which does the thinking
(the mind)

Figure 4.5 The "three souls"

Nutrition is the blunt instance of this work. The material object is literally incorporated through metabolic activity. Perception, the reception of the forms of objects without the matter, requires a greater degree of complexity and organization than nutrition, and hence is the province only of animals and not plants. The sense organs of the animal have a specific structure allowing them to be affected by a limited set of sensible objects. The eye is an animated chunk of matter constituted such as to be able to receive a specific range of light. Too much and the eye will be destroyed (424a29, 429b1); too little, and the eye cannot see.

Thinking, by contrast, has an intelligible rather than a material object, and this is "somehow in the soul itself." Teasing out the meaning of this phrase is too big a job for this chapter. Instead, we must be content here only to note again that however obscure Aristotle's explanation of thinking is, and however great the differences are between it and perceiving, there is nonetheless a clear analogical structure unifying all the workings of the soul. Thinking is a kind of affection. As in perception, the mind receives forms.[23] Doing so, the mind is at work. The critical difference between thinking and perceiving is shown by the following line of argument. Since the mind "thinks everything," it must potentially be everything. In turn, this implies that, before it thinks, it can actually be nothing in particular. Except for its capacity to receive intelligible forms, it has no nature of its own. Because it is "unmixed" with anything actual it partakes in nothing bodily. Thus, it is "separate" (429a18–b5).

Again, what "separate" means has been debated for centuries. For our purposes here consider only two points. First, as mentioned above, the actuality–potentiality relationship analogically binds the various faculties of the soul together. Even taking into account the extraordinary perplexities surrounding Aristotelian mind, eating, perceiving, and thinking are all instances of the soul at work becoming actually like that which is potentially like.

What is unique about thinking is that the potentially unlike – namely, intelligible forms – and that which thinks, the mind ([2] and [3] in the diagrams above), are "somehow" one and the same. For this reason, those who call the soul "the place of forms" (429a28) are not wrong, at least not when referring to "passive mind" (430a24).

Because in all of nature, an active element or pole must accompany such a passive one, there must also be an active correlate to "passive mind." Presumably this would be "active mind," which, even though he does not use this exact phrase, Aristotle seems to discuss in Book III, chapter 5. This too is described as "separate" (430a17). What this "active mind" is, and how it relates to "passive mind," is far from clear. Nonetheless, this much seems to hold: when it comes to thinking, all three of the components of the analogical scheme – the (1), (2), and (3) in the diagrams above – "somehow" take place within the mind. For this reason, unlike eating and perceiving, we are not dependent on the presence of external objects, and thus we can think whenever we want.

To summarize this complicated discussion of the relationship between the soul and the world as explicated in *On the Soul*: Because we are linked to the world in an actually-unlike/potentially-like relationship, the soul can become identical to its objects. It can receive forms, both perceptible and intelligible. And these forms can be named by the "spoken words" of our languages. For this reason, human beings are at home in the world, and Aristotle has confidence in our capacity to apprehend it truthfully.

To appreciate just how uniquely ancient such "theoretical confidence" really is, one need only compare it with the attitude towards the external world adopted by René Descartes (1596–1650), one of the great founders of modern philosophy. In his work *Discourse on Method*, Descartes argues that in order to achieve the truth the following methodological principle must be adopted: "to include nothing more in my judgments than what presented itself to my mind with such clarity and distinctness that I would have no occasion to put it in doubt." In other words, in order for something to be counted as true, it must be incapable of being doubted. On the basis of this extreme criterion, all information gathered from the senses must be rejected as being false, because the senses are never completely reliable. (When my eye is infected, for example, I may well see objects poorly and so misidentify them.) As Descartes puts it, "since our senses sometimes deceive us, I decided to suppose that nothing was exactly as our sense would have us imagine."[24]

What Aristotle takes for granted – namely, that by and large we accurately perceive things as they are in themselves – is doubted by Descartes at the outset of his project. What Descartes fears – that our ordinary experience with the external world may be riddled with error and that, in fact, it is immensely difficult to prove that it exists at all – Aristotle does not worry about. Recall the following comment he makes in the *Physics*: "It would be ridiculous to attempt to prove that nature is, for it is apparent that there are many such kinds of beings." Aristotle is confident that the way things "appear" tells us much about they way they are, and so to doubt the existence of the external world would be foolish. The epistemological problems that have come to dominate much of modern and contemporary philosophy – principally, how does the human mind access the world external to it, which is sometimes known as the "mind–body" problem, or the problem of "subjectivity" – are simply not items on Aristotle's agenda.

We conclude this section by returning to a passage from *Metaphysics* Book I.

All human beings by nature desire to know. A sign of this is our liking of the senses; for even apart from their usefulness we like them for themselves, and most of all the sense of sight, since not only in order to get something done, but even when we are not about to do anything at all, we prefer seeing more than the rest. The cause of this is that of all the senses this one especially makes us into knowers and makes plain many distinctions. (980a20–7)[25]

The ability to perceive is not only beneficial, but essential to human survival. If we could not see, we would miss doors and bump into walls. If we could not feel heat, we would not pull our hands away from a fire and our skin would burn. But, says Aristotle, even apart from their obvious usefulness, "we like" our senses. There are moments when we simply enjoy looking at the sky, or smelling a fragrance, or feeling the wind on our skin, even if these sense perceptions do not immediately benefit us. This is a "sign," a piece of evidence, that by nature we are receptive to, and welcoming of, the world around us. In this regard, far and away the paradigmatic sense is sight, for more than any other it "makes plain many distinctions." Entering a dark room filled with tables and chairs, we would have to grope and stumble and slowly feel the various objects before knowing what they were. If the room is well lit, however, and our sight is good, we can almost immediately distinguish the tables from the chairs, and so we quickly sit on the latter.

Sight reveals distinctions. Or, to use the all-important word Aristotle learned from his teacher Plato, it reveals "forms." We can easily distinguish a chair from a table: they look different. They have different shapes. Of all the senses, sight, best at apprehending forms, "makes us into knowers," because the natural world is divided into forms. Plants are not animals, dogs are not cats, men are not women. The goal of the philosopher is to understand and to appreciate the heterogeneity of the world. The fact that "we like" our senses, especially vision, and sometimes we simply enjoy looking at things even if there is no need to, is evidence that this goal is an altogether natural one. There is, then, a seamless continuum, from eating a cookie, to smelling a flower, to looking with interest at the differences between cats and dogs, to understanding the formal structures of reality.

Teleological Ethics

a) Moral virtue

The previous two sections sketched Aristotle's conception of nature and of the soul. We learned that his is a richly intelligible world, exemplified best by living beings whose organic structure is teleological, and in which the human animal is thoroughly at home. So far, then, we have largely been exploring the "Presocratic" or theoretical side of Aristotle. The works discussed above – principally the *Physics*, but also *On the Soul, De Interpretatione*, and *Metaphysics* – continue the project Thales inaugurated: to offer an account of nature or of reality.

Aristotle, however, went far beyond his predecessors because he combined the Presocratic project with the Platonic concern for human excellence; for, in other words, ethics and politics. To these "practical" works – whose subjects include human action (*praxis*) and values – we must turn next. We begin with a look at the *Nicomachean Ethics*. It opens with a sentence that will suggest a major theme of this section: Aristotle's practical philosophy emerges organically from his theoretical work.

> Every art [*technê*] and every investigation, and similarly every action and choice, seem to aim at some good; hence the good has been well described as that at which everything aims. (1094a1–3)[26]

We are on familiar teleological ground. When we act, we do so for reasons; namely, in order to attain some "end" or "good." So, for example, Bob goes to his job flipping burgers in order to make some money. Money is the good, the *telos*, at which he aims. His job is the means by which he hopes to attain his end. Thus, when Aristotle says the good is "well described as that at which everything aims," he implies that human life is thoroughly purposive or teleological.

The next point Aristotle makes – as equally commonsensical as the first – is that goods and ends are hierarchically ordered. Bob flips burgers in order to make money. But his goal in making money is to buy a car. As such, the car is a higher-order good than the money. It too, however, is a means to a higher end: driving fast on the highway. In turn, this is a means to an even higher end: reducing the amount of time it takes him to get to the beach. The sequence goes on.

The question Aristotle next poses is, does this sequence of means and ends terminate, or does it go on forever? If it does terminate, it would have to do so with an end that is not a means to anything higher, but instead is good in itself. But does such a "highest good" exist? Aristotle thinks so:

> If then among our actions there is some end which we wish for because of itself, and because of which we wish for everything else, and if we do not choose everything because of something else – since if we did it would go on indefinitely, and as a result desire would be empty and vain – clearly this would be the highest good. (1094a18–22)

Aristotle's argument is indirect: it begins by assuming that the means–end sequence proceeds indefinitely (or infinitely), which is the opposite of his own position. Imagine Bob flipping burgers in order to make money, to buy a car, to drive fast, and on and on without end. If this were the case, then desire, indeed life itself, would be "empty and vain." No end would have any value, or even be a real end, because it would only be a means to something else. To formulate this point in slightly mathematical terms, if the sequence of means and ends were infinite, then no single item in the sequence gets any closer to the end and so has more value than any other. All would be "divided by" infinity, and so their value would be effectively negated. If the sequence of means–ends did not terminate, then life would indeed be "empty and vain," meaningless and pointless. What Aristotle leaves out of this argument is his implicit presupposition: life is not meaningless. Therefore, he concludes, there must be a termination point, a "highest good."

Aristotle feels no need to make explicit what in fact is the crucial premise of his argument: life is meaningful, desire is not empty. He can leave this unstated because he takes it to be so apparent. The discussions of the previous two sections suggest why. For Aristotle life – whether of a human being or a plant – has "meaning." As was discussed in the Introduction, this word, so famously associated with philosophy, has two basic senses. The first is the semantic, as in "'table' means a piece of furniture with a flat top placed horizontally on legs." There is also the purposive sense: "I meant to turn the lights off." Both senses are operative in the phrase "life has meaning." Life is both purposive and its purposive structure can be explained or articulated. Aristotle takes this as a given, and he does so because he takes his bearings from what is "apparent" (*phaneron*), or the phenomena. Human beings take their lives to have meaning. When Bob gets up in the morning, he dutifully trudges off to work. He does so because he cares about making some money, for his goal of buying a car matters to, is meaningful to, him. If he did not feel this deep in his bones he would stay in bed. His going to work is thus evidence that desire, as it is experienced by actual human beings, is surely not empty or vain.

Believing he has demonstrated the existence of a highest good, an end choiceworthy in itself, Aristotle goes forward to explain what it is. Such an explanation, he thinks, will be extremely useful. Just as an archer must see the target well in order to hit it, so must a human being, who is ultimately aiming for the highest good, understand what it is. It is surprisingly easy to give it a name: "both the majority of people and those who are refined call [the highest good] happiness" (*eudaimonia*: 1095a19).

If I ask Bob, "why are you flipping burgers?," the content of his answer ("to make money") is different from the content of the question ("burgers"). This is the case with all goods or ends, except the final one. Bob wants money in order to buy a car, and a car in order to get to the beach quickly. But when this sequence comes to a halt, then the content of the question and the answer will merge. So, if I push Bob hard enough, asking him "why do you want to get to the beach?" and so on, eventually he will answer "because I want to be happy." If I then ask him, "but why do you want to be happy?," his answer will be "because I want to be happy." There is nothing else to say. Happiness is the final and highest good, for the sake of which we do all else.

Unfortunately, identifying happiness as the highest good does little to advance our knowledge of it. Most people already know this (1097b22), and so it is little more than a platitude. Aristotle proposes a strategy with which to push the inquiry forward. "Perhaps [happiness] will become more clear if the function of human being could be grasped" (1098b24–5). This should be puzzling. Why, in order to discover what happiness is, must we inquire into the human "function"? As usual, a clue comes from the Greek. The word *ergon* is related to an old friend, for it is at the root of *energeia*, translated above as "actuality," but literally coming closer to "being-at-work." An *ergon*, then, is a "work, a deed, an action." The reason so many translators use the English "function" is found in the following passage:

> Just as there is apparently a function of the eye, the hand, the foot, and in general of each of the bodily parts, may we also attribute to a human

being some function besides all of these? What then would this be? For living is apparently shared with plants, and something special is being sought. For this reason both nutrition and growth should be eliminated. Next would come some sort of life of sense perception, but this appears to be common to the horse, the ox, and every animal. What remains is some sort of life of action belonging to that which has reason [*logos*]. (1097b30–98a4)

The function, the special work, of the eye is to see; the function of the hand is to grasp. Similarly, Aristotle suggests, the human being as a whole must have a work proper to it. This function cannot be nutrition or perception, for (as we know from *On the Soul*) human beings share these activities with plants and animals. The only function unique to humans is rational work or *logos*.

To understand better why Aristotle turns to "function" in order to comprehend happiness, we need to examine the Greek word *eudaimonia*. While "happiness" is the regular translation, it is somewhat misleading. The Greek begins with *eu*, a prefix meaning "well," which is still found in English words like "euphemism" and "euthanasia." A *daimon* is some sort of "spirit." *Eudaimonia*, then, means "a spirit in good shape," and can also be translated as "prosperity," or even better "flourishing." Unlike our word "happiness," *eudaimonia* thus refers to an objectively positive condition, rather than to a merely subjective one. To clarify, imagine this scenario: your friend Sue is the ultimate slacker. She sleeps 18 hours a day, and spends most of the remaining 6 eating and drinking. Her family is wealthy enough for her not to take a job, she is of cheerful temperament, and always seems, when awake, to be smiling. You are quite puzzled by her demeanor, and so you ask, "are you happy?" She says "yes." You, a hard-working person who sleeps only 6 hours a day, are skeptical and so ask again, "are you *really* happy?" Again she answers "yes," and she does so with a sincerity you believe.

The question is, can Sue be wrong about her experience and sensation of her own happiness? To use a slightly technical word, is happiness an "incorrigible" experience, one incapable of being corrected and about which one cannot be wrong? Some experiences are clearly of this sort. Consider pain. If your head aches, and I ask you, "does it hurt?" and you answer me as honestly as you can, "yes it does," you cannot be wrong. If you feel yourself to be in pain, then you really are in pain. By contrast, if I ask you, "what's the matter?"

and you answer, "I have a brain tumor," then you might well be wrong. If you go to the hospital and have the proper tests, the existence of a brain tumor can be ruled out. Your belief in a brain tumor is thus corrigible. But your sensation of pain, assuming you have reported it as honestly as you can, is not.

Generally, our word "happiness" suggests something incorrigible. By contrast, Aristotle's *eudaimonia*, here best understood as "flourishing," is distinctly corrigible. Sue is simply wrong about her own condition. She thinks she is happy, and she surely feels a certain contentment or pleasure, but she is not really flourishing. She has not actualized her full potential as a human being, for she is not hard at work doing what human beings are uniquely and naturally suited to do, namely engaging in rational activity.

The next step is this: the concept of an *ergon* leads directly to, is paired with, the concept of *areté* or "excellence." If I can determine the *ergon* of an object, I can determine its *areté*. So, for example, I know the function of my glasses: to improve my vision. Because I know this, I can determine whether my glasses are good or even excellent. If I can see distant objects clearly when I am wearing them, then I have a good pair of glasses.[27]

With these terms in place, Aristotle's definition of happiness should make sense: "it is a certain kind of activity of the soul expressing excellence" (1099b26).

We have now followed Aristotle in the first five steps of his *Ethics*. He (thinks he) has shown that (1) human life is purposive; (2) there is a highest purpose or good; (3) this is happiness; (4) in order to understand happiness one must comprehend the human function, which in turn discloses our appropriate excellence or virtue; (5) this function is rational activity. The next step is obvious: Aristotle must tell us what rational activity is. He begins by dividing it into two kinds: "one as obeying reason [*logos*], the other as thinking and having reason" (1098a5).

This division can best be understood by considering the relationship between a parent and a child, or a teacher and a student. The former gives commands to the latter who, if all goes according to plan, will obey. It may seem strange to attribute rational activity to the latter, for "obeying" may seem to be passive. But for Aristotle obedience, while not the highest expression of rational work, is nonetheless a form of it. This is because it takes reason both to comprehend a command and to understand that one ought to obey it. It is reasonable, for example, for a university student to follow the "commands" of the professor written on the course syllabus. Presumably, the professor knows her subject, as well as how to teach it, and the student only stands to benefit from "obeying." As a result, both teacher and student actualize their rational capacities insofar as each executes their side of the pedagogical bargain.

To the two forms of rational activity, each of which is an inflection of the human function, correspond two kinds of excellence or virtue. As Aristotle puts it, "virtue, then, is of two sorts, intellectual virtue and moral virtue" (1103a15). The former is the actualization of the part which itself has reason and the latter the part conceived as able to obey reason. By means of this distinction Aristotle organizes most of the *Nicomachean Ethics*. Books II–V are about moral virtues, Book VI and X (at least chapters 7 and 8) are about intellectual virtues. (Books VII–IX are more difficult to classify.) He offers the following as a preliminary way to differentiate the two: "Intellectual virtue mostly come from teaching . . . while moral virtue results from habit" (1103a15–17).

Intellectual virtue would include excellence in physics, mathematics, and philosophy itself, each of which needs to be taught, and to which we will turn at the end of this section. For the moment, we will concentrate on moral virtues such as courage, temperance, and justice, all of which arise from habit. To appreciate the implications of this assertion, we need only to reflect on what a habit is. As usual, the way to do this is to bring to mind something familiar; say, the way you arrange your clothes before you go to sleep. It is likely you put them in almost exactly the same place every night. Perhaps you hang them neatly and put them in the closet; or perhaps you throw them into a pile near the foot of the bed. In either case, no real thought is involved. The action has been repeated so many times that by now it feels almost automatic. This, however, it is not. The action of the alarm clock is automatic. The machinery is set to sound the alarm at 7 A.M., and unless there is a mechanical or electrical breakdown it will do this. However automatic it feels, the habitual pattern of arranging your clothes is not equivalent to the workings of a clock: you can do otherwise if you choose to. Similarly, a habitual action is not involuntary as are breathing or blinking one's eyes. Even if it is difficult, it is not impossible to break one's habits. On the other hand, a habitual action is not fully self-conscious either. Before I reach to take a fourth piece of chocolate cake, I may pause and deliberate whether I should do so or not. The subsequent action, assuming I am following the directives of my reasoning, is one fully illuminated by reflection. By contrast, the habitual act of arranging my clothes before bed takes place in gray light. It is somewhere in-between full self-conscious and automatic or involuntary behavior.

Parents (or a community of elders), if they are doing their job properly, attempt to instill good habits in their children. Perhaps as a child you were required to wash the dinner dishes. After a while, this became "second nature," and so you have continued the practice ever since. Washing the dishes is now so familiar to you that doing so is almost pleasurable, while failing to do so generates small sparks of discomfort. If washing the dinner dishes is a good habit, then it provides an example of what Aristotle means by moral virtue and why he conceives of it as the excellence or actualization of the "obeying" side of our rational capacity. By citing three specific moral virtues, Aristotle expresses his general point this way: "we become just by doing just actions, temperate by doing temperate actions, courageous by doing courageous actions" (1103b1). One becomes just not by taking a course titled "A Theory of Justice" or answering Socrates' "what is it" question. Instead, moral virtues arise from repeated patterns of behavior, frequently imposed by external constraint, which eventually become so thoroughly integrated into one's daily routine that they are pleasant to perform. If, for example, someone "stands firm against terrifying situations and enjoys it, or at least is not pained by it, then he is courageous" (1104b7).

Still, moral virtues, as closely related as they are to habit, may seem too passive or mindless to qualify as genuine expressions of excellence. Unlike Plato, however, on this score Aristotle has moderate expectations and he is willing to designate ordinary people as virtuous, and habit is the middle ground, the gray area, occupied by most of us most of the time. To illustrate this distinction between the two philosophers, imagine someone asking you, "why do you wash the dishes every night? Why not just leave them at the table?" You, along with most dishwashers, will be hard pressed to provide an adequate reply. After all, you have done so all your life and have rarely wondered why. Now imagine you have invited Socrates over to dinner. When you jump up and take the dishes to the sink he asks you, "why are you doing that?" You answer, "because it's a good thing to do and I think I should." He responds, "Ah, so you think it's a good thing to do. This means that you must know what goodness itself is. After all, you've just shown me an example of it. You can't identify a particular without knowing the universal of which it is an example. So, tell me: what is the good itself? And if you can't answer that question, put down those dishes, and have another cup of coffee, and start talking with me."

From Aristotle's perspective, Socrates has over-intellectualized moral virtue. There is no need to know what the good itself is – there is no need to be a philosopher – in order to be helpful and wash the dishes. One simply needs to have been brought up properly by one's parents and community.

Two additional points are suggested by this discussion of habit. First, unlike the great moral philosophers of modernity (especially Kant), Aristotle does not place a high premium on freedom. For example, he says this: "The legislator makes the citizens good by habituating them" (1103b3). This is an important clue not only to the difference between ancient and modern ethics, but also to the divergence of their political philosophies. Aristotle requires the legislator, and by extension the city, to "make" the citizens good. Conceivably there could be a law stipulating that all citizens must hang their clothes up neatly every night. Such external constraints would be designed to inculcate good habits. We of the modern world would find such regulations insufferable. By our lights, the essential purpose of the state is not to make us good, but to allow citizens the freedom to pursue whatever conception of the good they deem to be their own. For Aristotle, the relationship between city and citizen is more like that between a concerned parent and a child.

Second, because it depends so greatly on habits, and because these in turn depend on the presence of external authorities capable of inculcating habitual patterns of behavior, attaining moral virtue requires some luck. Children do not choose the communities in which they are raised, and no one chooses their parents, so if moral virtue requires one to be well raised, it cannot entirely be a matter of choice or personal responsibility. (Williams 1981 offers an extensive discussion of "moral luck.")

Our habits coagulate and they become our "character." (The Greek for "habit" is *ethos*, the root of our "ethics," while the related word *êthos* means "character.") As familiar as this notion may appear to be, it is also surprisingly elusive. First, consider how difficult it is to assess someone's character. Imagine that Bob has just given some money to his impoverished friend Sue. Even if we agree that his was a generous action, we cannot conclude from this that he is, in fact, a generous man. He may have given his money to Sue in order to secure some benefit from her in the future, or to impress his other friends. He may have done so while suffering from an acute headache that caused him to act erratically. He may have just won the lottery, and with so much money to burn it was effortless for him to fork over a bit of it.

Clearly, then, observation of a single action is insufficient to draw conclusions about someone's character. Instead, it requires a great deal of time, and the judgment one makes is always somewhat precarious. If for the past 20 years Bob has been generous through thick and thin, when he had headaches and when he was feeling fine, perhaps he really is a generous man. Only someone knowing him well, however, is in a position to make this judgment about him. Even then, the judgment is never completely certain. People surprise us all too often.

Because his is a teleological ethics, and emerges from an understanding of the human function, which in turn is derived from an understanding of human nature and form, Aristotle's ethics, unlike most modern moral theories (especially those of Kant and Mill), centers around character. The central ethical question for him is not, "is this particular action the right one to perform?" but "what sort of human being should I aspire to be?"

To continue this line of thought, we turn next to Aristotle's definition of moral virtue.

> Virtue is a characteristic involving choice, consisting in observing the mean relative to us, a mean which is determined by the sort of reasoning which a man of practical wisdom [*phronimos*] would use to determine it. (1107a1–4)

Moral virtue is a "characteristic": it belongs to our characters. Furthermore, it involves choice. Only insofar as one chooses one's actions can they be evaluated morally. If, for example, I am constrained to perform an act against my will, or if I inadvertently or unknowingly do something without intending to, I cannot be held morally responsible for it. The crux, however, of Aristotle's definition of moral virtue is the notion of the "moral mean." To explain, he compares it with the arithmetical mean. Both are in-between the two extremes of "too much" and "too little." But they are different as well. The arithmetical mean can be determined by a mechanical decision procedure, or an algorithm. If 2 is one extreme and 10 the other, then the mean is computed by adding them together and dividing by 2. The answer is 6. This procedure is invariant and generates the right answer every time. The "moral mean," by contrast, is "relative to us." It is located within a human context.

The example Aristotle uses to illustrate the mean comes from the question, "how much should a person eat?" Assume 2 units of grain is too little to sustain a human being, and 10 is too much. The right answer to our question falls somewhere in-between, but there is no algorithm with which to determine what exactly this is for any given person. For instance, Milo the wrestler (1106b3) may well need 8 or 9 units, and skinny Bob may only require 3. When it comes to humans the mean, what is just right, is variable. To return to the example of generosity: assume Bob, who is rich, wants to help and be generous towards his friend Sue, who is poor. How should he go about doing this? How much money should he give her? If he gives too much, the gift may be counterproductive. Sue may be offended by it, or feel belittled, and then reject the gift altogether. If he gives too little, the amount may not meet her needs. Bob must give neither too little nor too much, but just the right amount. But how much is this? It depends on, it is relative to, the character of Sue, and how she reacts to gifts.

"Relative" is something of a dangerous word here, for it is famously associated with the Sophists. Aristotle is not, however, advocating Sophistic relativism. This is clear when he says that the mean is "determined by reason." In other words, when it comes to the question, "how much money should Bob give to Sue?," an objectively right answer is available. Although it is determined rationally, this answer cannot be generated by an algorithm. Instead, it takes good judgment, an excellent eye for human needs, or what Aristotle calls "practical wisdom" (*phronêsis*).

"Practical wisdom" is an intellectual virtue (and is discussed in Book VI), but it functions as a bridge to the moral virtues. It includes within it all the moral virtues, as well as the intellectual capacity to correctly determine the "mean relative to us." As Aristotle puts it, it is "a truthful, rational, practical condition concerning human goods" (1140a21). Those who have it are good human beings who want and attempt to do the right thing, and in addition are astute enough to hit the mean on a regular basis; to determine, in other words, what in making practical decisions is neither too much, nor too little. They are inclined to act virtuously, as well as intelligent enough to do so effectively.

To close this section, consider Aristotle's definition of one particular moral virtue.

> Courage is a mean with respect to fear and confidence (1115a7) . . . he is courageous who endures and fears the right things, for the right reason, in the right way, and at the right time, and who displays confidence in a similar way. (1115b17–20)

The courageous man feels fear, but resists it and so endures in the performance of his action. Not all fears, however, should in fact be resisted. Imagine you are in a region of Africa where malaria is rampant. In such a place it may well be wise to be afraid of mosquitoes. As a result, someone facing a swarm of mosquitoes who felt no fear and so chose not to run away, would be fearing too little, and would be excessively bold rather than genuinely (virtuously) courageous. On the other hand, if someone who lives in London, where mosquitoes almost never carry infection, flees from a single insect buzzing around his ear, he is behaving in a cowardly fashion. Again, courage is fearing the right things at the right time in the right way: not too much, not too little.

But what exactly is the meaning of this "right" mentioned several times in the paragraph above, and where does it come from? It emanates from the mean, which in turn is "determined by the sort of reasoning which a man of practical wisdom [*phronimos*] would use to determine it." The definition of courage can now be revised: it is fearing those things the man of practical wisdom would fear, when, for, and in the way he would fear them. This may seem circular. "What is courage," you ask. For the answer, you must look to the *phronimos*, to the virtuous man. "Yes," you respond (thinking perhaps of Meno's paradox), "but how can I identify the virtuous man without knowing what virtue is, or even having practical wisdom myself?"

It is actually quite difficult to untangle this dilemma. Suffice it to say here that Aristotle's *Ethics* is of a piece with the rest of his philosophical works. He is consummately "theoretical," a word whose root is the Greek *theorein*, "to look at, to view." In this regard, recall the enormous premium Aristotle places on sight in *Metaphysics* I: more than the other senses it "makes us into knowers and makes plain many distinctions." Just as *The Parts of Animals* is a treatise whose goal is to make clear the organic parts and the teleological structures of animal life – to let them show themselves as they are in themselves through the medium of *logos* – so too the *Ethics* shows and points the reader towards the *phronimos*. The book, however, is not a training manual in virtue, but a philosophical work whose goal is to illuminate the nature of, and so the *telos* of, human *praxis*. It does not offer a recipe or a set of guidelines on how to become courageous or attain practical wisdom. Instead, it "makes plain" the distinction between a courageous man, and the two extremes flanking him: the coward and the overly bold. Not everyone will be able to recognize the picture Aristotle draws. But for those of us lucky enough to have been raised properly, to be disposed towards virtue, and to have the intelligence to work our way through the *Nicomachean Etihcs*, his words will ring true.

b) Intellectual virtue

As with any good student, Aristotle is not afraid to criticize his teacher. At times, Plato seems to recognize only one form of human excellence: the philosophical. In the *Apology*, for example, Socrates famously says, "the unexamined life is not worth living for a human being" (38a). As he suggests in the parable of the cave, only a life illuminated by the bright sunlight of reason can liberate us from the obscurity of images, and so is truly desirable. By contrast, Aristotle attributes a significant role in the formation of moral virtue to habit, and by doing so challenges this view. An ordinary, and so relatively unreflective, person can, if raised properly by attentive parents in a decent *polis*, lead a life well worth living. Such a rehabilitation of the habitual nature of moral virtue seems to promise a conception of human excellence far more expansive than the one offered by Plato, for it will embrace even the nonphilosophical.

Still, the apple does not fall too far from the tree. In Book X of the *Nicomachean Ethics*, in one of the most controversial passages in his entire corpus, Aristotle seems to return to his Platonic roots. For here he proclaims that the best life of all is found in the use of one's mind, or as he puts, in the life of "study" or, more literally, "theory" (*theôria*).

> If happiness, then, is activity expressing virtue, it is reasonable for it to express the supreme virtue. This would be the virtue of what is best.

The best is mind . . . Therefore, complete happiness would be the actuality of this expressing its proper virtue; and this is the actuality of theory. (1177a12–18)

Aristotle lists several reasons why the theoretical life is best and happiest of all.

1. It is the actuality of the mind, which in turn is what is supreme in us and which studies the most supreme objects.
2. We can "study" (or "theorize") more continuously than we can do anything else.
3. Theoretical activity is most pleasant.
4. It is most self-sufficient; in other words, it has the least need of external goods or human assistants.
5. "Theory is liked because of itself alone"; it generates no benefit other than itself.
6. It is most leisurely.
7. The theoretical life actualizes what is most divine in us.
8. It actualizes what human beings in fact are, namely mind (1177a20–78a3).

Let us begin with the notion of "leisure" (point 6). Constrained by neither the clock nor by external demands, leisure is free time during which we are able to do just what we want. It is a time for fun or play or whatever work we value and enjoy for its own sake. The Greek for "leisure" is *scholê*, the root of our word "school." This may be surprising, since for most people today going to school hardly seems leisurely. Indeed, the modern school (and university) is often intensely laborious, with a stated purpose of preparing students to enter the workforce. In other words, our conception of education is largely technical: the knowledge accrued by the student is meant to be usefully applied. By contrast, for Aristotle, "school" is a place for the leisurely exploration of whatever it is in the world we find fascinating or inspiring. Intellectual, or specifically "theoretical," activity is not for the sake of application in some useful domain, but a form of work human beings do when they have free time and are flourishing. Just as we like our senses, especially vision, even when they generate for us no benefit, so too do we like "theorizing" simply for itself (point 5).

In *Metaphysics* Book I, Aristotle offers a brief history of philosophy. He claims that people began to ask the question "why?" and then began to seek causes and to develop the sciences, only when they had leisure. For example, "mathematics arose first in Egypt; for there members of the priestly class were allowed to be at leisure" (981b22). The search for causes only commences when people are allowed to pursue questions because they are compelled by interest alone. This is particularly true of philosophy: "human beings," Aristotle says, "first began to philosophize even as they do now, because of wonder" (982b12). Intellectual inquiry begins in a state of amazement. The world strikes us as full of wonders, and if we are lucky enough to live in a city which has reached a sufficiently high level of prosperity, and which is at peace, we will be drawn, by our very nature, to think about them. Philosophy, far from being a tedious or required subject at the university, is voluntary and so more akin to play than to labor.

The "theoretical life," Aristotle asserts in defending its supreme excellence, is most "continuous" (point 2). In other words, it is least likely to be interrupted. Unlike a life spent pursuing money or politics or fame, a theoretical life does not essentially depend on external circumstances or support. While it may be helpful to have "colleagues" (1177a32), ultimately the life of the mind depends largely on one's internal resources. For this reason, it is not only most "self-sufficient" (point 4), but most pleasant as well (point 3). In actualizing our capacity to study the world, we attain our *telos*. Just as a plant in full bloom, or a mature animal at the peak of its vitality, flourishes, so too does a human being in the altogether pleasant act of "theorizing."

The last two items on this list (7 and 8) might seem difficult to reconcile: theoretical activity is described as both somehow "divine" as well as most fully human. A reconciliation is, however, forthcoming: the most complete human life, Aristotle seems to believe, is one spent in trying to overcome its own humanity, in becoming "divine." As he puts it, even if it is happy, "the life expressing the other kind of virtue," namely moral or practical virtue, is so only in a "second best" sort of way. "For these [practical] forms of actuality are human" (1178a10), while theoretical activity, which aims to understand the world as a totality, leaves the all too human concerns of the city far behind.

This passage has caused scholars no end of consternation. (See Kraut 1991, pp. 1–9 for a representative discussion of it.) By relegating the life of moral or practical virtue to "merely" human status, while elevating the life of the mind to the "divine," Aristotle seems to betray the wonderful generosity he otherwise expresses towards ordinary

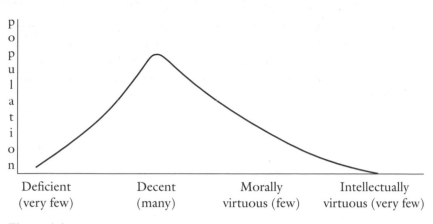

Deficient   Decent   Morally   Intellectually
(very few)   (many)   virtuous (few)   virtuous (very few)

Figure 4.6

human decency. He seems to open up a gap between theory and practice, and perhaps more insidiously (or "Platonically") between those merely "human" people who spend their time taking care of our practical affairs, and those who are nearly "divine" because they are engaged in the theoretical work of studying the world. To elaborate, the bell curve again comes in handy (see figure 4.6).

The curve drawn here recalls its previous two usages (figures 4.1. and 4.2), both of which represented the teleological development of an individual. As with every animal, human beings have a *telos* given to them by their nature, and which functions normatively. If an eagle cannot fly, it is an inferior member of its species. If Sue is a slacker who does little more than sleep and drink, she is incompletely human. By contrast, those flourishing, mature adults actualizing their capacity for hard rational work are excellent. This third use of the curve (figure 4.6) shows the (rather rough) sense in which for Aristotle ontogeny, the lifecycle or teleological development of a single organism as it moves towards achievement of its proper form (figure 4.2), recapitulates phylogeny, the development of a species. Just as over the course of an individual's life there is a high point, so too over an entire population a few are high, most are middling, and some are inferior. In terms of their moral development, most people are pretty decent. They obey the laws, take care of their families, and go about their daily business in a habitual and effective, if unreflective, manner. A smaller number actually attain moral virtue, with some even achieving "practical wisdom." A much smaller number are genuinely rotten, and an even smaller number engage in the life of the mind.

The bell curve visually depicting Aristotle's teleological conception of nature – whether it does so in terms of the development of an individual or of the distribution of excellence across a population – reveals serious problems when it is considered within the context of his *Ethics*. Why can only a very few attain complete excellence? Is Aristotle a terrible elitist, who thinks some people are so deficient that it is permissible to treat them badly or even turn them into slaves? Because the very young have not yet fully developed their rational capacity, and the very old are losing theirs, is it legitimate to discard such members of the community if it becomes convenient or cost-effective to do so? If those living the divinely theoretical life are so superior to those poor souls who are "merely human," and who thus can at best hope to achieve practical virtue, should they be given places of privilege in a city? Finally, does this distinction between intellectual and moral virtue open up a disturbing gap between theory and practice? Is Aristotelian theorizing useless and just an excuse for self-absorption? After all, it requires the luxury of leisure, brings no immediate benefit, and alone is liked for its own sake. What value then could this putatively most excellent work possibly have for others? To address these questions, we turn next to Aristotle's *Politics*.

Natural Politics

a) The political animal

> Since we see that every city is a community and every community is constituted for the sake of some good (for everybody does everything for the sake of what seems good), it is clear that all communities aim for some good. And the most authoritative of all communities, which embraces all the others, aims for the most authoritative of all goods. This is what is called the city and the political community. (*Politics*, 1252a1–6)[28]

This passage puts us again on familiar teleological ground. Human communities are natural and so aim at some good. The largest and most important of all communities is the *polis*, the city. It is the *telos* of the following subcommunities from which it emerges:

1) The *family*: the primal human community is composed of male and female, "those who cannot exist without each other"

(1252a26). The *telos* of this community is reproduction, the most basic requirement of the species.

2) The *household* is composed of those naturally suited to rule and those naturally suited to be ruled (a distinction we will discuss shortly), and its goal is one step beyond reproduction: "survival" (1252a31).

3) The *village* is a combination of several households. Its *telos* goes beyond daily or even short-term survival (1252a17). The village looks to the future and its long-range enhancement.

4) The *city* is formed from a number of villages. "It comes to be for the sake of living, but is for the sake of living well. Therefore, if the prior communities are by nature, so too is every city by nature, for it is their *telos*, and nature is *telos* (1252b27–32).

The city develops organically from smaller subcommunities, each of which arises in order to fulfill a human need. Initially, in the family and household, humans gather together simply to survive and then maintain themselves. Ultimately, however, we enter into political communities because we need to flourish. The city provides us with the conditions under which we can strive not merely for the preservation of life (as a modern thinker such as Hobbes might have it), but for the attainment of the good life. Being a citizen, then, belongs to human nature. Or, as Aristotle puts it, "apparently the city is among those beings that are by nature, and human being is by nature a political animal" (1253a4). He elaborates in the following:

> Why a human being is more of a political animal than any bee or other gregarious animal is clear. For nature, as we say, does nothing in vain, and alone among the animals human beings have rational speech [*logos*]. While voice signifies pleasure and pain, and so belongs to the other animals . . . rational speech is for the purpose of clarifying what is advantageous and what is harmful, and hence what is just or unjust. For this is unique to human beings in comparison with the other animals: they alone have a perception of good and bad and justice and injustice, and so on. When a community shares in these it produces a household and a city. (1253a7–18)

Just as wings do for a bird, *logos* characterizes our species. Since "nature does nothing in vain," this attribute must play some role in fulfilling our organic structure. Its purpose (actually, one of its purposes) is to articulate and thus make possible the sharing of values, and hence the political community itself.

Aristotle continues: "The city is by nature prior to the household and to each one of us as individuals" (1253a19). "Prior" here is not meant historically: families and households came into being before cities did. Instead, the word signifies that being a citizen is more basic to the human animal, closer to its *telos*, than is being an individual. As always, this sort of teleological statement has normative implications. In this case, if people fail to be actively political – if they, for example, fail to identify their interests with those of the city, and simply conceive of themselves as detached individuals – they betray the nature of the human species, and thereby fall short. As Aristotle later puts it, someone removed from the city is "either a beast or a god" (1253a29). Gods have no need for cities: they are self-sufficient. Nor are beasts political: they have no *logos*. Only humans make cities, and in doing so they actualize their nature.

In saying this, Aristotle reflects a belief common in antiquity (and quite foreign to those held today). As I mentioned in chapter 2, the Greeks, and especially the Athenians, were intensely political and strongly identified themselves with their *polis*. To cite again the famous words of Pericles, "the very men who take care of public affairs look after their own at the same time . . . For we think that a man who does not take part in public affairs is good for nothing."

When Aristotle describes someone who is apolitical as either "a beast or a god," his mention of the latter returns us to the issue of "theory and practice" broached in our discussion of *Nicomachean Ethics* Book X. There the theoretical life was described as "most divine" and the practical one was relegated to secondary status. Somehow, then, the philosopher who studies the world is both in the city as an ordinary human being, but outside of it as well. This dilemma has not yet been resolved, and we will turn to it shortly.

Central to Aristotle's conception of the household, which functions as a unit in the development of the city, is slavery, an institution utterly unacceptable in the contemporary world, but common in Ancient Greece. A slave is a human being who has been reduced to a thing, an animate piece of property or tool. How could a thinker as sophisticated and generous, and as apparently humane, as Aristotle defend a practice which to us is self-evidently repugnant?

The first point to note is that Aristotle does not defend or justify all forms of slavery, only what he calls "natural slavery." In ancient Greek warfare, if one city conquered another, it would often kill the men and enslave the women and children. Such is the institution of "legal" or "conventional" slavery. It is the result of political and military force and is oblivious to the quality of the people enslaved. By contrast, the salient feature of the natural slave is precisely his unique quality. He is by nature constituted to receive orders and so is benefited by being a slave.

> For being able to use thought to see ahead is characteristic of one who rules and is master by nature, while being able to labor with the body is characteristic of the one who is ruled and is by nature a slave. In this way, the interests of both master and slave are served. (1251a31–3)

The rational capacity of a natural slave is so limited that he does not have the foresight to make decisions for himself. He needs someone to think for him, which is precisely what the master does. Aristotle justifies making this rather uncomfortable distinction in the following way:

> It is apparent that it is by nature and advantageous for the body to be ruled by the soul, and for the emotional part to be ruled by what has mind and by the rational part, while it is harmful for their relationship to be equal or reversed. This holds true for both human beings and the rest of the animals. For tame animals are better in their nature than wild ones, and it is better for all of these to be ruled by human beings . . . Furthermore, the male relates to the female as better does to the worse, and the ruler does so to the ruled. And so it must go for all of humankind. Therefore, those who are as different [from other human beings] as the soul is from the body or humans from beasts – and if using the body is their proper work [*ergon*], and if this is the best that can come from them, then this is the condition they are in – are slaves by nature . . . For someone is a slave by nature who is capable of belonging to another . . . and who participates in reason only to the extent of perceiving it, but does not have it . . . That some are free and others slaves by nature, and that for these slavery is both advantageous and just, is evident. (1254b5–1255a3)

The ruler–ruled relationship exists throughout nature. Most striking is the case of the soul and the body. A healthy adult is able to exert a significant measure of rational control over his appetites and passions. Those who cannot do this are manifestly deficient. Because the soul of the natural slave is unable to rule his body, he stands to be benefited from the reception of orders from a master. Indeed, this becomes the essential criterion of a natural slave: he must be bene-fited by being a slave. If he is not, as of course the vast majority of the human race would not be, there is no justification for enslaving him.

The argument above leads to what is perhaps a surprising implication: Aristotle's defense of slavery provides, somewhat covertly but also quite powerfully, a critique of the institution as it actually existed in ancient Greece. (Lear 1988, p. 197 makes this point.) As suggested, it leads to the conclusion that the vast majority of people enslaved under the conventions of Ancient Greek warfare, virtually none of whom would be naturally deficient, suffer an injustice. Still, even if his defense of slavery can be transformed into this sort of critique, Aristotle is surely no egalitarian. Some people simply are superior to others. Unlike contemporary moralists, Aristotle would not agree that all people, simply by virtue of being human, deserve freedom, autonomy, and equal respect. Because his conception of the *polis* takes its bearings from nature, which is teleological and thus hierarchically organized, his conception of the citizenry is analogously stratified.

To illustrate, consider the familiar cliché, "a woman's place is in the home." Most of us find it obnoxious. Aristotle, however, would take it to be obvious. After all, he asserts that "the male relates to the female as better does to the worse." Just as the natural place of fire is up in the heavens, and that of water is down here on earth, a woman belongs in the home. Because of her natural limitations, this is where, and only where, she flourishes and can actualize her potential for excellence. Incapable of participating in either politics or philosophy, and superior to a slave, she is best suited to manage the household.

This example shows how potentially dangerous Aristotle's naturalized politics can become. If a woman's place is in the home, then what is to stop someone from declaring that members of a specific ethnic group belong behind a computer screen, while others should be working out in the fields? Much better, an opponent might well maintain, and much safer, is to begin by affirming human equality: no one belongs anywhere in particular. People should end up where their talents take them and where they want to end up. Such, at least, is one familiar, and particularly modern, response to Aristotle.

Nonetheless, his sense of naturalized politics should not be altogether discarded, and in fact if it is revised (by, for example, eliminating his bias against women) it can be useful even today. This is because, as he so often does, Aristotle challenges a contemporary orthodoxy, one we take for granted, and yet often feel discomforted by.

As discussed throughout this chapter, the notion of "place" is central to the *Physics*. As opposed to the Democritean, and then the modern, notion of an infinite space, and a homogeneous conception of matter in motion, Aristotle's forms are stable, his cosmos is limited, and natural beings have a place. Fire belongs above with the stars, while the earth, center of our lives, is below. The various beings in the world fit together to form a hierarchically organized and beautiful whole. From this conception of nature his political views emerge. In a parallel fashion, the basic political views of modernity emerge from its conception of the universe. Just as, since the "scientific revolution," space has been conceived as infinite and placeless, with no "up" or "down" to limit it, and no *telos* to give it meaning, so too human beings face the unlimited possibility of freedom. No one belongs anywhere, and no place is essentially different from another.

On the one hand, the equality and social mobility made possible by removing the natural constraints intrinsic to the Aristotelian scheme can be inspiring and full of hope. And yet, faced with such limitlessness, more than a few have felt a cold shudder. Perhaps the first to do so was Pascal who, writing in 1660, famously said, "the eternal silence of these infinite spaces frightens me" (Pascal 1941, p. 75). More recently, Alasdair MacIntyre's *After Virtue*, written in 1981, expressed a powerful longing for a return to the Aristotelian conception of virtue, an ethical concept that, as we have seen, depends on his notion of form and so, by extension, on his understanding of nature in general.

Today, many of us are regularly confronted, and disturbed, by the phenomenon of "globalization." The music being listened to, the shirts being worn, the food consumed, the TV screens being watched, are the same whether one is in Lagos or Boston, Frankfurt or Beijing. Driven by the imperatives of commerce, the world increasingly looks like one gigantic marketplace. Everywhere there are gas stations, satellite hookups, internet chat rooms, and hamburgers for sale. In the age of the jet plane, massive waves of immigration, and the cell phone, national boundaries seem to be losing their significance. No one belongs anywhere in particular.

To return to our earlier example: in many (but far from all) countries throughout the world a woman's place is no longer said to be in the home. She, like all of us, is free to roam. Again, such freedom, and the equality attendant upon it, is often delicious and rewarding. Far from the confines of a traditional society, in which daughters are expected to replicate the lives of their mothers, and boys those of their fathers, and the elders expect to be buried in ancestral ground, ours is increasingly a world of ceaseless change and rapid transformation. Fewer and fewer people live in the same village or city as did their parents. Instead, they move to the megacities of Cairo, or Mexico City, Bombay, or Los Angeles. Whatever positives are attached to these phenomena, they also can be debilitating. Detached from the traditional bonds – whether they were national or cultural, political or religious, familial or tribal – that helped connect the previous generations to one another, many a globalized soul is helplessly stuck in an urban slum far from home. Those lucky enough to have been born in a "developed" country often spend their days shopping like mad, endlessly gabbing on cell phones, and flying effortlessly from one continent to another. And not a few such souls become lonely, lost, and desperate. The need for alternative visions has never been greater.

Aristotle, with his teleological physics and his conception of politics corresponding to it, offers an alternative. Even if we can hardly return to the ancient *polis* – and certainly few women, for example, would want to – thinking about Aristotle's *Politics* can nonetheless be invigorating. It offers a vision of a cosmos in which, so unlike our own, human beings have a place and so are at home.

b) Best life; best city

As Socrates does in Plato's *Republic*, in Book VII of the *Politics* Aristotle sketches what he takes to be the best of all possible cities. Before doing so, however, he requires a prior question to be answered: "It is necessary for one about to conduct the appropriate inquiry into the best regime first to determine what the most choiceworthy life is" (1323a14–16). To understand the best city, one must first understand the best life.

(For the reasons alluded to above, it should be clear that this is a sentiment with which modern political thinkers would disagree. The guiding principle of the modern "liberal" state is to protect the liberties of the citizens and, rather than guiding them towards any particular conception of the "most choiceworthy life," allow them to pursue any version of the good they choose.)

There are two candidates for the best life: "the political or practical," and the "one released from all externals, namely the theoretical life, which some people say belongs only to the philosopher" (1324b28). The previous sections have prepared us to understand why these two are preeminent. On the one hand, in *Politics* I, Aristotle identifies human being as an animal political by nature. As a result, and in keeping with traditional Greek values, he counts a life spent performing civic duties as excellent. On the other hand, in *Nicomachean Ethics* X, Aristotle defends the life of theory, which is more divine than human, as the best of all. Yet again, we have returned to the conflict between "theory and practice."

Resolution finally arrives in Book VII of the *Politics*. Here Aristotle argues that while theoretical activity is indeed the highest and most esteemed of all, it is not without political or practical value. This is because the theoretical life provides the entire city with a *telos*. Even though the majority of citizens cannot afford to spend their time studying the world, and even though in his leisurely pursuit of the truth the philosopher stands apart from the tedious labors and distractions of daily routine, it is nonetheless in the city's interest to support the theoretical life. To explain why, Aristotle argues somewhat indirectly; that is, by showing the unacceptable consequences of assuming the opposite of what he wants to demonstrate.

Imagine the political life were the best available to human beings. Even more drastically, imagine that the city, with its commitment to practice and utility, were to denigrate and refuse to support what it takes to be the useless pursuits of the philosopher. If so, Aristotle argues, then the horizons of the city would shrink, and it would become a world or end unto itself. As a result, it could have only one goal, one animating principle, namely to reproduce or expand itself. Aristotle thinks this is actually the case in some cities:

> While most laws in most cities are pretty haphazard, if any of them do have laws directed at any one goal, they would all aim for domination. For example, in Sparta and Crete the educational system has been designed with an eye to making war. (1324b5–9)

"Domination" or power is the ultimate purpose of many an actual city. Since they conceive of no value, indeed no reality, other than themselves, the best such cities can aspire to is their own expansion. Aristotle counts this as a disaster. He voices his displeasure in the following passage:

> It would seem to be utterly absurd if the work [*ergon*] of the politician were to study how to rule and dominate neighboring cities, and to do so whether they are willing or unwilling to be ruled. (1324b22–6)

Aristotle expresses his opposition to the view that political (or economic) expansion is the aim of the city – a view he thinks is conceptually generated by counting the practical rather than the theoretical life as best – through a deceptively simple motto: "Peace is the goal [*telos*] of war, and the goal of labor is leisure" (1334a10). The first half may seem trivial, but regrettably it is not. Cities like Sparta and Crete operate with no *telos* beyond themselves and are consequently unable to envision a peaceful, stable existence in which their citizens are not battling to get bigger, but enjoying what they have and flourishing in leisure. Their only reason for being is to impose their will on others, but when they succeed in doing so, they have no idea or vision of the sort of life they wish to impose. Such cities act according to the Heraclitean dictum, "war is the father of all, the king of all." For them there is nothing but the hard labor and restless pursuit of expansion. By contrast, Aristotle proposes that leisure, freedom from external constraint and distraction, is the goal of labor. Yes, we must live in a well-governed city whose economy is sufficiently prosperous to allow its citizens to live securely and in material comfort. Yes, we must have armies to defend our borders and politicians to labor for the well-being of the community. But when all of this hard work is completed, there is a payoff: free time during which intellectual inquiry can begin. The goal of war, and the only reason to engage in it, is to live in peace and to provide the conditions for flourishing. Cities like Sparta and Crete, bereft as they are of philosophy, have no inkling of what to do with themselves when they are not burdened with the business of war.

To reiterate the contemporary parallel: in the age of globalization, most countries, especially the "advanced" ones, are much like Sparta and Crete, for their conception of the good is dominated by the goal of economic growth. As a result, economics, rather than political philosophy, has become the subject to be studied in order to rule a city well. Aristotle would find this backwards, since for him economics should be subordinated to politics. The goal of the former is to provide the conditions required for the preservation of life, while the job of the latter is to provide the conditions under which citizens can lead the good life. This distinction, between life and the good life, is altogether crucial for Aristotle, but largely missing in contemporary political thought. For example, many political economists will take lifespan, a sheerly quantitative measure, to be the crucial indicator of a well-functioning society, and relentless growth the sole measure of an economy's success. Such a view, which is quintessentially modern, can provide no answer to the question, "when is enough enough?" It is unable to determine when the resources of a community are sufficient to allow the citizens to flourish, because it is bereft of any substantive notion of flourishing. By contrast, Aristotle, equipped as he is with his teleological conception of human nature, argues that a political community should stop growing when it is sufficiently strong to defend its borders and so can live peacefully, has rulers who care about the common good, and can provide its best citizens with the leisure they require to pursue their theoretical activities.

Unfortunately, most men, as Aristotle understands full well, cannot tolerate leisure. In a grim assessment, he says "war compels men to be just and temperate, while the enjoyment of good fortune and having leisure while at peace makes them aggressive" (1324–7). Most men, especially high-energy ones, get bored easily and so cannot stand free time. They are restless and need to move. In times of peace and prosperity, they do not know what to do with themselves. And so if they are rich, they will try to get even richer. Even if they are already powerful, they will still start fights. One way or another their restless energy will burn, and Aristotle is not hopeful about the outcome. In contrast, during times of war, constraints are automatically put in place to control, and to provide an outlet for, such men. They are forced to discipline themselves and moderate their own ambitions by the demands of their commanders. By serving their city, rather than themselves, they are given the opportunity to show courage and vent their aggression in a controlled manner, one which will not tear the city itself apart. In short, Aristotle identifies war as the only arena in which most men can achieve some measure of *aretê*. Regrettably, only a few can actually flourish in times of peace and leisure, for only a few have intellects sufficiently powerful to discipline and enable themselves to enjoy their time studying the world which, for them, is full of wonders.

The philosopher – self-sufficiently engaged in an activity valuable in itself – appreciates the beauty, order, and variety of nature, and does not study with an eye towards usefully applying the knowledge he gains. Such a life, to a Cretan or a Spartan or a contemporary American, will seem useless and even unrecognizable. Aristotle, however, sees it as the *telos*, not only of an individual, but of the city itself. When a citizen lives a theoretical life, and thereby fully actualizes the capacity nature has given to our species, he or she exemplifies the extent of human possibility. Such people send a message to the rest of the citizens: "there is something beyond the ordinary labor of your daily lives, and the wars you fight to defend your city. There is a payoff, namely peace and the leisure needed to study, and thereby appreciate, the world in which we all, regardless of what city we come from, live." When theory is despised, as it was in Sparta and Crete – and as it increasingly is in our own society in which technology is prized above all other intellectual pursuits – when leisure is pilloried by a community, such as our own, which is relentlessly dominated by the work ethic, when philosophy is trivialized, as it too often is in today's universities, then the human community as a whole has lost something of practical importance. The theoretical life tokens the possibility and goodness of leisure and peace. Without it, there is nothing but expansion and the drive for power. For this reason, cities should attempt to create the conditions in which philosophy is possible. Such, at least, is Aristotle's attempt to reunite theory with practice. Guided by these sorts of reflections, he says this:

> In fact, it would be possible for a single city, which clearly would have to be governed well, to be happy in itself, if it were possible for such a city to live somewhere by itself with excellent and serious laws in place. The organization of such a political system would not be directed at war or the domination of others. (1325a1–4)

It is probably impossible, as Aristotle understands, for any city in the "real" world to "live somewhere by itself," and no doubt this is even more true in the age of the globalized modern state. Still, with these remarks he sketches an ideal, one which emanates from the basic ingredients of his worldview. Simply put, for Aristotle human life has meaning. It is purposive, and its purposiveness can be rationally comprehended. The "function" of the human animal is rational activity, and its *telos* is to achieve excellence in it. By contrast, the modern western worldview – whose germs can be found in Democritus, Heraclitus, and Empedocles, and which comes to fruition in Galileo, Newton, and Darwin – is meaningless. Any given human life in an infinite universe of homogeneous matter in motion is ultimately no better than any other. When this conception is transferred to the political level, as it has been over the course of the centuries, nothing remains for a city to do but get bigger or die. In the face of this lamentable condition, Aristotle's alternative, as unrealistic and antiquated as it may seem, is well worth retrieving . . . even today.

Conclusion

Aristotle is the hero of our story because he is the culmination of the dialectical development of Ancient Greek Philosophy sketched in this book. In a nutshell, he accomplishes this by combining the Presocratic study of nature with the Platonic commitment to human excellence and the Forms. He weaves together the strands of thought bequeathed to him by his predecessors, patiently contributes his own remarkable insights, and the result is a massive tapestry, a comprehensive *logos* of both human being and the world.

Aristotle never responds to the views of his predecessors by simply declaring them false. Recall what he says: "Truth is like the proverbial door which no one can miss." No one can get everything wrong because human beings are naturally disposed towards finding the truth. Virtually everybody, then, gets something right. The failure of the Presocratics was not that they were wrong, but that they were not right enough. Their views were partial and thus one-sided because they excluded human experience and practice, *doxa* and the phenomena of ordinary life, from their purview. On the other hand, recall Aristotle's statement that with Socrates "investigation into nature stopped, and philosophers turned to the study of practical virtue and of politics." This ignoring of nature was as equally one-sided as the exclusive concentration on it. Aristotle's solution, his own *logos*, follows a middle, and thereby more comprehensive, path. He is devoted, as much as any thinker has ever been, to a study of nature, but this includes, indeed takes its bearings from, human nature.

Aristotle is superbly dialectical. For example, Milesian thinkers such as Thales and Anaximenes conceived of the *archê* as a determinate substance. Anaximander, by contrast, found it in "the indeterminate." Aristotle preserves something positive in both sides of the debate. By associating matter with potentiality – for matter is neither a "this" nor a "that," but potentially is either – he acknowledges the reality of the indeterminate. By affirming the natural priority of form, which, because it is responsible for a thing's being a "this" or "that," is the basis of actuality, he recognizes the ontological role of determinacy. He has, with these two moves, synthesized the opposing views of Thales and Anaximander.

Another example: Plato's Forms, those universals accessible only to the philosopher whose intellect has been prepared by a rigorous training in mathematics, are separate from the particulars participating in, and so gaining their reality from, them. By contrast, Aristotle reunites form and particular. The rabbit standing before me is both an individual as well as a member of a species. In seeing it, then, I see more than a raw particular; I see a rabbit, a living being with an intelligible, and thus universal, form. Aristotle retains, but dialectically modifies, the Platonic notion of Forms. He brings them down to earth.

Perhaps the most striking instance of the dialectical middle way is found in Aristotle's treatment of the soul, the *psuchê*. According to the tenets of Presocratic materialism, notably those of Democritus, the soul is nothing more than matter in motion. On the other extreme, for Plato it is an immortal and separate being which exists "itself by itself." The Aristotelian definition of soul is in-between. It is "the actuality of a natural, organic body potentially having life." Soul is neither a separate, immaterial thing, nor a chunk of matter, but the work, the activity, of a living being interacting with the world around it.

A last example, which we have just finished discussing: Presocratic theory, their *logos* of *phusis*, was far removed from practice, the active life of citizens in the *polis*. For Plato, theory and practice seemed to merge in the person of the "philosopher-ruler" of the *Republic* who, having seen the "Form of the Good," returns to the cave in order to illuminate it. Like his teacher, Aristotle affirms the practical value of the philosopher, but he does not follow the extreme recommendation that the philosopher should actually be placed in charge of the city. Instead, the value he identifies in the theoretical life is based precisely on the fact that it is separate from political concerns. By living a life of leisure, by studying the world thoughtfully and appreciatively, the philosopher provides a *telos* for the entire city. His life is a reminder that human existence has a purpose, that labor is for the sake of leisure, and war is for the sake of peace. Without the philosopher to provide this model, the city never knows when "enough is enough" and so has nothing to aim for but the indefinite expansion of itself.

We close by returning to the well-known quotation from Alfred North Whitehead with which this book began: "the safest general characterization of the European philosophical tradition is that it consists in a series of footnotes to Plato." Given the extraordinary level of *aporia*, or "perplexity," found in the dialogues, what Whitehead must have meant is that Plato raised all the basic questions that human life inevitably will provoke us to ask, and which philosophers have pursued for over two millennia. Aristotle, however, went one step further: he offered a comprehensive set of answers to his teacher's questions. Many of his answers – his geocentrism, his claim that species are eternal and nature teleological, his defense of the "natural place" occupied by women and slaves – are outdated today, for they have been overwhelmed by the past 400 years of philosophical and scientific development in modern western culture. But has there only been progress, or has much been lost along the way? Whether exemplified by the extraordinary advances made in the laboratory of human reproduction, or the titanic power of weapons of mass destruction, the staggering reach of contemporary technology, based on a thoroughly non-Aristotelian physics, is often demoralizing and sometimes terrifying. The reduction of all forms of reality to invisible particles in motion threatens to denude the world of its beautifully ordered heterogeneity. The replacement of the soul with neurons firing in the brain threatens to rob our ordinary experience of its meaning. The proud declaration of human freedom and autonomy, on which we base so much of our political and ethical thinking, runs the risk of leaving us placeless and alone.

As Husserl put it some 70 years ago, the "European sciences," and hence western culture itself, is facing a "crisis." Failure to think critically is an abdication of responsibility. This book has been animated by the conviction that Aristotle's answers, precisely because they are outdated, can and should become a valuable resource for the contemporary critic. Perhaps at no time in the history of western culture has there been a more pressing need to retrieve them.

Notes

1 I remind readers that Aristotle's treatment of his predecessors has been severely criticized, especially by Kingsley 2002.

2 In fact, most scholars believe that Aristotle's writings are highly edited versions of his lecture notes.

3 The citation is from *Table Talk*, vol. 1, July 2, 1830. Thanks to Peter Murphy and Alan White of Williams College for this information.

4 Translation is from Irwin & Fine 1996.

5 This is overstated. More properly, Plato writes dialogue in which his character Socrates frequently articulates a rationalist position.

6 Translation is my own. The Greek text is Ross 1998.

7 On the relationship between Democritus' "void" and space see Koyré 1968. The title of this valuable book, *From the Closed World to the Infinite Universe*, precisely expresses its subject, namely the transformation of the Aristotelian world into the modern one of Galileo and Newton.

8 This phrase, used by centuries of thinkers, particularly astronomers, who were influenced by him, was inspired but not actually coined by Aristotle.

9 I largely follow the translation of Irwin & Fine 1996.

10 Actually, the Greek verb is *legetai*, "it is said." This means, however, "it is said by us."

11 Translations come from Peck 1998. I substitute "beautiful" for his "admirable," which is how he translates *kalon*.

12 Citations from Spinoza come from the Appendix to Book I of his *Ethics*.

13 Citations are from *New Organon* I.45 and I.41.

14 Translation is my own. The Greek text is Peck 1990.

15 Translation is from Irwin & Fine 1996.

16 This is from the footnote to the first paragraph of the "Historical Sketch" that opens Darwin's *The Origin of the Species*.

17 The Greek text is Cook 1996.

18 The Greek text is Ross 1963.

19 Aristotle also uses the word *entelecheia*, inside of which is found the word *telos*.

20 Actually, he uses "grammar" as his example here. This is a little harder to work with, for the Greek word *grammatikê* means both "grammar" in our sense, as well as "the ability to spell." Since he later cites arithmetic (417a32), I import it here.

21 Because Aristotle's embryology places such emphasis on the "male seed" it has regularly been criticized by feminists as being reflective of his, and his culture's, enormous sexism. For a thorough discussion, see Tress 1992.

22 Sense perceptions supply the "raw material" for thought. They are, however, particular, while thought is of universals. How the universal is "extracted" from the particular is a central, and highly technical, issue for Aristotle that cannot be addressed in this short book. Readers should begin with *Metaphysics* I.1, and *Posterior Analytics* II.19.

23 In fact, it receives these forms from perception through the mediation of "imagination," as explained in *On the Soul* III.3.
24 The text is Descartes 1980, pp. 10 and 17.
25 The Greek text is Ross 1970.
26 The Greek text is Bywater 1962.
27 An easy objection can be brought against this. What if I believe the function of my glasses is to enhance my appearance, and not just assist my vision? In other words, Aristotle may be overconfident in his ability to ascribe functions to things.
28 The Greek text is Ross 1988.

References

Ahrensdorf, P. 1995: *The Death of Socrates and the Life of Philosophy*. Albany: State University of New York Press.

Bacon, F. 1955: *The Selected Writings of Francis Bacon*. New York: Random House.

Benson, H. 2000: *Socratic Wisdom*. New York: Oxford University Press.

Bloom, A. (tr.) 1991: *The Republic of Plato*. New York: Basic Books.

Brickhouse, T. and Smith, N: 2002: *The Trial and Execution of Socrates*. Oxford: Oxford University Press.

Burkert, W. 1972: *Lore and Science in Ancient Pythagoreanism*, tr. E. Minar. Cambridge, MA: Harvard University Press.

Burnet, J. (ed.) 1967: *Platonis Opera*. Oxford: Clarendon Press.

Burnyeat, M. 1976: Protagoras and Self-Refutation in Later Greek Philosophy. *Philosophical Review* 85: 44–69.

Bywater, I. (ed.) 1962: *Aristotelis Ethica Nicomachea*. Oxford: Clarendon Press.

Cohen, S., Curd, P., and Reeve, C. (eds. and tr.) 2000: *Readings in Ancient Greek Philosophy*. Indianapolis: Hackett.

Collobert, C. 2002: Aristotle's Review of the Presocratics. *Journal of the History of Philosophy* 40: 281–95.

Cook, H. (ed. and tr.) 1996: *Aristotle: On Interpretation*. Cambridge, MA: Harvard University Press.

Crick, F, 1994: *The Astonishing Hypothesis: The Scientific Search for the Soul*. New York: Scribner.

Darwin, C. 1925. *The Origin of Species*. New York: Carlton House.

Derrida, J. 1976: *Of Grammatology*, tr. G. Spivak. Baltimore: Johns Hopkins University Press.

Descartes, R. 1980: *Discourse on Method*, tr. D. Cress. Indianapolis: Hackett.

Diels, H. and Kranz, W. (eds.) 1922: *Die Fragmente der Vorsokratiker*. Berlin: Weidmannsche Buchhandlung. Rev. ed. 1961.

Evelyn-White, H. (tr.) 1977: *Hesiod: The Homeric Hymns and Homerica*. Cambridge, MA: Harvard University Press.

Feyerabend, P. 1978: In Defence of Aristotle. In G. Radnitsky and G. Andersson, eds., *Progress and Rationality in Science*. Boston: Reidel, pp. 144–80.

Fish. S. 1989: *Doing What Comes Naturally*. Durham, NC: Duke University Press.

Fowler, H. (tr.) 1982. *Plato's Phaedrus*. Cambridge, MA: Harvard University Press.

Furth, M. 1987: Aristotle's Biological Universe. In A. Gotthelf and J. Lennox, eds., *Philosophical Issues in Aristotle's Biology*. Cambridge: Cambridge University Press.

Galileo, G. 1960: *The Assayer*, tr. S. Drake. Philadelphia: University of Pennsylvania Press.

Gallop, D. 1980: *Plato's Phaedo*. Oxford: Clarendon Press.

Gotthelf, A. and Lennox, J. G. (eds.) 1987: *Philosophical Issues in Aristotle's Biology*. Cambridge: Cambridge University Press.

Griswold, C. (ed.) 1988: *Platonic Writings/Platonic Readings*. New York: Routledge.

Griswold, C. 1999: Relying on Your Own Voice. *Review of Metaphysics* 53: 283–307.

Guthrie, W. K. C. 1962–81: *A History of Greek Philosophy*. Cambridge: Cambridge University Press.

Guthrie, W. K. C. 1988: *The Sophists*. Cambridge: Cambridge University Press.

Hammond, N. and Scullard, H. 1970: *The Oxford Classical Dictionary*. Oxford: Clarendon Press.

Heidegger, M. 1962: *Being and Time*, tr. J. Macqauarrie and E. Robinson. New York: Harper.

Hesiod. 1977: *The Homeric Hymns and Homerica*, tr. H. G. Evelyn-White. Cambridge, MA: Harvard University Press.

Hett, W. (tr.) 1957: *Aristotle: On the Soul*. Cambridge, MA: Harvard University Press.

Howland, J. 1991: Re-Reading Plato: The Problem of Platonic Chronology. *Phoenix* 45: 189–214.

Hume, D. 1975: *A Treatise of Human Nature*, ed. L. A. Selby-Bigge. Oxford: Clarendon Press.

Husserl, E. 1970: *The Crisis of European Sciences an Transcendental Philosophy*, tr. D. Carr. Evanston, IL: Northwestern University Press.

Hyland, D. 1984: *The Question of Play*. Lanham, MD: University Press of America.

Hyland, D. 1992: *The Origins of Philosophy*. Atlantic Highlands, NJ: Humanities Press.

Inwood, B. 2001: *The Poem of Empedocles*. Toronto: University of Toronto Press.

Irwin, T. and Fine, G. (tr.) 1996: *Aristotle: Introductory Readings*. Indianapolis: Hackett.

Kahn, C. 1960: *Anaximander and the Origins of Greek Cosmology*. New York: Columbia University Press.

Kahn, C. 1979: *The Art and Thought of Heraclitus*. Cambridge: Cambridge University Press.

Kerferd, G. B. 1981: *The Sophistic Movement*. Cambridge: Cambridge University Press.

Kingsley, P. 2002: Empedocles for the New Millennium. *Ancient Philosophy* 22: 333–414.

Kirk, G. S. 1954: *Heraclitus, the Cosmic Fragments:* Cambridge: Cambridge University Press.

Kirk, G. S., Raven, J. E., and Schofield, M. (eds. and tr.) 1983: *The Presocratic Philosophers*. Cambridge: Cambridge University Press.

Klein, J. 1975: *A Commentary on Plato's Meno*. Chapel Hill: University of North Carolina Press.

Koyré, A. 1968: *From the Closed World to the Infinite Universe*. Baltimore: Johns Hopkins University Press.

Kraut, R. 1991: *Aristotle on the Human Good*. Princeton: Princeton University Press.

Lear, J. 1988: *Aristotle: The Desire to Understand*. Cambridge: Cambridge University Press.

Lombardo, S. (tr.) 1982: *Parmenides and Empedocles*. San Francisco: Grey Fox Press.

MacDowell, D. (ed. and tr.), 1982: *Gorgias: Encomium of Helen*. Bristol: Bristol Classical Press.

MacIntyre, A. 1981: *After Virtue: A Study in Moral Theory*. Notre Dame: University of Notre Dame Press.

Mendelson, M. 2002: *Many Sides: A Protagorean Approach to the Theory, Practice, and Pedagogy of Argument*. Dordrecht: Kluwer.

Miller, M. 2001: 'First of all': On the Semantics and Ethics of Hesiod's Cosmogony. *Ancient Philosophy* 21: 251–76.

Modrak, D. 2001: *Aristotle's Theory of Language and Meaning*. Cambridge: Cambridge University Press.

Monoson, S. 2000: *Plato's Democratic Entanglements: Athenian Politics and the Practice of Philosophy*. Princeton: Princeton University Press.

Mueller, I. 1992: Mathematical Method and Philosophical Truth. In R. Kraut, ed., *The Cambridge Companion to Plato*. Cambridge: Cambridge University Press.

Nehamas, A. 1975: Plato on the Imperfection of the Sensible World. *American Philosophical Quarterly* 12: 105–17.

Nehamas, A. and Woodruff, P. (tr.) 1989: *Plato's Symposium*. Indianapolis: Hackett.

Nietzsche, F. 1962: *Philosophy in the Tragic Age of the Greeks*, tr. M. Cowan. Chicago: Gateway.

Nietzsche, F. 1989: *The Genealogy of Morals*, tr. W. Kaufmann. New York: Random House.

Nussbaum, M. 1985: *Aristotle's De Motu Animalium*. Princeton: Princeton University Press.

Nussbaum, M. 1986: *The Fragility of Goodness*. Cambridge: Cambridge University Press.

Nussbaum, M. and Rorty, A. (eds.) 1992: *Essays on Aristotle's De Anima*. Oxford: Clarendon Press.

Osborne, C. 1987: *Rethinking Early Greek Philosophy*. Ithaca: Cornell University Press.

Owen, G. E. L. 1975: "Tithenai ta Phainomena." In J. Barnes, ed., *Articles on Aristotle*, vol. I. London: Duckworth.

Pascal, B. 1941: *Pensées*, tr. W. Trotter. New York: Random House.

Peck, A. (tr.) 1990: *Aristotle: Generation of Animals*. Cambridge, MA: Harvard University Press.

Peck, A. (tr.) 1998: *Aristotle: Parts of Animals*. Cambridge, MA: Harvard University Press.

Popper, K. 1950: *The Open Society and Its Enemies*. Princeton: Princeton University.

Press. G. (ed.) 2000: *Who Speaks for Plato?* Lanham, MD: Rowman & Littlefield.

Roochnik, D. 1990: *The Tragedy of Reason*. New York: Routledge.

Roochnik, D. 1996: *Of Art and Wisdom*. State College: Pennsylvania State University Press.

Roochnik, D. 2001: Socrates' Pedagogical Flexibility: Two Case Studies. *Teaching Philosophy* 24: 29–45.

Roochnik, D. 2002: Metaphysics and Pronouns at *Phaedo* 74b7-9. In W. Welton, ed., *Plato's Forms: Varieties of Interpretation*. Lanham, MD: Lexington Books.

Roochnik, D. 2003: *Beautiful City: The Dialectical Character of Plato's Republic*. Ithaca: Cornell University Press.

Rorty, A. (ed.) 1992: *Essays on Aristotle's De Anima*. Oxford: Clarendon Press.

Rorty, R. 1980: *Philosophy and the Mirror of Nature*. Princeton: Princeton University Press.

Rorty, R. 1982: *Consequences of Pragmatism*. Minneapolis: University of Minnesota Press.

Rosen, S. 1987: *Plato's Symposium*. New Haven: Yale University Press.

Ross, W. D. (ed.) 1963: *Aristotelis De Anima*. Oxford: Clarendon Press.

Ross, W. D. (ed.) 1970: *Aristotle's Metaphysics*. Oxford: Clarendon Press.

Ross, W. D. (ed.) 1988: *Aristotelis Politica*. Oxford: Clarendon Press.

Ross, W. D. (ed.) 1998: *Aristotle's Physics*. Oxford: Clarendon Press.

Sacks, O. 1987: *The Man Who Mistook his Wife for a Hat and Other Clinical Tales*. New York: Perennial.

Schiappa, E. 1991: *Protagoras and Logos*. Columbia: University of South Carolina Press.

Searle, J. 1993: Rationality and Realism: What is at Stake? *Daedalus* 122: 55–84.

Smith, N. 1996: Plato's Divided Line. *Ancient Philosophy* 16: 25–47.

Soble, A. (ed.) 1989: *Eros, Agape, and Philia*. New York: Paragon.

Spinoza, B. 1970: *The Ethics*, tr. A. Boyle. New York: Dutton.

Sprague, R. (ed.) 1990: *The Older Sophists*. Columbia: University of South Carolina Press.

Stone, I. 1988: *The Trial of Socrates*. Boston: Little, Brown.

Strauss, L. 1964: *The City and Man*. Chicago: Rand McNally.

Tigerstedt, E. 1977: *Interpreting Plato*. Stockholm: Almqvist & Wiksell.

Tress, D. 1992: The Metaphysical Science of Aristotle's *Generation of Animals* and its Feminist Critics. *Review of Metaphysics* 46: 307–41.

Versényi, L. 1963: *Socratic Humanism*. New Haven: Yale University Press.

Vlastos, G. 1983: The Socratic Elenchus. *Oxford Studies in Ancient Philosophy* 1: 27–58.

Vlastos, G. 1991: *Socrates, Ironist and Moral Philosopher*. Ithaca: Cornell University Press.

Whitehead, A. N. 1969: *Process and Reality*. New York: Free Press.

Williams, B. 1981: *Moral Luck*. Cambridge: Cambridge University Press.

Woodruff, P. (ed. and tr.) 1993: *Thucydides on Justice, Power, and Human Nature*. Indianapolis: Hackett.

Wright, M. (ed. and tr.) 1985: *The Presocratics*. Bristol: Bristol Classical Press.

Index

beings, 18–19, 21–2, 26–7, 30, 32, 41

causes, 98–100, 177–88, 212
cave, allegory of, 151–3, 210
chance, 61–2, 181–2
Cicero, 86
city (*polis*), 69, 143, 147, 149–50, 214–16
consciousness, 95
contingency, 72–3
convention (*nomos*), 52–3, 54, 71–2, 78
cosmos, 168, 185, 219–20

Darwin, C., 182–4
deconstruction, 74–6
definitions, 82, 85, 110
democracy, 73–4, 103, 109, 150, 152–7
Democritus, 50–8, 67, 96, 98–9, 167, 169, 171, 179–80, 219, 226
Derrida, J., 38, 74
Descartes, R., 197
dialectic, 7–8
Diogenes Laertius, 24
divided-line, 128–32, 151
doxa ("opinion," "appearance"), 42, 45, 47, 49, 51, 53, 57, 58–9, 77–9, 113, 150–1, 169, 187, 225

elementalists, 49–64
eliminativism, 56
Empedocles, 58–63, 67, 180–4
empiricism, 23, 45, 52, 163
Epicurus, 57
epiphenomenalism, 95–7, 107
eros, 14–17, 20, 134–46
essence, 82, 84
eternity, 46
evolution, 60–2

Fish, S., 74–6
flux, 33–4, 37, 39, 105–6
folk psychology, 97
forms, 110–12, 117–19, 126, 131, 133, 145–7, 152, 161–2, 174–6, 178, 182–3, 187, 194, 198, 219, 225–6

Galileo, G., 54
genetics, 125–6
globalization, 219–20, 222–3
God, 26–7, 30, 46, 63, 67
Good, the, 132–3, 137–8, 147, 155, 226
Gorgias, 100–1, 106–7, 109, 113, 187

habit, 204–6, 210
happiness (*eudaimonia*), 137, 201–4, 210–11
hedonism, 58
Hegel, G. W. F., 7
Heraclitus, 31–41, 44, 49–50, 67, 105–6, 119, 222
Hesiod, 12–17, 24, 31, 134–5, 148
Homer, 12, 26, 76
Hume, D., 55
Husserl, E., 4–6, 170, 227
hylomorphism, 175–6

images, 129–30, 151
Indefinite, the, 22, 21–2, 27–8, 31, 36

leisure, 211, 214, 222–3
logos ("rational account," "language"), 4, 12–14, 16, 31, 34–5, 37, 45, 47–8, 71, 75, 77, 94, 100, 113, 141–6, 160, 187, 202–3, 215–16
Lucretius, 57–8